HANDBOOK OF
MICROCOMPUTER–BASED
INSTRUMENTATION AND CONTROLS

HANDBOOK OF MICROCOMPUTER–BASED INSTRUMENTATION AND CONTROLS

JOHN D. LENK

Consulting Technical Writer

PRENTICE–HALL, INC., *Englewood Cliffs, N.J. 07632*

Library of Congress Cataloging in Publication Data

Lenk, John D.
  Handbook of microcomputer-based instrumentation
and controls

  Includes index.
  1. Process control—Data processing.
  2. Microcomputers. I. Title.
  TS156.8.L46   1984   629.8'95   83-3270
  ISBN O-13-380519-0

Editorial/production supervision and
  interior design: Ellen Denning
Manufacturing buyer: Anthony Caruso

© 1984 by Prentice-Hall, Inc., Englewood Cliffs, New Jersey 07632

Printed in the United States of America

10 9 8 7 6 5 4 3 2

ISBN 0-13-380519-0

PRENTICE-HALL INTERNATIONAL, INC., *London*
PRENTICE-HALL OF AUSTRALIA PTY. LIMITED, *Sydney*
EDITORA PRENTICE-HALL DO BRASIL, LTDA., *Rio de Janeiro*
PRENTICE-HALL CANADA INC., *Toronto*
PRENTICE-HALL OF INDIA PRIVATE LIMITED, *New Delhi*
PRENTICE-HALL OF JAPAN, INC., *Tokyo*
PRENTICE-HALL OF SOUTHEAST ASIA PTE. LTD., *Singapore*
WHITEHALL-BOOKS LIMITED, *Wellington, New Zealand*

This book is happily dedicated to Irene, Karen,
Tom, Brandon, Justin,
Cathy, and Michael. And a special dedication to our little Lambie.

CONTENTS

PREFACE

This book is a "crash course" in digital or microcomputer-based instrumentation and control systems. The book is written with five classes of readers in mind. First, there is the engineer who must design with (and program) microcomputer-based systems. Next is the technician who must service digital instrumentation and control systems. Then there is the programmer/analyst who wants to relate programs and software to microcomputer-based equipment. Finally, but not of least importance, are students and hobbyists who want an introduction to microprocessor-based equipment.

The various classes of readers start from a different learning point. Obviously, engineers and technicians understand electronics, but they may have little knowledge of programmed devices or no knowledge of control and instrumentation systems. Programmer/analysts may be expert in computer language and systems but know nothing of control and instrumentation systems, particularly microprocessor-based systems. The student/hobbyists may have only an elementary knowledge of electronics and no understanding of digital or programmed equipment.

This book bridges the gaps by bringing all these readers up to the same point of understanding. This is done in a unique manner, following the tradition of the author's best-sellers. The descriptions of how the devices operate are technically accurate (to satisfy the technicians and engineers) but are written in simple, nontechnical terms wherever possible (for the benefit of programmers/students/hobbyists).

The first half of the book is devoted to the basic elements and theory of both instrumentation/control equipment and microcomputers. This first half is written in review or summary form to cover the widest possible range of subjects. The second half of the book describes actual control and instrumentation systems now in use throughout the industry. The second half also describes the programs and programming methods for this equipment. Thus, the book gives the reader both a detailed look at the real world of microcomputer-based instrumentation and control, and the background necessary to understand the equipment.

Chapter 1 provides an introduction to microprocessor-based control and instrumentation systems.

Chapter 2 reviews and summarizes the sensing elements and transducers found in control and instrumentation systems. The chapter also describes the basics of signal conditioning, measurement circuits, and control elements (actuators, transmitters, etc.) common to typical industrial control automation systems.

Chapter 3 reviews and summarizes microcomputers and microprocessor-based digital equipment. Although the review is thorough, the subjects discussed in this chapter are those necessary to understand the equipment described in Chapters 4 and 5.

Chapter 4 discusses and actual system that combines the two basic functions of control/instrumentation (Chapter 2) and microcomputer operation (Chapter 3).

Chapter 5 discusses how the system discussed in Chapter 4 can be programmed to perform the various control and instrumentation functions. The discussion includes block diagram descriptions, programming techniques, and sample programs for the system.

Many professionals have contributed their talent and knowledge to the preparation of this book. The author gratefully acknowledges that the tremendous effort required to make this book such a comprehensive work is impossible for one person, and he wishes to thank all who have contributed directly and indirectly.

Special thanks are due to the following: Dick Harmon and Glenn Green of Hewlett-Packard; Lothar Stern of Motorola Semiconductor Products, Inc.; Debra Siefert of Tektronix; Steve Bourque of Texas Instruments Incorporated; and Cheryl Gartenberg of United Technologies Mostek.

The author extends his gratitude to Dave Boelio, Hank Kennedy, John Davis, Jerry Slawney, Art Rittenberg, and Don Schaefer of Prentice-Hall. Their faith in the author has given him encouragement, and their editorial/marketing expertise has made many of the author's books best-sellers. The author also wishes to thank Joseph A. Labok of Los Angeles Valley College for his help and encouragement.

JOHN D. LENK

1

INTRODUCTION TO MICROCOMPUTER–BASED INSTRUMENTATION AND CONTROLS

Microcomputer-based instrumentation and control systems can be very complex, or relatively simple, depending on the application. For example, at the relatively simple end of the scale, the fuel injection system of an automotive engine contains sensors to monitor engine and driving conditions such as compression, altitude, rotation, and speed. Information from those sensors is converted into control signals by a computer or computer-like device such as a microprocessor or controller. In turn, the signals are converted into commands that control the engine's performance. The commands regulate fuel air-gasoline mixture, amount of fuel, rate of fuel flow, and so on. Thus, the engine is controlled or adjusted for optimum performance despite constantly changing operating conditions.

For an example of a more complex control and instrumentation system, consider an automated plant such as a petroleum refinery. The basic elements of such a system are shown in Fig. 1-1. Special devices called *transducers* or *sensors* (or possibly "pickups," although that is a slang term) are installed at many points along the refining process. The transducers measure the conditions or state of *process variables* at those points. Typical process variables could include temperature, pressure, rate of flow, chemical content, density, and so on, of the petroleum being refined. Any deviation from normal measurement (abnormal temperature, incorrect pressures, etc.) must be corrected instantly to

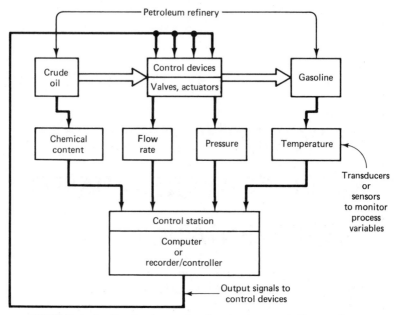

FIGURE 1-1   Basic elements of an instrumentation and control system for a petroleum refinery.

keep the petroleum flowing without interruption and to ensure that the refinery output is of proper quality.

The output from each transducer or sensor is transduced, or converted, to a corresponding signal (usually electric but possibly pneumatic in some older systems) and sent to a control center. That is, a process variable (temperature, pressure, etc.) is converted to a corresponding electrical signal in a form that can be accepted by a control station or device.

There are many types of control stations. In the older, noncomputer systems, some form of *recorder-controller* is often used as the basic element. A recorder-controller prints a continuous record of the condition or state of a process variable and compares the condition with a normal or desired value (often called a *set point*) expected at that stage in a process. Any deviation from normal produces an output signal from the recorder-controller that corresponds to the *amount of deviation* as well as the *phase of deviation*. That is, the signal indicates whether the condition or state of the process variable is above or below the value indicated by the set point, and by how much. The recorder-controller output signal is sent to an *actuator* such as an electromagnetic valve or possibly a motor-driven device, which restores the process variable to the normal value.

In a large control system such as a petroleum refinery, there usually is a complex interrelationship among the process variables. This means that if one variable changes, that change usually affects all other variables. For example, an increase in the temperature of a liquid in a refining tank could also raise the pressure on that liquid in the tank. Thus, if one variable changes, the set point of all the controllers should be readjusted to compensate for those changes. So complex is the interrelationship, however, that even an experienced operator cannot make all the readjustments required for the most efficient and profitable operation.

To overcome these problems, some form of digital computer is used in most present-day control and instrumentation systems. These can be conventional larger computers or the new and smaller microcomputer or minicomputer. Similarly, there are some systems that use a microprocessor-based instrument as the basic control element. Whichever type of computer is used, signals from the transducers are converted to corresponding numerical quantities that are fed to the computer. This relationship is shown in Fig. 1–2. That is, a physical quantity (pressure, temperature, etc.) is converted to an electrical signal by the transducer. In turn, an electrical signal is converted to a numerical quantity in a form suitable for the computer.

Because of the high speed involved, the computer or microprocessor-

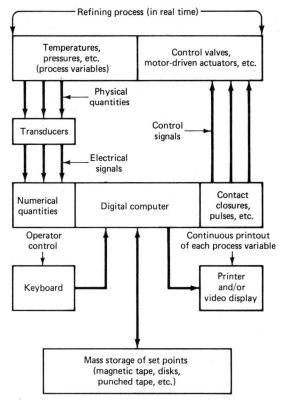

FIGURE 1-2 Basic elements of a computer-based instrumentation and control system.

based controller is able to calculate the effects of every change in the interrelationship among the variables and quickly produce output signals that adjust the set point of each controller to produce the most efficient operation. In the more sophisticated systems discussed in this book, the computer replaces the older recorder-controller completely. In these advanced systems we describe here, the computer continuously prints out the condition or state of each process variable (usually on a printer similar to that of a business computer or work processor), stores the various set points in memory (typically on magnetic tape, disks, and punched tape), and adjusts the set points as required. The computer then compares the input signals from the transducers with the readjusted set points and sends appropriate signals to the various actuators.

1-1 RELATIONSHIPS AMONG THE ELEMENTS OF A MICROCOMPUTER-BASED CONTROL AND INSTRUMENTATION SYSTEM

There are at least three, and possibly four, elements in any control and instrumentation system, in addition to the basic control element (computer, microprocessor, etc.). These elements include the sensing elements or transducers, the measurement and signal conditioning elements, the control devices or actuators, and possibly instrumentation devices.

1-1.1 Sensing Elements and Transducers

A typical automatic control system starts with a primary sensing element (sensor or transducer) that senses a condition, state, or value of a process variable and produces an output that reflects a condition. Typically, the electrical signal output is an *analog* of the process variable condition. For example, the output could be a voltage where 1 volt represents 1 pound of pressure, or a current where a 1-milliampere change in current represents a 1-degree change in temperature. There are many types of transducers used in present-day control systems. Among them are sensors of motion and force (acceleration, attitude, displacement, force, torque, pressure, speed, velocity, strain), fluid conditions (flow, pressure, and liquid level), humidity, moisture, light, radioactivity, temperature, and sound. Such transducers are discussed in Chapter 2. Although every possible type or variation of transducer or sensor cannot be included in one book, the coverage does include a full cross section of transducers used in present-day control systems. For a more complete presentation of transducer basics, your attention is called to the author's *Handbook of Controls and Instrumentation* (Englewood Cliffs, N.J.: Prentice-Hall, Inc., 1980).

1-1.2   Measurement and Signal Conditioning Elements

Measurement is an important part of any control and instrumentation system. For example, we measure the temperature and pressure of a process variable, the rate of flow, the acidity, and much more. The measurement is needed not only to learn the condition or quantity of a variable, but also to get a value that can be compared with a standard value (the set-point value) to obtain an *error signal*. The error signal is used to operate an actuator, which causes the process variable to return to a predetermined value.

In a typical control system, we start by using a sensor to translate the condition or quantity of a process variable to an electrical or pressure output signal. Chapter 2 concerns some of the methods generally used to measure such signals. Typical values to be measured include current, voltage, resistance, capacitance, inductance, frequency, and pulse rate. In microcomputer-based systems, the measurement process also involves conversion from analog values (where voltage represents pressure, etc.) to digital values, and vice versa. This is because computers use digital pulses, and require both analog-to-digital (A/D) and digital-to-analog (D/A) circuits. The basic functions of such circuits are discussed in Chapter 2.

1-1.3   Control Devices and Actuators

In most instances, the final stage of any control system consists of (1) a switch or contact that may be opened or closed, (2) a valve that may be fully opened or closed or adjusted to some position between the two extremes, (3) an electromagnetic device that may be energized by an electrical current to perform some mechanical or electrical function, and (4) a motor that may be started, stopped, or reversed (typically in steps) or whose running speed may be varied.

Between a primary sensing element, which initiates a control function, and a final actuator there may be many control elements, each performing a definite function in the system. Such devices are switches, valves, solenoids, relays, electron tubes, and (in most present-day systems) solid-state control elements. Chapter 2 covers some of the most commonly used elements, explains their operation, and shows how they fit into modern control systems.

1-1.4   Instrumentation, Readout Devices, and the Computer

In a sense, all the devices described in this book could be called instruments or instrumentation. However, we reserve these terms to those devices that indicate, transmit, or record signals between other elements in a system. In older and simpler systems, the indicators are basic pressure gauges, thermometers, electrical meters, panel lights that indicate an event (such as a red light that flashes when the fluid in a tank has reached a certain level), and similar devices. In computer-based systems, the indicators usually take the form of digital readouts, or possibly displays on a video terminal, or a printout on an output printer. In Chapters 4 and 5 we discuss a system where the printout is on a desk-top calculator (which also functions as the controller terminal).

Because of the complexity of even a simple microcomputer, a full description of computers is beyond the scope of this book. However, Chapter 3 discusses the elements of microcomputers, particularly as they apply to a control and instrumentation system. For a full presentation of modern computer basics, your attention is called to the author's best-selling *Handbook of Microprocessors, Microcomputers, and Minicomputers* (Englewood Cliffs, N.J.: Prentice-Hall, Inc. 1979) or the *Handbook of Digital Electronics* (Englewood Cliffs, N.J.: Prentice-Hall, Inc., 1981).

If you are already familiar with the basics of control and instrumentation systems, including transducers, signal conditioning, and actuators, you can skip Chapter 2. Similarly, if you fully understand microprocessor-based computer systems, you can pass over Chapter 3. However, it is recommended that you at least skim through these two chapters before getting into detailed discussions of present-day systems and circuits found in the remaining chapters.

1-2 TYPES OF CONTROL AND INSTRUMENTATION SYSTEMS

Each industry or specialized field has its own set of automatic control systems suited to its particular requirements, and there are many variations of each system. However, all control systems (both computer and noncomputer types) fall into either of two general groups: *open-loop* or *closed-loop* systems. Furthermore, these two basic groups can be classified as *continuous* or *discontinuous* systems. In the following sections, we describe each of these four basic systems, followed by an explanation of a simple yet complete system that incorporates all the basic elements of a typical microcomputer-based control and instrumentation system (sensor, signal conditioner, indicator, recorder, controller, actuator, etc.).

1-2.1 Basic Discontinuous Open-Loop Control System

In any open-loop system, a controlling device operates independently of a process variable that is being controlled. An example of a discontinuous open-loop system is shown in Fig. 1–3. The switch is the controlling device. The room temperature is the "process variable." When the switch is closed, current flowing through the heater raises the room temperature. When the switch is opened, the room temperature starts to fall. Because operation of the switch is not af-

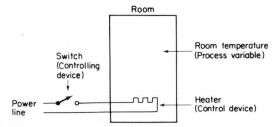

FIGURE 1-3   Basic discontinuous open-loop control system.

fected by room temperature (or the condition of the process variable) the system is open-loop. Similarly, because the control circuit can be opened and closed, the system is discontinous.

1-2.2   Basic Continuous Open-Loop Control System

A basic continuous open-loop system is shown in Fig. 1-4. Here the variable resistance is the controlling device. The resistance controls the amount of current flowing through the heater. In turn, the amount of current determines the room temperature. Again, the condition of the process variable (room temperature) does not affect operation of the controlling device (variable resistance), so the system is open-loop. However, because the control circuit is always closed and in operation, the system is continuous.

In most continuous open-loop systems, a *calibrated controlling device* must be used to place the process variable at the desired value. In the example shown in Fig. 1-4, the dial that operates the variable resistance can be calibrated in terms of desired room temperature. However, variations such as opening and closing windows and doors to the room affect such calibrations. From a practical standpoint, the variable resistance has no means for sensing such changes and making adjustments to meet them.

In most control systems, it is usually desired that the process variable be kept at a constant value. If an open-loop system such as that shown in Fig. 1-4

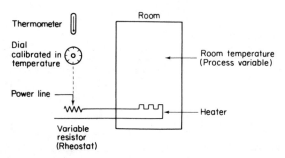

FIGURE 1-4   Basic continuous open-loop control system.

is used, an *indicating device* such as a thermometer must be used to show the condition of the process variable (room temperature) at all times. Then an operator must be posted at the controlling device to decrease the variable resistance (thus increasing current flow and heat) should the room temperature fall below the desired value (set point) or to increase the variable resistance should the temperature rise above that value.

1-2.3   Basic Discontinuous Closed-Loop Control System

An obvious disadvantage of an open-loop system is the lack of automatic control. That is, the process variable (or room temperature in our case) is not monitored constantly and is not maintained at a desired value, except by a human operator. Even a simple closed-loop system can overcome that disadvantage. Take the example of Fig. 1–5, which is a simplified version of a typical thermostat-controlled room heater. In this case, a gas heater is used. The flow of gas to the burners is controlled by a valve, which, in turn, is operated by current through a thermostat. (As a matter of interest, the current is usually generated by a *thermocouple* placed next to the heater's pilot element. Thermocouples are discussed in Chapter 2. For now, we are interested in how the gas burners are controlled by a thermostat.)

As shown in Fig. 1–5, a thermostat (or controlling device) is a bimetallic strip that bends in accordance with the temperature to which it is subjected. Two different metals are bonded together. Each metal expands and contracts (with changes in temperature) at a different rate, so the strip tends to bend when

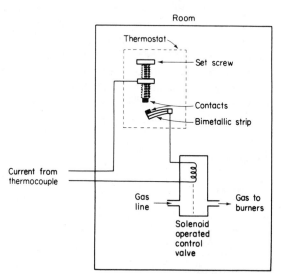

FIGURE 1-5   Basic discontinuous closed-loop control system.

temperature changes. The thermostat is mounted inside the room, usually on a wall away from the heater register. A setscrew, shown in Fig. 1–5, is adjusted so that *at the desired temperature* the contact points barely touch, and the circuit to the heater valve is completed. The desired temperature is thus the set point.

As room temperature rises above the set point, the bimetallic strip bends farther from its existing position, the contact points separate, and the circuit to the heater control valve is opened. The control valve then shuts off gas to the burners, and room temperature begins to drop. When room temperature drops below the set point, the bimetallic strip straightens enough so that the contact points touch once more. The circuit is now completed, the control valve opens, gas is applied to the burners, and the room temperature rises toward the set point. In this way, the room temperature is kept constant within a narrow *range* or *band*.

The system shown in Fig. 1–5 is an example of *fully automatic control.* The controlling device, or thermostat, compares the actual value of the process variable (room temperature) with the value corresponding to the set point. Any difference, or deviation, is noted, as well as the phase of the difference (whether the actual value of the process variable is greater or less than the value corresponding to the set point). The controller then acts in a direction to reduce the deviation to zero.

The system of Fig. 1–5 uses *feedback,* or the feeding back of energy from the process variable to the controlling element. In this case, it is the heat with the room that is applied (or fed back) to the thermostat. Because of this feedback, also known as an *error signal,* the closed-loop system lends itself to automatic process control, thus eliminating the need for a human operator. In addition to reducing costs, this is generally more reliable since the factor of human fatigue is absent, and control is possible under conditions where a human operator could not function rapidly enough or where the environment is hazardous.

1–2.4 Basic Closed-Loop System with Microcomputer Control

Now let us consider a system that corresponds more closely to those found in present-day industry or other control applications. An example of such a system is shown in Fig. 1–6. Here, the system involves keeping the temperature of a process variable (a liquid in this case) at a constant temperature. The liquid flows through a container that is heated by steam. Passage of steam to the jacket surrounding the container is controlled by a valve. In turn, the valve is controlled by the system shown in Fig. 1–6.

A transducer senses the condition of the process variable. In our system, the transducer is used to sense the temperature of the liquid, and to produce a corresponding electrical signal. That signal is applied through a scanner or multiplexer (MUX) to a signal conditioner. The scanner or MUX makes it

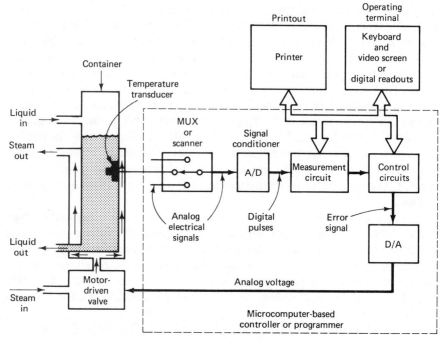

FIGURE 1-6   Basic closed-loop system with microcomputer control.

possible for the controller to sample the signals of many transducers throughout a complex system. Rotary switches are used as scanners in older systems. Present-day control systems using solid-state electronic scanners can sample hundreds (or possibly thousands) of process variables (transducer outputs) in 1 second.

The signal conditioner shown in Fig. 1–6 between the transducer and the measurement circuits of the microcomputer-based controller or programmer is A/D, analog-to-digital. This is because the transducer produces an electrical voltage or current, whereas the controller responds only to digital pulses. Note that the signal conditioning process can be performed in the transducer itself, or in the controller, or in both, depending on the system. In many cases, signal conditioning is a simple matter of converting from a low voltage (typically a few millivolts produced by a transducer) to a higher voltage (typically 5 V, used by many present-day microcomputers) or conversion of direct current to alternating current, and vice versa. In microcomputer-based systems, signal conditioning always involves both A/D and D/A conversion.

The measurement circuit within the controller or programmer compares the digital pulses representing the process variable with a set point or other reference. Typically, some form of *terminal* is used to set and operate the controller or programmer. In some cases, the terminal is the same as for any other type of computer, complete with keyboard and video screen. In other cases, the terminal has digital readouts and a keyboard. Similarly, there are controllers or programmers that have their own controls and do not require any form of terminal. Chapters 4 and 5 describe a system where a *multiprogrammer* is operated by a desk-top *calculator* which has both indicator (digital readout) and recorder (paper printout) functions.

No matter what system is used, the signal from the measuring circuits is applied to the control circuits within the controller or programmer, as shown in Fig. 1–6. The control circuits also receive set-point or reference signals (from the terminal or other operating controls, such as the keyboard of a calculator) that correspond to the predetermined values at which the process variables are to be kept. The controller or programmer circuits compare the two signals and, if there is a difference or deviation between them, determines the amount and phase of the deviation.

In simple terms, the controller or programmer determines if the value of the process variable is greater or less than the set-point value. The control circuits then generate an error signal (in the form of digital pulses) that corresponds to the amount and phase of the deviation. This error signal is converted to an analog voltage suitable to operate the motor-driven valve. Depending on the phase of the error signal, the opening of the valve is increased or decreased, thus permitting more or less steam to flow to the container steam jacket so as to increase or decrease the value of the process variable (the temperature of the liquid in our case).

Circuits within the controller or programmer act to reduce the deviation to zero. Thus, if the actual value of the process variable rises a certain amount above the set-point value, the valve is closed and the steam is cut off. As a result, the process variable (liquid temperature) starts to decrease. When this value falls below the set-point value, the valve is opened and steam flows to rise again. In this way, the process variable value (temperature) is kept constant between predetermined limits, or within an *error band.*

It is often desirable to keep a continuous written record of the process variables. For that reason, the measurement signals applied to the terminal (video screen or digital readout) are also available to other permanent recording instruments. The output printer shown in Fig. 1–6 is quite common, and provides a written record similar to that of a word processor or electric typewriter. Other common recorders are magnetic tape or disk recorders (to provide permanent magnetic storage) or an X–Y plotter (to provide a permanent graph). In the system described in Chapters 4 and 5, the paper tape of the calculator provides a permanent record of all process variables.

2

ELEMENTS OF CONTROL AND INSTRUMENTATION SYSTEMS

In this chapter we review and summarize the sensing elements and transducers found in control and instrumentation systems. We also describe the basics of signal conditioning, measurement circuits, and control elements (including actuators and transmitters) common to typical industrial automation systems.

2-1 BASIC MEASURING AND CONTROL SYSTEMS

As shown in Fig. 2-1, a basic measuring system consists of a transducer, which converts the quantity or condition to be measured (the *measurand*) into a usable electrical signal. Note that the terms *transducer* and *sensor* are often interchanged, both in this book and in the control/instrumentation field. Specifically, a transducer is the complete device used to provide an output in response to a specific measurand. A sensor is the element in a transducer that actually senses the measurand. Thus, a transducer may only contain a sensor. More likely, the transducer contains both the sensor and the transducing element, and may even contain the signal conditioning circuits.

Sometimes a transducer signal output is usable "as is." Most often, however, a transducer signal is modified by signal conditioning circuits. For a

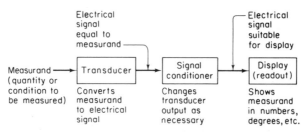

FIGURE 2-1   Basic electronic measuring system.

simple measuring system such as that shown in Fig. 2–1, the conditioned signal is then applied to a display, such as an analog or digital meter, chart recorder, or numerical printout, where the measurand appears in readable form such as numbers, degrees, and so on.

For a control system such as that shown in Fig. 2–2, the output of the signal conditioner is applied to a controller or other control device. In turn, the controller produces an output (based on the measured input) to operate control devices such as valves, actuators, motors, and so. For example, in a very simple control system, a transducer measures pressure in a tank and produces a corresponding output that is applied to a controller through signal conditioning circuits. The controller then operates a valve that controls the pressure in the tank. With such a closed-loop system (Chapter 1), tank pressure can be maintained at any desired value within certain limits.

Signal conditioning circuits can be part of a transducer or controller, or both. There are two basic reasons for such variety. First, a controller may be a simple electromechanical device such as a relay, or a very complex unit such as a digital computer (in the case of this book, a microcomputer based on operation of a microprocessor). The signals required by each of these controllers are quite different. A relay can be operated with simple d-c voltage from a resistance-type transducer, but a microcomputer requires a digital pulse input.

Second, even if only one controller is used, there are many types of transducers that must be reconciled to a common input. For example, assume that a controller requires a d-c input and that some of the transducers in the control system produce an a-c output. Under these conditions, the a-c outputs must be *rectified* and *demodulated* to direct current. Or, assume that a controller requires signals in the 5–V range, and that some of the transducers produce outputs in the millivolt range. Obviously, these signals must be *amplified* to the 5-V range.

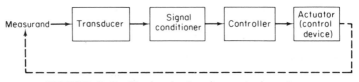

FIGURE 2-2   Basic electronic control system.

2-2 BASIC TRANSDUCER DEFINITIONS AND METHODS

In this section we describe how a transducer can be classified or described, and summarize all the transduction methods in common use.

2-2.1 Describing a Transducer

There are many ways to describe a transducer. One way is to answer the following questions.

1. What is the *measurand,* or what is to be measured by the transducer (acceleration, motion, etc.)?

2. What is the *transduction principle* or the nature of operation (resistive, capacitive, etc.)?

3. What is the *sensing element* (bellows, moving arm, etc.)?

4. What is the *measuring range,* or upper and lower limits of the measurand to be measured (± 5 g's of gravity, $\pm 50°$ of angular rotation, etc.)?

5. What is the *output signal range,* or upper and lower limits of the output signal (± 5 V dc, 0 to 10 mV, etc.)?

6. What are the *special features,* if any (signal conditioning circuits as part of the transducer, waterproof case, etc.)?

2-2.2 Summary of Transduction Methods

The following is a summary of the transduction or sensing methods in common use. Some specific examples of transducers using these sensing methods are discussed beginning in Sec. 2-3.

Resistive Transduction. As shown in Fig. 2-3, the measurand is converted into a change of resistance. The resistance change can be in either a conductor or a semiconductor and can be accomplished by various means. The most common means of changing resistance is by sliding a wiper or contact arm along a resistance element. Other ways to change resistance include drying or wetting of materials such as salts, applying mechanical stress, and heating or cooling a resistance element.

Strain-Gage Transduction. The strain gage is a special form of resistive transducer, as shown in Fig. 2-4. Here, the measurand is converted into resistance change by mechanical stress or strain. Typically, a strain-gage transducer is used in a *bridge circuit,* a fixed reference or excitation voltage is applied, and the output is a variable voltage. The amplitude of the variable voltage indicates the amount of strain. Either a-c or d-c excitation voltages

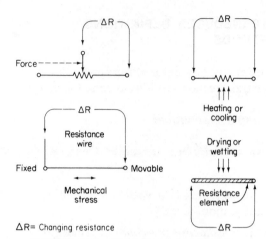

FIGURE 2-3   Resistive transduction.

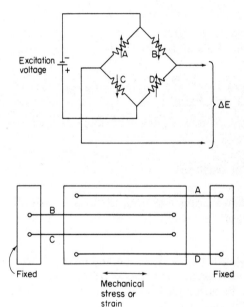

FIGURE 2-4   Strain-gage transduction.

can be used, depending on what is required at the output (to match other transducers in the system).

Figure 2–4 shows both the physical construction and the schematic wiring of a bridge-type strain-gage transducer. The upward arrows on the schematic indicate increasing resistances, and the downward arrows show decreasing resistance. Note that resistances A and D increase but resistances B and C decrease for a strain in one direction. If the direction of strain is reversed, the resistance changes reverse (A and D decrease, B and C increase). These resistance changes cause the output voltage to change polarity. Thus, output voltage indicates both direction and amount of strain (as shown by the polarity and amplitude of the voltage, respectively).

Potentiometric Transduction.   As shown in Fig. 2–5, potentiometeric transduction is another form of resistance transducer. Here, a resistance element is connected as a potentiometer, rather than as the simple variable resistance shown in Fig. 2–4. In the circuit of Fig. 2–5, movement of the wiper arm causes a change in the ratio (*resistance ratio*) between the resistance from one end of the element to the wiper arm, and the resistance of the total element. For a typical application, an a-c or d-c reference voltage is applied, and the output is a *voltage ratio*. For example, if the reference voltage is 10 V and the arm is at the halfway (50%) point on a resistance element, the output is 5 V. If the arm is moved up to the 75% point by the measurand, the output is 7.5 V.

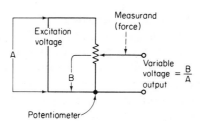

FIGURE 2–5   Potentiometric transduction.

Capacitive Transduction.   As shown in Fig. 2–6, the measurand is converted into a change of capacitance. A capacitor consists essentially of two conductors or plates separated by an insulator or dielectric. In a capacitive transducer, the change of capacitance occurs typically when a displacement of a sensing element causes one plate to move toward or away from the other plate. Sometimes the moving plate is the sensing element (such as when one plate is formed by a diaphragm). In other cases, both plates are stationary, and the change occurs in the dielectric, such as when the dielectric is a liquid that rises and falls between the plates. Capacitive transducers are often used in a bridge circuit similar to that of Fig. 2–4, with an a-c excitation voltage applied.

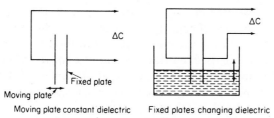

FIGURE 2-6 Capacitive transduction.

Inductive Transduction. As shown in Fig. 2-7, the measurand is converted into a change of self-inductance of a single coil. This change in self-inductance is usually done by displacement of the coil core, which is linked or attached to a mechanical sensing element. Inductive transducers are often used in bridge circuits similar to that of Fig. 2-4, with an a-c excitation voltage.

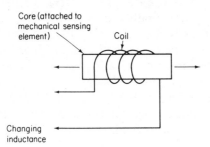

FIGURE 2-7   Inductive transduction.

Electromagnetic Transduction. As shown in Fig. 2-8, the measurand is converted into a voltage induced in a conductor by a change in magnetic flux. This transducer is thus self-generating and needs no excitation voltage. Change in magnetic flux is usually done by relative motion between a magnet or a piece of magnetic material and an electromagnet (which is a coil with iron or other magnetic metal core). Phonograph pickups and magnetic microphones are common examples of electromagnetic transducers. A microphone converts (transduces) sound waves into a signal voltage. A phonograph pickup converts mechanical motion (caused by the pickup moving over the record surface) into voltage.

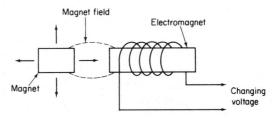

FIGURE 2-8   Electromagnetic transduction.

Reluctive Transduction. As shown in Fig. 2-9, the measurand is converted into an a-c voltage change by a change in the reluctance path between two or more coils, with a-c excitation applied to the coil system. Generally, reluctive transducers are used in bridge circuits or as *differential transformers*. Change in reluctance is generally done by displacement of a magnetic core (sometimes called the *armature*) linked to a mechanical sensing element. Reluctive transducers require an a-c excitation voltage.

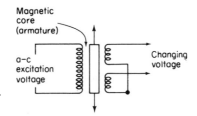

FIGURE 2-9 Reluctive transduction.

Piezoelectric Transduction. As shown in Fig. 2–10, the measurand is converted into a voltage generated by crystals (when mechanically stressed). In some piezoelectric transducers, the electrostatic charge between the two plates (which compress the crystals) is changed by the measurand. Mechanical stress is developed by tension, stress, compression, or bending of the crystals between the plates. In turn, these forces are exerted by the sensing element connected to the plates. Piezoelectric transducers are self-generating and thus require no excitation voltage.

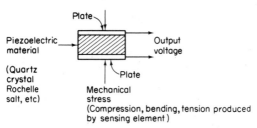

FIGURE 2-10 Piezoelectric transduction.

Photoconductive Transduction. As shown in Fig. 2–11, the measurand is converted into a change in resistance (or the reciprocal of resistance, which is conductance) of a semiconductor material (silicon, selenium, germanium) by a change in the amount of light striking the material. In some photoconductive transducers the change of light is produced by a moving shutter between a light source and the semiconductor material. The shutter is linked to a sensing element. In other photoconductive transducers, the resistance change is produced entirely by a change in light surrounding the semiconductor material. Photoconductive transducers are often used in bridge circuits with d-c excitation.

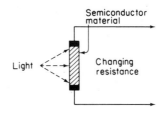

FIGURE 2-11 Photoconductive transduction.

Photovoltaic transduction.   As shown in Fig. 2–12, the measurand is converted into a voltage generated when light strikes the junction between certain dissimilar materials in a photovoltaic transducer. Since photovoltaic transducers are self-generating, no excitation voltage is required, so they can be used for the direct measurement of light intensity. In some transducers, the photovoltatic element is used with a fixed light source and a moving shutter operated by the measurand sensing element.

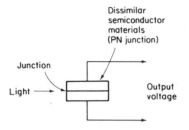

FIGURE 2-12   Photovoltaic transduction.

2-3   MOTION AND FORCE SENSORS

Motion and force sensors can be classified by the method of sensing or by the condition they sense. In this section we use the latter classification and discuss devices that sense linear motion, angular motion, speed of rotation, compression, tension, torque, acceleration, vibration, and attitude.

2-3.1   *Linear-Motion Sensors*

The *linear-motion potentiometer* shown in Fig. 2–13 is the most basic type of linear-motion sensor, and operates by converting linear motion into changes in resistance. The slider is moved over the resistance element by means of an arm

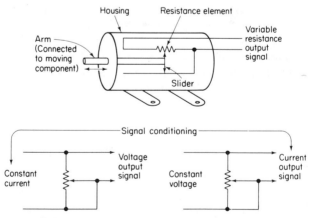

FIGURE 2-13   Linear-motion potentiometer.

connected to the moving component. As the slider is moved by the arm, the resistance of the potentiometer is varied. The resistance change is an indication of the amount of linear movement, whereas the direction of movement is indicated by whether the resistance is increasing or decreasing.

The *linear-motion variable inductor* shown in Fig. 2–14 is another basic type of linear-motion sensor. Here, the inductance of the device is increased as an iron core is moved farther into the coil, and reduced as the core moves out of the coil. Since movement of the core is determined by the motion of a moving component, the inductance changes are proportional to the linear motion of the component, and the direction of these changes (increasing or decreasing) is an indication of the direction of motion.

The sensor of Fig. 2–14 can also be used as an inductor in the frequency control circuit of an oscillator as shown in Fig. 2–15. The output frequency of the oscillator varies in accordance with linear motion. A large change in frequency indicates a greater amount of motion. Similarly, the direction of frequency change (increasing or decreasing) indicates the direction of motion.

Linear motion can be converted to corresponding changes in capacitance by means of a *linear-motion variable capacitor,* shown in Fig. 2–16. The direction of motion is detected by an increase or decrease in capacitance, while the change in capacitance is proportional to the amount of movement. The sensor of Fig. 2–16 can also be used in the frequency control circuit of the oscillator. The circuit is the same as shown in Fig. 2–15 except that the inductor is fixed and the capacitor is variable.

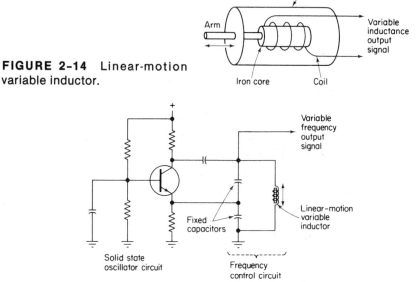

FIGURE 2–14 Linear-motion variable inductor.

FIGURE 2–15 Using a linear-motion variable inductor in an oscillator frequency control circuit.

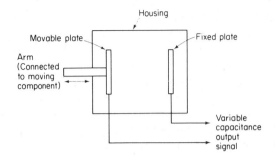

FIGURE 2–16   Linear-motion variable capacitor.

The *linear variable differential transformer* (LVDT) shown in Fig. 2–17 is another widely used linear-motion sensor. As the core is moved back and forth by the moving component, the transformer produces an a-c output signal that reflects the amount and direction of the component movement. Some systems require a d-c output voltage signal to match the output signals of other transducers. In such a case, a signal conditioning circuit (known as a *phase-sensitive demodulator*) similar to that shown in Fig. 2–18 can be used. When the core is in the null or center position, the voltage across the resistors are equal and opposite, producing a net output of zero. Any physical displacement of the core causes the voltage across one resistor to increase, with a corresponding decrease in voltage across the other resistor. The difference between the two voltages appears across the output terminals and produces a measure of the physical position of the core (and the moving component). The amplitude of the d-c voltage indicates the amount of deviation from the null or center position. The polarity of the d-c output indicates the direction of movement from the null position.

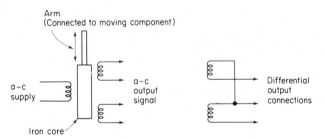

FIGURE 2–17   Linear variable differential transformer (LVDT).

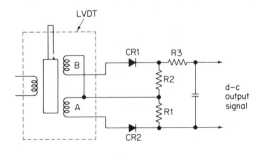

FIGURE 2–18   LVDT with d-c output signal.

2-3.2   Angular-Motion Sensors

The *angular-motion potentiometer* shown in Fig. 2–19 is the most basic of the angular-motion sensors. The potentiometer of Fig. 2–19 resembles the linear-motion potentiometer shown in Fig. 2–13 except that the resistance element is circular instead of straight. The slider is mounted on a shaft, and as the shaft is rotated the slider moves over the resistance element. The resistance of the potentiometer changes in proportion to the angular motion, and the direction of rotation is determined by whether the resistance is increasing or decreasing.

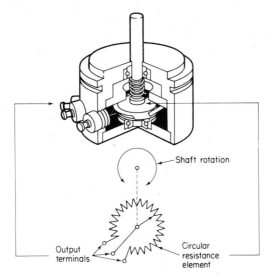

FIGURE 2-19   Angular-motion potentiometer.

The *angular-motion variable capacitor* shown in Fig. 2–20 is another basic angular-motion sensor. The capacitance is a function of the degree of angular rotation, since the rotating component is coupled to the capacitor shaft. The direction of rotation is determined by whether the capacitance is increasing or decreasing.

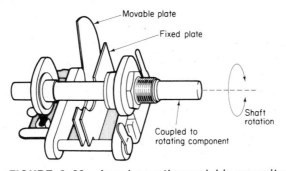

FIGURE 2-20   Angular-motion variable capacitor.

The *rotary variable differential transformer* (RVDT) shown in Fig. 2–21 is a variation of the LVDT described in Sec. 2–3.1. With the RVDT, the core is cam-shaped and is rotated between the transformer windings by means of a shaft. Both the amount of angular motion and the direction are obtained from the voltage and phase of the RVDT output signal (which is often coverted to direct current using a phase-sensitive demodulator similar to that of Fig. 2–18).

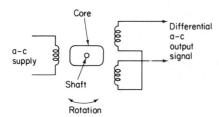

FIGURE 2-21   Rotary variable differential transformer (RVDT).

The *variable-reluctance transducer* shown in Fig. 2–22 is another angular-motion sensor somewhat like the RVDT. Any rotary displacement of the shaft and armature from the null position results in a differential-voltage output. The amplitude of this voltage is directly proportional to the amount of displacement. The phase of the output voltage indicates the direction of the angular displacement. As in the case of the LVDT and RVDT, a signal conditioning circuit is used in systems that require a d-c voltage output.

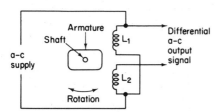

FIGURE 2-22   Variable-reluctance transducer.

2-3.3   Speed of Rotation Sensors

There are a number of methods for sensing the speed of rotation of some rotating component, such as a motor. One of the most basic methods is the *electrical tachometer* shown in Fig. 2–23. Here, the shaft of the rotating component is coupled to the shaft of a small d-c generator. The output voltage of the generator is fed to a voltmeter. The scale of the voltmeter is calibrated in units of rpm (revolutions per minute). With the electrical tachometer, an increase in rotational speed produces a higher voltage, which, in turn, appears as a higher-rpm indication.

The *rotating disk and light sensor* shown in Fig. 2–24 is another method for measuring speed of rotation. When the disk is rotated so that a hole appears

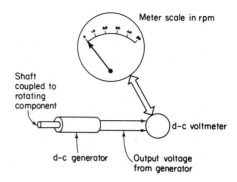

FIGURE 2-23 Electrical tacho-meter.

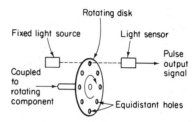

FIGURE 2-24 Speed of rotation sensor using rotating disk and light sensor.

between the sensor and the light source, the sensor produces an output voltage. If the disk is rotating steadily, the sensor produces "pulses" of voltage (one pulse for each hole). These pulses are similar to the voltage pulses found in computers and other digital electronic equipment. The pulses can be converted to an rpm indication by a frequency-measuring device or counter such as that described in Sec. 2-13.

The *magnetic pickup* shown in Fig. 2-25 is one of the most common methods of measuring speed of rotation. When the wheel is rotated and the teeth pass through the magnetic field around the coil, a voltage pulse is induced in the coil. The frequency of the pulses depends on the number of teeth and the speed of rotation. Since the number of teeth is known, the pulse frequency can be related directly to rpm, and can be converted directly to rpm when a counter (Sec. 2-13) is used.

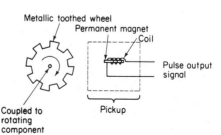

FIGURE 2-25 Speed of rotation sensor using magnetic pickup.

2-3.4   Compressor Sensors

One of the most common compression or force sensors is the *bonded wire strain gage,* shown in Fig. 2–26. (Operation of a strain gage is described in Sec. 2–2.2 and shown in Fig. 2–4.) The strain gage of Fig. 2–26 consists of a length of fine wire arranged in the form of a grid and bonded to a paper or plastic sheet. A typical application that illustrates the operating principle of the bonded wire strain gage is that of the *load cell,* shown in Fig. 2–27. In this system the gage is cemented to the side of a steel column. In turn, the column is enclosed in a metal housing so that only the end of the column protrudes through the top.

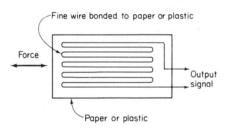

FIGURE 2-26   Bonded wire strain gage.

When heavy pressure is applied to the top, the column and the strain gage cemented to the side are compressed. As the strain gage is compressed, the length of its wire is shortened and its cross-sectional area is increased, producing a decrease in strain gage wire resistance. Load cells are generally used to measure relatively large forces, and are usually found with bridge-type signal conditioning (as shown in Fig. 2–4).

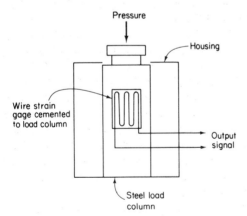

FIGURE 2-27   Load cell strain gage.

Unbonded Wire Strain Gages.   Gages such as that shown in Fig. 2–28 are often used to measure small amounts of force. When a force is applied through the rod to the spring, movement of the spring causes a corresponding movement of the posts. As a result, the strain (and the resistance) of the winding is changed, and the bridge becomes unbalanced, producing an output voltage that is proportional to the force.

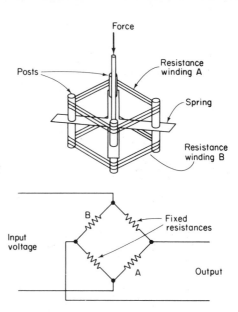

FIGURE 2-28 Unbonded wire strain gage.

Semiconductor Strain Gages. These are another form of force sensor. There are two basic types of semiconductor force sensors: the *piezoresistance* sensor and the *piezoelectric* sensor. Both types operate on the piezoeffect described in Sec. 2-2.2 and shown in Fig. 2-10. For the piezoresistance sensor shown in Fig. 2-29, the plates and silicon material become a variable resistance and can be connected in a typical bridge, as described for the wire strain gage. The applied force produces an output voltage (from the bridge) that is proportional to the amount of force. For the piezoelectric sensor shown in Fig. 2-30, a voltage (proportional to force) is developed across the plates. In some cases, the voltage can be used directly. For example, one way is to apply the voltage to a voltmeter having a scale marked in units of force (grams, ounces, etc.). However, since the voltage developed is very small, it is usually more practical to amplify the voltage through signal conditioning circuits (Sec. 2-13).

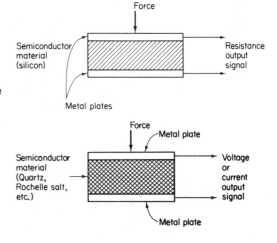

FIGURE 2-29 Piezoresistance (semiconductor) strain gage.

FIGURE 2-30 Piezoelectric (semiconductor) strain gage.

2-3.5 Tension Sensors

Bonded and unbonded wire strain gages can be used as tension sensors. The crane scale shown in Fig. 2–31 is an example of how a bonded strain gage can be used to measure the tension produced by a given load on a crane. In this case, the strain produced by the heavy load stretches a metal column to which the strain gage is cemented. Semiconductor strain gages, both piezoresistance and piezoelectric, can also be used as tension sensors.

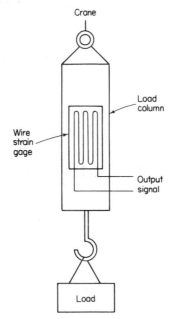

FIGURE 2-31 Tension sensor (crane scale).

2-3.6 Torque Sensors

As rotary motion is applied to a shaft, a twisting force called torque is imparted to the shaft. A bonded wire strain gage can be used as a sensor of that force as shown in Fig. 2–32. As the shaft is rotated, the twisting action of the torque stretches the wire of the gage, changing the resistance. Note that in this torque

FIGURE 2-32 Torque sensor.

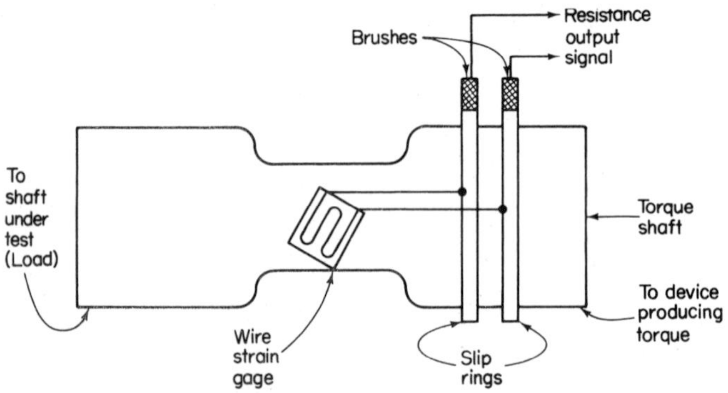

sensor system, the ends of the strain gage are brought out to the external circuit by means of slip rings and brushes similar to those used on an a-c motor or generator (permitting the shaft to rotate without snapping the connection leads).

2-3.7 Acceleration and Vibration Sensors

Where automatic control is required of vehicles such as rockets, unmanned aircraft, or space probes, there must be some method for sensing and measuring the force of acceleration. This is generally done by means of acceleration sensors or *accelerometers*. The basic sensing element of most accelerometers is a *seismic mass,* also known as a *proof mass.* Usually, the mass is restrained by a spring and a damping system as shown in Fig. 2-33. When acceleration is applied to the accelerometer, the mass moves relative to the case as shown. When acceleration stops, the spring returns the mass to its original position.

The seismic mass of a linear accelerometer is typically a circular or rectangular body, arranged to slide along a bar and restrained from motion in all directions except the sensing axis. Note the black/white circular symbol shown on the mass in Fig. 2-33. That symbol is commonly used to point out the location of the seismic mass gravitational center. Figure 2-34 shows a typical *resistance accelerometer* design. Damping is used to minimize vibration-induced noise in the output due to wiper whipping and large changes in contact resistance between the wiper and the resistance element. Similarly, there are

FIGURE 2-33 Basic acceleration sensing elements.

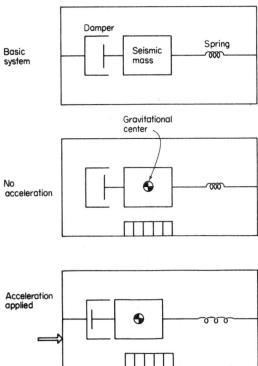

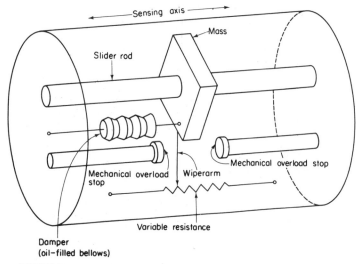

FIGURE 2-34 Typical resistance accelerometer design.

overload stops to limit wiper travel if acceleration exceeds the accelerometer range.

In addition to the basic resistance accelerometer, there are *reluctance, strain-gage,* and *piezoelectric* accelerometers used in control and instrumentation systems. Typical piezoelectric accelerometers are shown in Fig. 2-35. These designs are commonly used for vibration sensors but can also be used in other linear applications. Note the arrow and " + " symbol on the outside of the case. The arrow indicates the *sensing axis* of the accelerometer (the direction

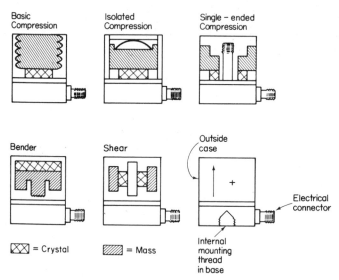

FIGURE 2-35 Typical piezoelectric accelerometer designs.

in which acceleration is measured). The " + " symbol indicates the direction in which the case must be accelerated to get an output of positive polarity. (In all the Fig. 2–35 designs, the sensing axis is at right angles to the base, and the crystals are polarized so as to minimize any output due to acceleration along all other axes.) As the base of the accelerometer is accelerated in the direction indicated by the " + " symbol, the force exerted by the mass on the crystal is increased, due to the inertia of the mass, which tends to oppose the acceleration. Since the mass is a fixed quantity, the increase of the force that the mass exerts on the crystal is proportional to acceleration. Thus, the output voltage produced by the crystal is proportional to acceleration.

Accelerometers can also be used effectively to *monitor vibration*. When a moving body is subject to vibration, that body is, in effect, accelerated alternately in one direction and then the other. Thus, a basic accelerometer can be used effectively as a *vibration sensor*. The piezoelectric sensors of Fig. 2–35 can be used as vibration sensors. There are versions of both inductive and capacitive vibration sensors. One of the most common types of vibration sensor uses a linear variable differential transformer (Fig. 2–17). Such a vibration sensor is shown in Fig. 2–36. Here, the core of the transformer is maintained in its null position by means of rods connected to flexible reeds at either end. The core itself is the mass of this sensor. As the sensor moves up and down as a result of vibration, the output voltage from the transformer is an a-c signal. The phase of the signal shifts alternately in one direction and then the other, in response to each vibration. The magnitude of the output signal depends on the amplitude of the vibration. As in the case of other sensors using LVDT, the output signal of a vibration sensor may be rectified to produce a d-c voltage that is compatible with other sensors. The magnitude of the d-c voltage is an indication of vibration amplitude.

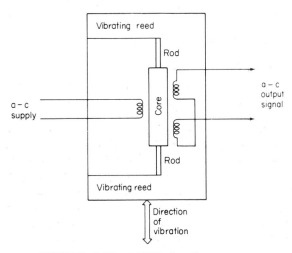

FIGURE 2-36 LVDT vibration sensor.

2-4   FLUID SENSORS

Fluid sensors can be classified by the method of sensing or by the condition they sense. In this section we use the latter classification to cover devices that sense the three most commonly measured conditions of fluid: *flow, pressure,* and *liquid level.*

2-4.1   Fluid-Flow Sensors

There are many processes that require a means for measuring fluid flow, and there are two conditions of particular importance. In one case it is necessary to measure the *total quantity* of the fluid flow. In the other case, the most important factor is the *rate of flow,* or the amount of fluid passing a given point during a given period of time. One of the most common methods for sensing the rate of fluid flow is to place an obstruction in the path of the fluid, and measure the difference is pressure before and after the obstruction using a *differential-pressure sensor* (discussed in Sec. 2–4.2). The obstruction causes a change in fluid pressure which is dependent on the rate of flow. By measuring the difference in pressure, before and after the obstruction, the rate of flow may be determined. The orifice plate and the venturi tube are common devices for this *indirect* rate of flow measurement. (Figure 2–37 shows a rate-of-flow sensor using a venturi and differential-pressure transducer.)

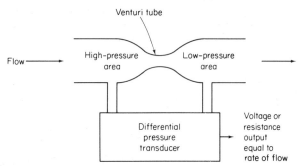

FIGURE 2-37   Rate-of-flow sensor using venturi tube and differential pressure transducer.

There are several methods for obtaining *direct measurement* of the fluid flow rate. Two of the most common methods involve a turbine flowmeter, and a magnetic flowmeter, both of which can be considered as rate-of-flow transducers or sensors. That is, with either device, the rate of flow is converted directly into a corresponding electrical signal.

The *turbine flowmeter* shown in Fig. 2–38 consists basically of a rotor mounted axially within a pipe between a set of bearings. As the fluid flows past a set of propeller blades mounted on the rotor, the rotor spins. The speed of rotation is directly proportional to the rate of flow through the pipe. The fixed

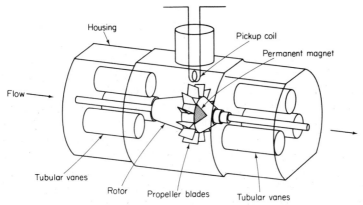

FIGURE 2-38   Turbine flowmeter.

tubular vanes at either side of the rotor reduce the swirling effect of the fluid, an effect that would interfere with the rotation. A small permanent magnet is mounted within the body of the rotor. As the rotor and magnet spin, a current is induced in a pickup coil within the housing, creating a magnetic field around the coil. As each propeller blade of the rotor passes the coil, the magnetic field around the coil is disturbed, thereby producing an electrical pulse in the pickup coil. The frequency of these pulses is directly proportional to the rate of flow through the pipe. By counting the number of pulses during a given period of time, the fluid flow rate can be determined. (Counting circuits and devices are discussed in Sec. 2–13.)

The *magnetic flowmeter* shown in Fig. 2–39 operates on the principle that a voltage is induced in a conductor when the conductor moves through a

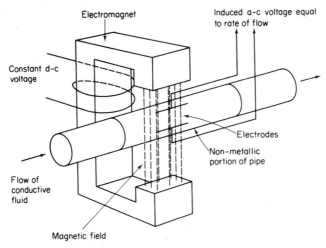

FIGURE 2-39   Magnetic flowmeter.

magnetic field. In the magnetic flowmeter, the constant magnetic field is provided by a steady direct current flowing through the coil of an electromagnet that surrounds the pipe. The fluid, which must be a conductive material, flows through a nonmetallic section of pipe located in the air gap of the electromagnet. The effective length of the conductor corresponds to the inner diameter of the pipe located in the air gap. Since this diameter is constant, the length of the conductor is constant. Thus, with the length of the conductor and the magnetic field both constant, the induced voltage depends on the speed with which the conductor cuts through the field (fluid rate of flow). The induced voltage in the conductor is picked up by means of two electrodes set in opposite sides of the nonmetallic section of pipe. The rate of flow is determined by measuring the voltage.

The *quantity-of-flow sensor* shown in Fig. 2–40 is typical of the sensors found in most residential water systems and in many corresponding industrial systems. The main element of this sensor is a moving disk which is arranged so that, when tilted to the left, the left-hand part of the chamber is filled with fluid and access to the exit pipe is shut off. The pressure of incoming fluid tilts the disk to the right, thus forcing the fluid to fill the entire chamber and opening access to the exit pipe. When the chamber is again emptied, the disk tilts back to the left and the entire process is repeated.

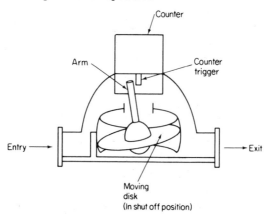

FIGURE 2-40   Quantity-of-flow sensor (water meter).

As the disk tilts from side to side, an arm operates a counting mechanism or switch. Since the capacity of the chamber is known, the quantity of fluid for each count can be determined. The number of counts per given period of time then indicates the quantity of flow for the same time.

2-4.2 Fluid Pressure Sensors

There are a number of different devices used for sensing or measuring the pressure exerted by a fluid. Some of the most common are the *bellows, Bour-*

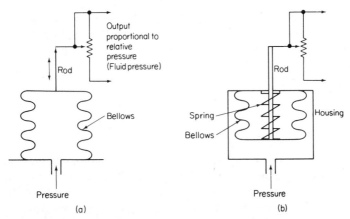

FIGURE 2-41 Basic bellows-type pressure sensor to measure relative (or fluid) pressure.

don tube, diaphragm, capsule, and *pressure cell* or *pressure transducer.* There are also a number of *differential-pressure* sensors.

The basic bellow pressure sensor shown in Fig. 2–41a consists of a cylindrical metal box with corrugated walls of thin, springy material such as brass, phosphor-bronze, or stainless steel and is generally used where the pressures involved are low. Pressure inside the bellows extends its length. Since the bottom end of the bellows is fixed, the travel of the rod connected to the top end of the bellows is directly proportional to the pressure within. The motion of this rod can be used to move the slider of a resistance element or other linear-motion transducer (Sec. 2–3.1). The electrical output signal from the resistive element is then proportional to the fluid pressure applied to the bellows.

The basic *Bourdon tube* shown in Fig. 2–42 consists of a tube with a flattened cross section made of a springy metal, such as phosphor-bronze or stainless steel, in the form of an incomplete circle. As the fluid pressure inside

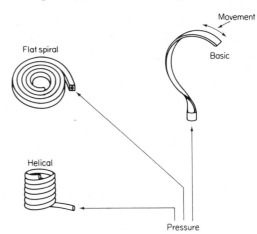

FIGURE 2-42 Basic Bourdon tube pressure sensors.

the tube is increased, the tube tends to straighten. As the pressure is reduced, the tube tends to return to its curved form. The position of the free end of the tube thus varies with changes in the fluid pressure. The motion of the free end can be used to operate a motion-sensing transducer to produce an electrical output.

The basic *diaphragm sensor* shown in Fig. 2–43a is a circular disk of thin springy metal firmly supported at the rim. As pressure is applied to one side of the diaphragm, the center is bent away from the pressure, moving the rod accordingly. Often, two or more diaphragms are joined to form a capsule as shown in Fig. 2–43b. The diaphragm sensor may also be combined with a transducer in a single unit as shown in Fig. 2–44. The diaphragm and fixed plate form the plates of a capacitor. When pressure is applied, the diaphragm is bent closer to the fixed plate, increasing the capacitance. The variable capacitance (which varies with pressure changes) is the output signal. Generally, capacitance output forms one leg of an a-c bridge circuit, as shown in Fig. 2–44.

There are many types of *pressure cells* and *pressure transducers*. The pressure transducer shown in Fig. 2–45 is often used to measure gas pressures such as those within the cylinder of an internal-combustion engine. The diaphragm end of the transducer is inserted through a threaded hole in the side

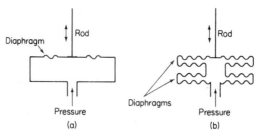

FIGURE 2-43 Diaphragm and capsule pressure sensors: (a) basic diaphragm; (b) capsule.

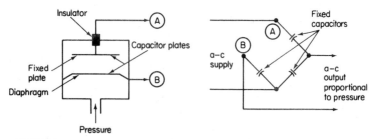

FIGURE 2-44 Diaphragm-type pressure sensor using capacitor transducer output.

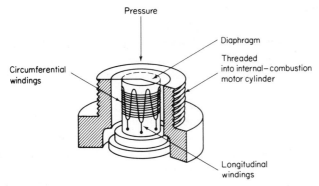

FIGURE 2-45 Pressure transducer for measurement of gas pressures.

of the cylinder. Pressure transducers are also used in automobile radiators. The pressure to be measured is imposed on the diaphragm and as the pressure increases, the cylindrical strain tube decreases in length while increasing in diameter. These dimensional changes are detected by the wire strain gages bonded to the strain tube. The resistance of the circumferential winding increases and the longitudinal winding decreases with an increase in pressure. These resistance changes, which are proportional to fluid pressure changes, are used as the output signal.

The three most common differential-pressure transducers are the *manometer, differential-bellows* and *differential-capsule* sensors. All three types produce an output that represents the difference between two pressures measured simultaneously. For example, two bellows elements may be combined to form a *differential-pressure sensor,* as shown in Fig. 2–46. The bellows elements are linked by a rod. Pressure A moves the rod to the right, and pressure B moves the rod to the left. The resultant movement of the rod is proportional to the differential between pressure A and pressure B. As the rod moves, an arm transmits the motion to an external transducer (such as a resistance element).

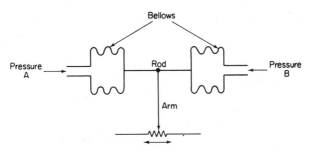

FIGURE 2-46 Differential-pressure transducer with two opposing bellows elements.

2-4.3 Liquid-Level Sensors

There are a number of different devices used for sensing or measuring the level of a liquid in a tank or other container. Some of the most common include the *pressure sensor, float-operated resistance element,* and *capacitive* or *conductive*-level sensors.

Any of the *fluid-pressure sensors* described in Sec. 2–4.2 can be used to measure liquid level by placing the sensor at the bottom of a tank or container as shown in Fig. 2–47. The pressure exerted on the liquid depends, in part, on the height of the liquid. Thus, by measuring the fluid pressure on the bottom, the level within the tank can be measured.

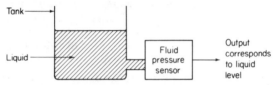

FIGURE 2-47 Liquid-level sensor using fluid pressure measurement.

The *float-operated resistance element* shown in Fig. 2–48 is the most common liquid-level sensor. As the liquid rises in the tank, the float (typically a hollow metal or plastic ball) is raised, and its arm causes the slider to move over the resistance element so that the resistance is increased. As the liquid level falls so does the float, and the resistance is decreased. Thus, the resistance is proportional to the level of the liquid in the tank.

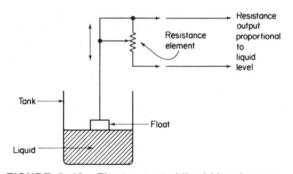

FIGURE 2-48 Float-operated liquid-level sensor.

The *capacitive liquid-level sensor* shown in Fig. 2–49 is the next most common liquid-level sensor. This device consists of an insulated metal electrode firmly fixed near and parallel to the metal wall of the tank. If the liquid is nonconductive, the electrode and tank all form the plates of a capacitor, and the liquid between them acts as a dielectric.

The capacitance depends, in part, on the height of the dielectric (or liquid) between the plates. The greater the height, the larger the capacitance, and vice

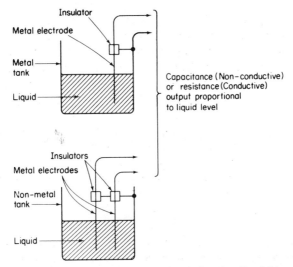

FIGURE 2-49 Capacitive and conductive liquid-level sensors.

versa. Thus, the capacitance is directly proportional to the level of the liquid in the tank.

The *conductive liquid-level sensor,* also shown in Fig. 2-49, is similar to the capacitive sensor except that the conductive sensor is used where the liquid is conductive. The conductive liquid acts as a variable resistance between the rod and tank wall. The resistance depends on the height of the liquid between the rod and tank. Where the tank is not made of metal, two or four parallel insulated rods, held a fixed distance apart, are used as the capacitor plates (or resistance element electrodes).

In some applications, it is necessary to sense when a liquid flowing into a tank reaches a predetermined level. When that level is reached, a control circuit may shut off or otherwise regulate the liquid flow.

The simplest of such devices is the *float switch,* shown in Fig. 2-50. The switch is controlled by the arm, rod, and float, which (in turn) is controlled by the liquid level. When the liquid level drops, so does the float. The arm is pulled down, and the switch is operated. When the liquid is nonflammable, a simple level-limit sensor can be made by using an electrode, as shown in Fig. 2-51. The electrode is set in the side of the metal tank at the desired level. When the liquid

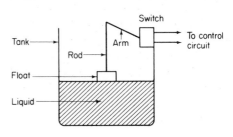

FIGURE 2-50 Float-operated liquid-level limit sensor (and control switch).

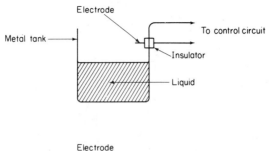

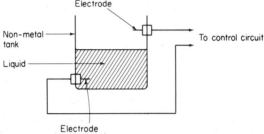

FIGURE 2-51 Simple liquid-level-limit sensors for nonflammable liquid.

reaches that level, contact is made between the liquid and the electrode to complete the control circuit. When the level drops below the electrode, contact is broken and the control circuit is opened. For this circuit it is assumed that the tank is made of metal and makes contact with the liquid. Where there is no such contact (glass or plastic tanks) the circuit is completed by extending another electrode into the liquid through the tank near the bottom.

2-5 MOISTURE AND HUMIDITY SENSORS

Moisture and humidity sensors can be classified by the method of sensing or by the conditions sensed. The two most common instruments used for moisture and humidity measurement are the *hygrometer* and the *psychrometer,* each using a different method of sensing. The most important conditions to be sensed are *relative humidity* and *dew point.*

   Relative humidity is the ratio (expressed in percent) of the water vapor (moisture) actually present in the air to water vapor required for saturation at a given temperature. For example, if a water-vapor count of 20 produces saturation at 25°C, and the actual count is 10 at that temperature, the relative humidity is 50%. A water-vapor count of 15 at 25°C indicates a 75% relative humidity. Relative humidity is always temperature dependent. *Dew point* is the temperature at which the saturation water-vapor pressure is equal to the partial pressure of the water vapor in the atmosphere. Dew-point measurement is a measure of the temperature of a surface at the instant when moisture (dew) is first precipitated on the surface as the surrounding surface is cooled. For example, assume that the temperature is decreasing and dew forms just as the temperature reaches 25°C. This indicates a dew point of 25°C.

2-5.1 Hygrometer-Type Sensors

A hygrometer measures humidity directly. Generally, a hygrometer is calibrated in terms of relative humidity, but can also be used to indicate absolute humidity. The most popular *resistive hygrometer sensors* are those in which a variation of relative humidity produces a variation in their resistance. This resistance change occurs in certain materials such as hygroscopic salts and carbon powder. These materials are usually applied as a film over an insulating substrate and are terminated by metal contacts as shown in Fig. 2–52. Lithium chloride is the most common hygroscopic salt. The resistance of lithium chloride changes when it is exposed to variations in humidity. The higher the relative humidity, the more moisture the lithium chloride absorbs and the lower its resistance. Thus, the resistance of the sensor may be used as a measure of the relative humidity of the air to which it is exposed. In addition to the resistance-type devices, there are dielectric-film, mechanical-displacement, oscillating-crystal, and aluminum oxide hygrometers.

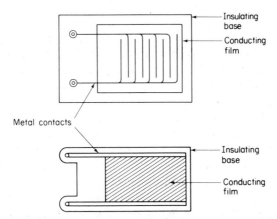

FIGURE 2-52 Resistive hygrometer sensors (chemical humidity-sensing elements).

2-5.2 Psychrometer-Type Sensors

The psychrometer is a humidity-measuring instrument which uses one *wet-bulb thermometer* and one *dry-bulb thermometer*. Typically, the thermometers are resistive or thermocouple, as discussed in Sec. 2–7. The dry-bulb thermometer measures ambient temperature. The wet-bulb thermometer measures temperature reduction due to evaporation cooling. Relative humidity is determined from the two temperature readings and a reading of the barometric pressure, usually by means of a *psychrometric table*. At any given ambient temperature (dry-bulb reading), the relative humidity decreases as the difference between the dry-bulb and wet-bulb readings increases.

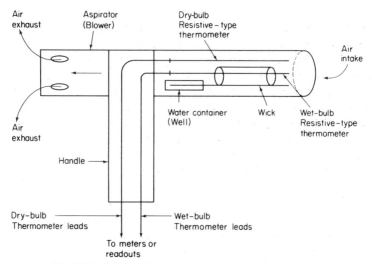

FIGURE 2–53   Portable psychrometer system.

Figure 2–53 shows the elements of a typical psychrometer system. These elements include two resistive-type thermometers. As discussed in Sec. 2–7, such thermometers produce a resistance output which varies with temperature and thus provides an indication of temperature. The system operates on the principle of cooling by evaporation. Moving air is used to produce evaporation but to keep moisture-laden air from blanketing the thermometers. The dry bulb is not affected by the moving air and registers the ambient temperature. However, the wet-bulb thermometer registers a lower temperature due to the evaporation of the water in the wick around the sensor. Since the cooling effect is a function of the relative humidity of the air (the lower the relative humidity, the faster the evaporation), the relative humidity may be determined by comparing the readings of the two thermometers. Figure 2–54 is a typical psychrometric table that shows the relative humidity at selected temperatures. For example, if the dry-bulb (ambient) temperature is 70°F and the wet-bulb

FIGURE 2–54   Partial psychrometric chart showing the relationships among relative humidity, ambient temperature (dry-bulb reading), and difference between dry- and wet-bulb readings.

Dry-bulb reading °F	Difference between dry-bulb and wet-bulb readings, °F			
	1	10	20	30
40	92	–	–	–
50	93	38	–	–
60	94	48	6	–
70	95	55	20	–
80	96	61	29	4
90	96	65	36	13
100	96	68	42	21
110	97	70	46	27

temperature is 1° less, the relative humidity is 95°F. If the wet-bulb temperature drops to 60°F with a 70°F dry-bulb temperature (a 10°F difference), the relative humidity is 55%.

2-5.3 Dew-Point Sensors

A dew-point sensor performs the function of temperature sensing as well as noting the change from vapor to liquid (instant-of-condensation-sensing function). Figure 2–55 shows the basic elements of a *resistive-type* dew-point sensor. The condensation surface is an insulating glass and epoxy disk. The condensation sensor is a resistive element in the form of a metal conducting grid embedded in the disk. The temperature-sensing function is provided by a thermocouple (Sec. 2–7) also embedded in the disk.

The disk is cooled from the side opposite the sensors as shown in Fig. 2–55. When the due point is reached, the resistance of the conducting grid changes drastically (usually unbalancing a bridge circuit). The temperature-sensing thermocouple provides an indication of the temperature at the dew

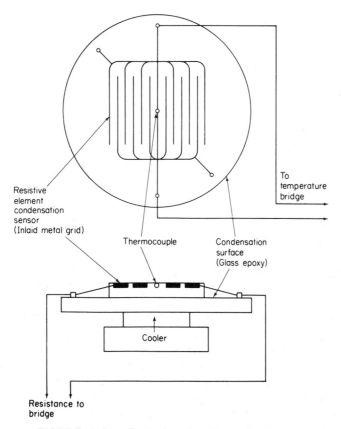

FIGURE 2-55   Resistive-type dew-point sensor.

point, as well as before and after the dew point is reached when the disk is cooled. In addition to the resistive-type instrument, there are *photoelectric-type* and *radiation-* or *nuclear-type* dew-point sensors.

2-6 LIGHT AND RADIOACTIVITY SENSORS

Both light and radioactivity are a form of radiation. Thus, the devices that sense light and radioactivity are, in effect, radiation sensors. In this section we consider sensors that can sense and measure the intensities of radiations, such as light and X-rays as well as nuclear radiations, so-called because they come from the nuclei of radioactive atoms. These nuclear radiations consist, for the most part, of beams of alpha, beta, and neutron particles and gamma rays.

2-6.1 Light Sensors

There are three basic types of light sensors: *photoemissive, photoconductive,* and *photovoltaic.*

The *phototube* shown in Fig. 2–56, once a commonly used light-controlled device (such as in alarms), is the most basic of the photoemissive light sensors. The output current of the basic phototube is very small, typically

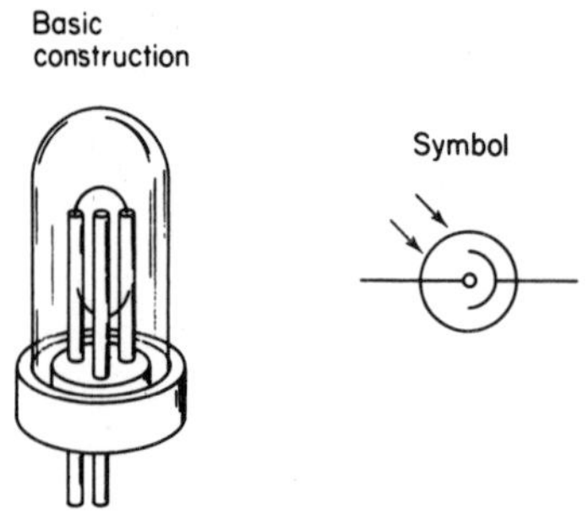

Basic
construction

Symbol

FIGURE 2-56 Construction and symbol for diode-type photo-tube.

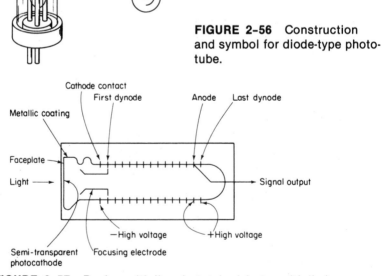

Cathode contact
First dynode
Anode   Last dynode
Metallic coating
Faceplate
Light
Signal output
—High voltage   +High voltage
Semi-transparent   Focusing electrode
photocathode

FIGURE 2-57 Basic multiplier phototube (photomultiplier).

a few microamperes, and often requires amplification. One method for increasing the current produced by a given amount of light is to use a *multiplier phototube* (also known as a photomultiplier tube), such as that shown in Fig. 2-57. In multiplier phototubes, the electrons emitted by the cathode are made to strike in succession a series of positive plates, called *dynodes,* before they reach the anode. As each electron strikes a dynode, a number of electrons are knocked off, thus increasing the current flow.

Figure 2-58 shows the most basic application of a phototube, that of controlling a relay. When the phototube is not exposed to any light, little or no current flows in the relay circuit. When light strikes the phototube cathode, current flows and the relay is operated (the normally open contacts close and the normally closed contacts open). Operation and control of relays is discussed further in Sec. 2-14.

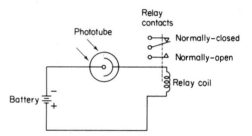

FIGURE 2-58 Basic application of phototube (relay control).

The phototube has generally been replaced by the photoconductive sensor. For example, the phototube of Fig. 2-58 can be replaced by a photoconductive sensor such as that shown in Fig. 2-59. Cadmium sulfide (CdS) and cadmium selenide (CdSe) are the most popular photoconductive materials because they are extremely sensitive to light changes, particularly in the visible-light region. When infrared light (specifically) is to be measured, lead sulfide (PbS) and lead selenid (PbSe) are used for the photoconductive material.

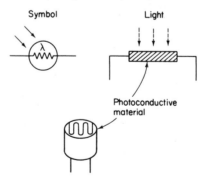

FIGURE 2-59 Construction and symbol for basic photoconductive light sensor.

Most semiconductor diodes and transistors are photosensitive. That is, current flow increases across the diode and transistor junctions when exposed to light. When used as light sensors, the diodes (called *photodiodes*) and transistors (*phototransistors*) are constructed so that the junctions are exposed to a maximum of light as shown in Fig. 2–60. (Note that the top of the photodiode enclosure is made of a transparent material such as clear plastic.)

Photovoltaic light sensors are self-generating (they produce current when exposed to light) and thus do not require a power source. For example, the battery of Fig. 2–58 can be eliminated, provided that the photovoltaic device produced sufficient current to operate the relay. The *solar cell,* so called because it is used to convert light energy from the sun into electrical power, is probably the best known photovoltaic device. Selenium and silicon are the most popular materials for photovoltaic light sensors (or *photocells*) when visible light is to be measured. Germanium can also be used but is better suited to measure infrared light. Figures 2–61 and 2–62 show the construction and symbols for typical silicon and selenium *photovoltaic cells,* respectively. Silicon cells are the most efficient, but selenium cells have characteristics more nearly like the human eye. Thus, selenium is often used in applications where the light sources are similar to those related to normal human vision (such as automatic camera light sensors).

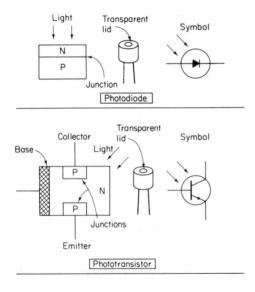

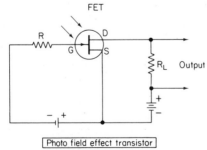

FIGURE 2-60 Construction and symbols for photoconductive-junction light sensors (photodiodes and phototransistors).

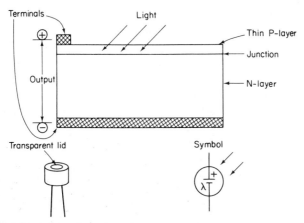

FIGURE 2-61 Construction symbol for silicon photovoltaic cell (photovoltaic light sensor).

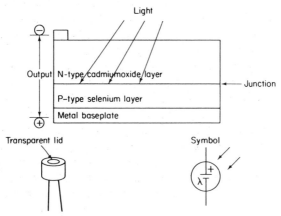

FIGURE 2-62 Construction and symbol for selenium photovoltaic cell (photovoltaic light sensor).

2-6.2 X-ray Sensors

Because of this penetrating power, X-rays are used for many industrial applications, such as detecting the level of liquids in closed tanks, and the thickness of rapidly moving sheets of material such as paper, plastic, or metal. There are two methods for sensing X-rays. One method depends on the fact that when X-rays strike certain materials, such as calcium tungstate, a visible glow of light is produced. The intensity of the glow, in turn, is measured by a photocell. This method of sensing X-rays is similar to the scintillation counter method of sensing nuclear radiation discussed in Sec. 2–6.3. The other method for sensing X-ray intensity makes use of the fact that X-rays affect a cadmium sulfide crystal in the same way as visible light (Sec. 2–6.1). The X-rays produce a sharp drop in the resistance of the crystal. If a steady voltage is applied across the crystal, the current produced varies in proportion to the intensity of the X-rays.

2-6.3 Nuclear Radiation Sensors

Nuclear or radioactive materials emit nuclear radiations, consisting of four parts. One part is the *alpha* particle, which is a helium nucleus consisting of two protons and two neutrons, and carries a positive charge. The second part is the *beta* particle, which is an electron and carries a negative charge. The third part is the *neutron* particle, which carries no electrical charge. The fourth part is the *gamma ray,* an electromagnetic wave somewhat similar to X-rays.

There are two basic methods for converting nuclear radiations into usable electric output signals. The first method, called *ionizing transduction,* depends on the production of an *ion pair* in a gaseous or solid material, and the separation of the positive and negative charges to produce a voltage. The second method, called *photoelectric transduction,* uses a *scintillator* material which generates light in the presence of radiation, and a light sensor which provides a voltage output proportional to the light.

Figure 2–63 shows the basic elements of a photoelectric radiation sensor, commonly called a *scintillation counter.* The scintillator material, usually crystals such as sodium iodide and zinc sulfide, produces a flash of light (called scintillation) each time the crystal is struck by an alpha or beta particle or a gamma ray (or by X-rays when certain kinds of crystals are used). The crystal scintillations are picked up by reflecting mirrors and send to the window of a photomultiplier tube through a Lucite rod. Each particle produces a pulse of anode current at the output of the phototube. The output is applied to a counter circuit (such as described in Sec. 2–13). The intensity of the radiation is found by counting the number of pulses during a given period of time.

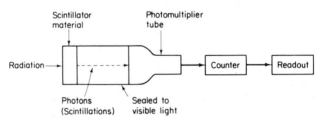

FIGURE 2-63 Basic elements of photoelectric radiation counter (scintillation counter).

There are three basic types of radiation sensors that use ionization: the *ionization chamber,* the *crystal sensor,* and the *semiconductor sensor.* The basic elements of all three sensors are shown in Fig. 2–64. In all three instances, the radiation breaks down part of the material into ion pairs with positive and negative charges. The resultant voltage or current is then measured to provide an indication or measure of the radiation.

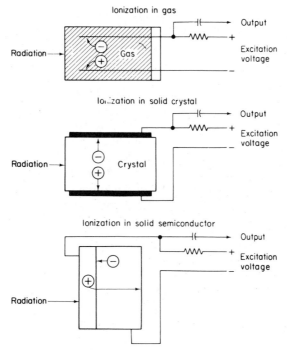

FIGURE 2-64 Basic elements of ionization-type radiation sensors.

Figure 2–65 shows the basic elements of a Geiger counter, which is probably the best known of the radiation sensors. The heart of the Geiger counter is the gas-filled Geiger–Müller tube. The anode of the tube is made positive and the cathode negative by means of a battery whose voltage is just below the ionization point of the gas. When radiation penetrates the window, some of the gas atoms are ionized, producing a pulse of current through load resistor R. A series of alpha or beta particles or bursts of gamma rays cause a series of current pulses to flow through the tube and the anode circuit. The output pulses are amplified and registered on some indicating devices as flashes of light or as

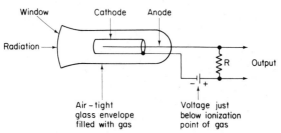

FIGURE 2-65 Geiger-Müller tube and basic circuit (Geiger counter).

clicks from a loudspeaker. By counting the number of flashes or clicks, it is possible to tell how many particles entered the tube during a given period of time, and thus obtain an indication of radiation intensity.

Because neutrons carry no electrical charge, they are difficult to detect. However, when neutrons strike the atom of a certain uranium isotope, the uranium atom splits into two or more parts. This splitting is known as *fission* and results in the release of radiation (alpha and beta particles and gamma rays) from the atom. Such radiation can be detected using the ionization or photoelectric (scintillation) sensors as described. A simple neutron sensor consists of a semiconductor junction diode, the top surface of which is coated with a very thin layer of uranium 235 as shown in Fig. 2–66. When the junction is struck by radiations resulting from fission (caused by neutrons striking atoms in the uranium 235 layer), the reverse current is increased. By measuring the change in current, the intensity of the neutrons may be determined.

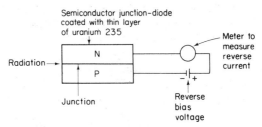

FIGURE 2–66   Neutron radiation sensor.

2-7 TEMPERATURE SENSORS

Temperature sensors are generally classified by the method of sensing. In this section we cover the six most commonly used methods for sensing temperature: *bimetallic, fluid-pressure, resistive, thermocouple, radiation,* and *oscillating crystal.*

2-7.1 Bimetallic Temperature Sensors

One of the most common bimetallic temperature sensors is the *thermostat.* Such thermostats are often used as *circuit breakers,* to provide protection against excessive current flow in an electrical circuit. Typically, circuit breakers are connected in series with the circuit to be protected, with the bimetallic strip in contact with one or more circuit terminals as shown in Fig. 2–67. As current flows through the strip, the resistance of the strip produces a certain amount of heat. If the current is normal (at or below the rating of the circuit breaker), the heat is not great enough to separate the contact points. Should the current rise above the rating, the heat becomes great enough to cause the strip to bend sufficiently to separate the contact point. The circuit is then opened, and the current flow stops.

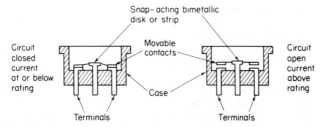

FIGURE 2-67 Bimetallic thermostat used as a circuit breaker.

2-7.2 Fluid-Pressure Temperature Sensors

When a fluid (liquid or gas) is heated, the fluid expands in direct proportion to the heat applied. The most common temperature sensor using the fluid-pressure principle is the familiar *mercury thermometer*. There are also electrical versions of mercury thermometers, such as the mercury thermostat shown in Fig. 2-68, used to control operation of an electrical heater. One problem of the mercury-in-glass system is very low current-handling capability, typically well below 1 mA. Thus, current is not sufficient to control a heater (to switch the heater on and off). The problem can be overcome by means of the circuit shown in Fig. 2-68. Here, a SCR (silicon-controlled rectifier) is used to amplify the current of a mercury thermostat and to carry the heavy current required by the heater. When the thermostat is open (low temperature with the mercury not touching both contacts simultaneously), capacitor *C* is in the circuit and charges each half-cycle of the a-c power. This triggers the SCR on each half-cycle and delivers power to the heater. When the thermostat is closed (high temperature with mercury touching both contacts simultaneously), capacitor *C* is shorted out of the circuit and cannot charge. The SCR can no longer trigger, and the heater shuts off. (SCRs are discussed further in Sec. 2-14.)

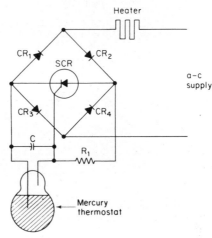

FIGURE 2-68 Electronic heater control.

2-7.3 Resistive Temperature Sensors

There are two basic types of resistive temperature sensors: the *conductive* type and the *semiconductor* type. Both types operate on the principle that the resistance of conductors and semiconductors changes with temperature.

The most common type of conductive temperature sensor is shown in Fig. 2-69. The temperature-sensing element is a coil of fine wire such as copper, nickel, or platinum. All of these metals have a *positive temperature coefficient* (they increase in resistance with increases in temperature). This resistance change results in bridge balance or unbalance, depending on the type of temperature-sensing system used. The temperature sensors such as shown in Fig. 2-69 are known as *immersion* or *probe* types, since they are designed to measure the temperature within inaccessible areas.

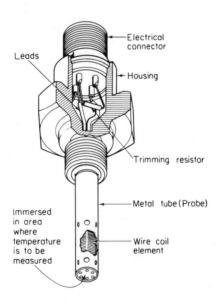

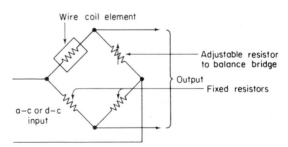

FIGURE 2-69 Immersion or probe-type conductive (resistive) temperature sensor.

The most common type of semiconductor temperature sensor is the thermistor shown in Fig. 2–70. Semiconductor temperature sensors generally have a *negative temperature coefficient* as shown by the curve of Fig. 2–70. Although thermistors come in various sizes and shapes as shown, they all contain a semiconductor of ceramic material made by sintering mixtures of metallic oxides such as manganese, nickel, cobalt, copper, iron, and uranium, formed into small glass-enclosed beads, disks, or rods. In addition to thermistors, semiconductor temperature sensors are made from germanium and silicon crystals, carbon resistors, and gallium–arsenide diodes. No matter what material is used, semiconductor temperature sensors often appear in bridge-type circuits.

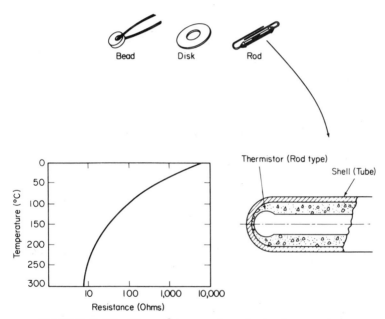

FIGURE 2-70 Thermistor semiconductor temperature sensor.

2-7.4 *Thermocouple Temperature Sensors*

Thermocouple temperature sensors are also known as *thermoelectric temperature transducers*. The basic thermocouple circuit shown in Fig. 2–71 consists of a pair of wires of different metals joined together at one end (the *sensing junction*) and terminated at their other end by terminals (the *reference junction*) which is maintained at a known temperature (*reference temperature*). The circuit is completed by a load, generally composed of a signal conditioning circuit. When there is a temperature difference between the sensing and reference junctions, a voltage is produced and flows through the load. This

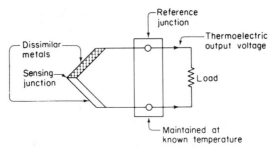

FIGURE 2-71 Basic thermocouple circuit.

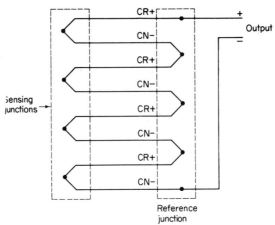

FIGURE 2-72 Immersion-type thermocouple probe.

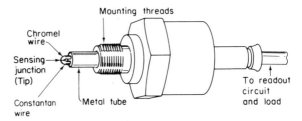

FIGURE 2-73 Typical Chromel-Alumel thermopile schematic.

characteristic is known as the *thermoelectric effect*. The thermocouple is generally encased in a metal tube for protection as shown in Fig. 2-72.

A *thermopile* is a combination of several thermocouples of the same materials connected in series as shown in Fig. 2-73, which is the schematic of a typical Chromel-Alumel thermopile. The output of a thermopile is equal to the output from each thermocouple multiplied by the number of thermocouples in the thermopile.

2-7.5 Radiation Pyrometer

Where very high temperatures such as those of metals being melted in an electric furnace are to be measured, most of the temperature sensors described thus far cannot be used because they would be destroyed by high heat. The radiation pyrometer, shown in Fig. 2-74, overcomes that problem. This pyrometer consists of a metal housing containing a fused-silica lens and a thermopile. The lens end is inserted into a small opening in the side of the furnace. Radiation from the heated material enters the lens and is focused on the thermopile. A cable at the other end of the pyrometer carries the generated voltage from the thermopile to signal conditioning or other measuring circuits.

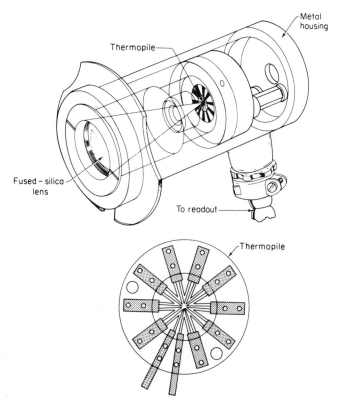

FIGURE 2-74 Radiation pyrometer.

2-7.6 Oscillating-Crystal Temperature Sensors

The quartz crystal used to control the frequency of oscillator circuits is temperature sensitive. That is, the frequency of oscillation is changed when the temperature of the crystal is changed. This condition can be used to measure temperatures in a range from about –40 to +230°C. A typical quartz crystal temperature sensor system is shown in Fig. 2–75. The crystal sensing element (a thin quartz crystal wafer) is contained in the tip of a probe connected by cable to the electronics unit (which contains a power supply, oscillators, signal conditioning, and display equipment). The frequency output, obtained by mixing the transducer-oscillator signal with a reference oscillator signal, is converted into a number of counts per unit of time (by a counter such as discussed in Sec. 2–13).

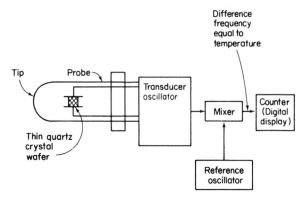

FIGURE 2-75 Quartz crystal temperature sensor system.

2-8 THICKNESS SENSORS

There are a number of sensors used to measure the thickness of materials in industrial applications. Thickness sensors can be magnetic, capacitive, soundwave or radiation types.

2-8.1 Magnetic Thickness Sensors

Figure 2–76 shows a sensor system used to measure the thickness of magnetic material. Since the material being measured is part of the magnetic circuit, the inductance of the coil (wound on an iron core) is determined (in part) by the thickness of the material. In the system of Fig. 2–76, the coil is made part of an

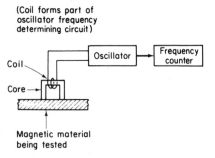

FIGURE 2-76 Sensor system used to measure thickness of magnetic material.

oscillator, the frequency of which depends on the coil inductance. By measuring oscillator frequency, the coil inductance (and thus the thickness of the material) is determined.

2-8.2   Capacitive Thickness Sensors

Figure 2–77 shows a sensor system used to measure the thickness of insulator material such as nonconducting plastic. With this system, metal plates are placed at either side of the material, forming a capacitor. Since the capacitance depends (in part) on the thickness of the dielectric, material thickness can be determined by measuring the capacitance. When the capacitance is made part of an oscillator, the oscillator frequency is determined by the capacitance, which, in turn, is a measure of the thickness.

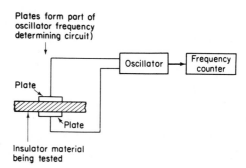

FIGURE 2-77 Sensor system used to measure thickness of insulator material.

2-8.3   Sound-Wave Thickness Sensors

Another type of thickness sensor uses ultrasonic vibrations. These are mechanical vibrations that use a gas, liquid, or solid as a medium and whose frequencies are beyond the audio range (that is, more than about 15,000 vibrations per second). The vibrations are produced by a transducer that converts the electrical output of an oscillator to ultrasonic vibrations of the corresponding frequencies. There are two basic types of ultrasonic transducers: *magnetostrictive* and *piezoelectric.*

Figure 2–78a shows a typical magnetostrictive-type sound-wave transducer consisting of a metal rod placed in a coil that is driven by oscillator signals. As a result of the alternating magnetic field generated by the coil, the rod alternately becomes longer and shorter at the frequency of oscillation. Since one end of the rod is fixed, the opposite end pushes and pulls on a plate or *diaphragm,* producing ultrasonic sound waves. In effect, the magnetostrictive transducer operates somewhat like a loudspeaker, but does not use exactly the same principle of operation.

Figure 2–78b shows a typical piezoelectric-type sound-wave transducer. As discussed, piezoelectric materials produce a voltage when they are com-

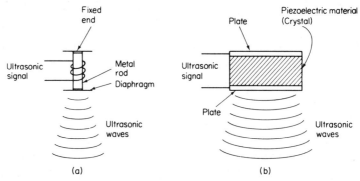

FIGURE 2-78 Ultrasonic transducers: (a) magnetostrictive; (b) piezoelectric.

pressed or mechanically vibrated. Similarly, when a voltage is applied to piezoelectric material (typically quartz crystal) the material compresses and expands. If the voltage is alternating at an ultrasonic frequency, the material compresses and expands at the same frequency. In effect, the piezoelectric material vibrates. These vibrations are transferred to a diaphragm to produce ultrasonic waves.

Figure 2–79 shows one way to use ultrasonic vibrations for the measurement of material thickness. Here, the transducer is placed on top of the material, so that the ultrasonic vibrations pass through the material to a flat surface. When vibrations strike the other side of the material, they are reflected back to the transducer from the surface. The time it takes for the vibrations to make one round trip depends, all other factors being equal, on the thickness of the material.

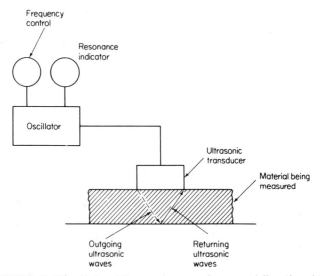

FIGURE 2-79 Using ultrasonic sound waves (vibrations) to measure thickness of materials.

A condition of *resonance* is produced if the material thickness is such that the time for one round trip is equal to the time of one cycle of ultrasonic vibration. Resonance occurs when the vibrations return at the exact time to reinforce outgoing vibrations. The exact timing depends on thickness and oscillator frequency. At resonance, there is a sudden change in the load that the transducer offers the oscillator. The change in load produces a corresponding change in oscillator current, and can be indicated by a meter or other indicator placed in the oscillator circuit. By noting the oscillator frequency at the point where the current change takes place, the time required for a round trip of the ultrasonic vibrations (and thus the thickness of the material) is determined.

2-8.4 Radiation Thickness Sensors

Figure 2–80 shows one system for measuring thickness by using a radiation sensor. Here a sheet material (plastic, paper, rubber, etc.) passes between a lower chamber containing a source of radiation (X-rays, gamma rays, beta rays) and an upper chamber containing one of the radiation sensors described in Sec. 2–6. As the radiation passes through the sheet material, some of the radiation is absorbed and, as a result, the radiation reading the sensor is less intense. The amount of absorption depends on the material density and thickness of the sheets. If the material and density are kept constant, the amount of radiation absorption varies directly with the thickness of the sheet. The radiation sensor can be calibrated in terms of thickness for various types of materials.

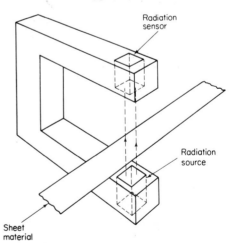

Radiation sensor

Radiation source

Sheet material

FIGURE 2-80 Using radiation sensor to measure thickness of materials.

2-9 PROXIMITY SENSORS

The proximity sensor is a device used to detect the proximity (or the absence) of a body. The speed-of-rotation sensor described in Sec. 2–3.3 is a form of proximity sensor. As shown in Fig. 2–25, the sensor consists of a coil wound on a small permanent magnet. When a metal object passes near the sensor (magnetic pickup) the magnetic field is changed, thus inducing a voltage pulse in the coil. A similar sensor may be used for many applications, such as counting metallic objects moving past the sensor on a conveyor belt. The sensor can also be constructed in the form of a tube, and used to count small metallic objects as they fall, one at a time, through the tube. In another example, a hollow magnetic pickup can be placed around a drill used for an automatic machining process. When the drill rotates, a voltage is induced in the coil. Should the drill break, absence of rotation within the pickup is sensed by the lack of induced voltage, and the machine shuts off automatically.

Figure 2–81 shows one of the many oscillator-type proximity sensors. Such sensors are sometimes called *capacitive relays,* and are frequently used as a safety device should the operators of machines place their hands into some dangerous area. The metal plate shown is placed at the dangerous area. Should the plate be touched, or even approached, the oscillator circuit is "grounded" through the operator's body, and is turned off (or there is a drastic change in the oscillator current to the control circuit). This causes a relay to operate some device, such as to turn off a motor.

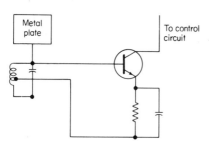

FIGURE 2-81 Oscillator-type proximity sensor using metal plate to stop oscillation.

2-10 DENSITY AND SPECIFIC GRAVITY SENSORS

Many industrial processes depend, in part, on the densities of liquids. An obvious method for measuring density is to weigh a known volume of a liquid. A simpler method is to use the *hydrometer,* which is a calibrated float. The function of a hydrometer is to measure *specific gravity,* which is the ratio between the weight of a substance and the weight of an equal volume of some other substance (usually water) that is used as a standard. The greater the density of a liquid, the less the hydrometer float sinks into the liquid. The density can be found by noting the calibration on the float (usually in terms of specific gravity with pure water as a reference) corresponding to the liquid surface. This is the method used to find the specific gravity of acid in a battery.

Figure 2–82 shows a variation of the hydrometer principle used as a density sensor. A float is weighted by a chain to sink to a predetermined depth in

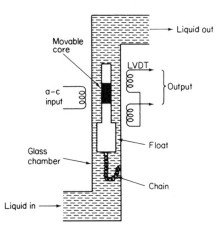

FIGURE 2-82 Hydrometer using LVDT to indicate density.

the liquid under test, flowing through a glass chamber. A rod attached to the top of the float carries the movable core of a linear variable differential transformer (Sec. 2-3.1). The transformer windings are wound around the outside of the glass chamber. The float is adjusted so that the transformer core is at the null position and the output voltage is zero. Should the density of the liquid increase, the float moves higher, the core is raised, and a differential output voltage is generated. The amplitude of the differential voltage is proportional to the rise of the core, and the phase is dependent on the direction of the core motion. Thus, the output voltage phase indicates whether the liquid is more or less dense than normal, whereas the voltage amplitude indicates the amount of density change or deviation from normal.

2-11 CHEMICAL SENSORS

Typical examples of chemical sensors include the pH (or *acidity/alkalinity*) sensor and the *thermal-conductivity gas analyzer*.

2-11.1 pH Sensor

The degree of acidity or alkalinity of any water-based solution is determined by the relative concentrations of *hydrogen* and *hydroxyl ions*. The solution is acidic when the hydrogen ions predominate. If hydroxyl ions are in the majority, the solution is alkaline. The hydrogen-ion concentration is measured on a scale (the pH *scale*) that ranges from 0 to 14, with 7 being neutral (equal hydrogen and hydroxyl ions). As the solution becomes more acid, the pH scale reading decreases below 7. As the solution becomes more alkaline, the pH scale reading increases above 7.

A pH measurement is obtained by immersing a pair of electrodes in the solution to be measured, and measuring the voltage across the electrodes as shown in Fig. 2–83 (similar to that action of a voltaic cell, where a pair of dissimilar electrodes are immersed in an electrolyte). In the pH cell, the *reference electrode* is at a constant voltage or potential, regardless of the pH. The potential of the *measuring electrode* is determined by the pH of the solution. Thus, the potential difference between the two electrodes depends on the pH. This potential difference can be measured by a voltmeter calibrated in terms of pH.

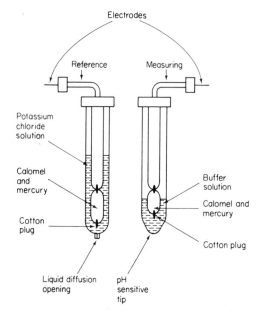

FIGURE 2-83   pH (acidity/alkalinity) sensor.

2-11.2   Thermal-Conductivity Gas Analyzer

Figure 2–84 shows the basic circuit for a thermal-conductivity gas analyzer. One common use for such analyzers is to measure air pollution or smog. Note that a balanced bridge circuit (Sec. 2–12) is formed, with two sensing resistors acting as balanced legs of the bridge. One sensing resistor is surrounded by the gas to be analyzed, whereas the other resistor is placed in a reference gas (such as oxygen, pure atmosphere, etc.). Where practical, both gases are maintained at the same pressure, water content, and so on.

The bridge is first balanced by exposing both resistors to the same gas. Current flows through both resistors, as well as through resistors R_1 and R_2. Resistor R_2 is adjusted for a "balance" or "zero set" condition on the meter. Then the resistors are exposed to the reference sample and gas sample. If the gas sample contains elements having a different thermal or heat conductivity than the reference sample, the bridge is unbalanced. In some cases, the meter reads out in terms of thermal conductivity. In other analyzers, the indication is on a GO–NO GO or a GOOD–BAD basis.

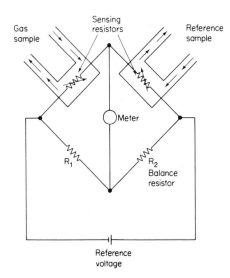

FIGURE 2-84   Basic thermal-
conductivity gas analyzer.

2-12   BASIC SIGNAL CONDITIONING CIRCUITS

The most common signal conditioning circuits involve some form of resistance networks. Less frequently, inductances or capacitances are used instead of resistors. In addition to these networks, there are four signal conditioning circuits or devices common to most transducers: *amplifiers, a-c to d-c converters, d-c to a-c converters,* and A/D or D/A *converters.*

2-12.1   *Resistance, Inductance, and Capacitance Signal Conditioning Networks*

Figure 2–85 shows the classic resistance networks found in signal conditioning circuits. These networks include the *voltage-divider, voltage-drop,* and *bridge* circuits.

The *voltage-divider* circuit of Fig. 2–85 consists of the transducer resistance element R, a fixed load resistance R_L, and an excitation voltage. The resistance of R is proportional to the measurand, the resistance of R_L is constant, and the output signal voltage is taken from across R_L. The output signal is proportional to the ratio of R and R_L, and thus to the measurand.

The *voltage-drop* circuit of Fig. 2–85 consists of the transistor resistance element R and a constant current source. The current source remains constant despite changes in R. Thus, since the voltage across a resistance (the output signal voltage in this case) is directly proportional to the product of current and resistance, the output signal is proportional to the value of R. If R increases due to a change in the measurand, the output voltage increases, and vice versa, making the output signal proportional to the measurand.

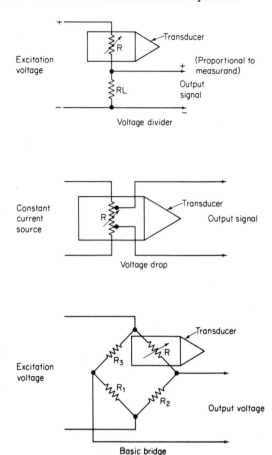

FIGURE 2-85 Resistance networks found in signal conditioning circuits.

The *bridge* circuit of Fig. 2–85 consists of the transducer resistance element R, two fixed resistances R_1 and R_2, an adjustable resistance R_3, and an excitation voltage. Element R forms one leg of the bridge and has a resistance proportional to the measurand. Resistor R_3 forms the opposite leg of the bridge and is adjustable to balance the bridge. If all resistances are equal, the output voltage is zero. Usually, R_3 is adjusted to produce a zero output voltage when the transducer element R is at midrange or at one end of the measurand range. When the measurand changes, the bridge is unbalanced (the ratios of the resistors are changed) and an output signal (proportional to the measurand) is produced. The bridge circuit not only indicates the amount of measurand change, but also indicates the polarity of that change.

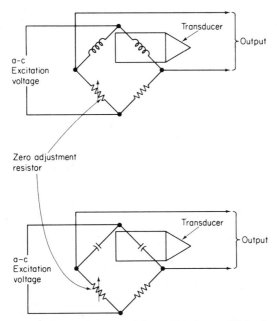

FIGURE 2-86 Balanced bridge signal conditioning networks for capacitive or inductive transducers.

When a transducer element is capacitive or inductive, a balanced bridge can still be used. However, the excitation must be alternating current as shown in Fig. 2–86.

2-12.2 A-C to D-C Signal Conditioning

The inductive and capacitive transducers of Fig. 2–86 require an a-c excitation signal, and the resistive transducers of Fig. 2–85 can be used with a-c excitation. When a d-c output signal is required, the signal conditioning circuit first produces an a-c output signal that is proportional to the measurand, and then converts it to a d-c output signal. This conversion function is known as *rectification* or *demodulation*. (In a strict sense, rectification is the conversion of a-c into d-c, whereas demodulation implies removing an a-c component from another signal. However, the terms are used interchangeably in transducer work.)

The *solid-state diode* is the most common rectifier or demodulator used in signal conditioning circuits. Figure 2–87 shows how the diode principle can be used to convert a-c into d-c in a signal conditioning circuit. The full-wave bridge rectifier of Fig. 2–87 is most often used in transducer work. With any of the circuits, current flows through the load resistor *R,* in one direction only, on both halves of the a-c signal cycle as shown by the arrows of Fig. 2–87.

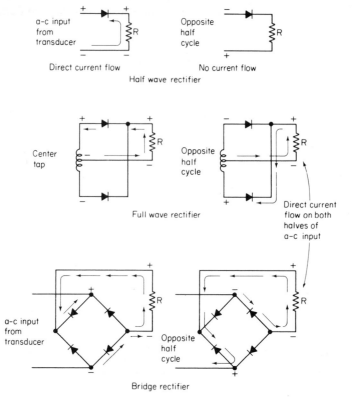

Half wave rectifier

Direct current flow — No current flow

Full wave rectifier

Direct current flow on both halves of a-c input

Bridge rectifier

FIGURE 2-87 Solid-state diodes used as rectifiers to convert a-c input from transducer to d-c output.

2-12.3 Amplifier Signal Conditioning Circuits

Another common signal conditioning circuit is the transistor amplifier, which is used to raise the level of transducer output signals. Transducers, particularly photovoltaic and piezoelectric, produce outputs in the millivolt range, whereas a typical microcomputer-based control system requires signals in the 5–V range. Transducer amplifier circuits can have discrete components, where each transistor and circuit part is a separate component, or integrated circuit (IC), where all parts are fabricated on one "chip." The trend today is to use IC amplifiers for signal conditioning of transducer outputs. We will not go into the basic theory of transistor amplifiers here. For a more comprehensive discussion of transistors and amplifiers, your attention is called to the author's best-selling *Handbook for Transistors* (Englewood Cliffs, N.J.: Prentice-Hall, Inc., 1976).

2-12.4 D-C to A-C Signal Conditioning

Sometimes it is necessary to convert direct current into alternating current. For example, assume that all but one of the transducers in a control system require d-c excitation voltages. The remaining one transducer requires an a-c excitation, and thus would require a separate power supply (which might be uneconomical or otherwise impractical). This problem can be solved by using a signal conditioning circuit that converts a d-c power supply (used for all remaining transducers) into an a-c excitation voltage for the one "odd-ball" transducer.

Figure 2–88 shows the circuit of a reluctive transducer that must be operated from a d-c supply and must produce a d-c output signal. The transducer produces an a-c output proportional to linear motion (Sec. 2–3). This a-c signal output is converted by the two rectifier circuits, as discussed in Sec. 2–12.2. The a-c excitation voltage from the transducer element is provided by the d-c to a-c *converter* or *inverter,* which consists essentially of two PNP transistors, a transformer, and two resistors.

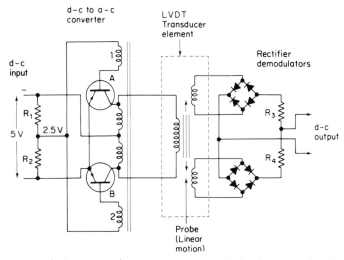

FIGURE 2–88 Reluctive transducer with d-c input and output.

Note that both transistors A and B are placed in a position to be turned on when the power supply is applied. That is, the emitters are connected to the positive end of the + 5-V supply, whereas the bases are connected to the junction of R_1 and R_2 through the transformer windings, placing a forward bias on both transistors. This forward bias turns on the transistor, and emitter–collector current flows through the center-tapped winding of the transformer, producing lines of force. These lines of force are picked up by the base windings 1 and 2, which are out of phase, so that one base receives a positive voltage when the other base is being driven negative, and vice versa.

Since transistors and transformer windings are never perfectly balanced, one transistor is driven into saturation, while the opposite transistor is cut off. When a transistor reaches saturation, and no further increases can occur, the lines of force collapse. This collapse produces a reverse in the voltage produced by the base windings 1 and 2, and the transistors switch states. The repeated rise and fall of the lines of force around the center-tapped winding generate an a-c voltage in the transformer secondary. This a-c voltage is used as the excitation voltage for the transducer element.

2-12.5 A/D and D/A Signal Conditioning

Transducers produce a voltage which is an analog of the condition or force they transduce (a voltage that represents the force or condition). As discussed in Chapter 3, microcomputer systems require digital inputs, rather than an a-c or d-c voltage, making it necessary to convert the analog voltage from the transducer into a corresponding digital value (A/D conversion). Similarly, the outputs from a microprocessor-based system are digital pulses which must be converted to voltages suitable for operating control devices (such as stepping relays, electromagnetic valves, etc.) Thus, D/A conversion is also required for most microprocessor-based systems.

There are several methods for converting voltage (or current) into digital form, and vice versa. Before discussing operation of these conversion circuits, let us review the signal formats found in microprocessor (Chapter 3) and other digital equipment. Although there are many ways in which digital pulses can be used to represent the 1 and 0 digits found in microprocessor equipment, there are three ways in common use. These are the NRZL (nonreturn to zero level), the NRZM (nonreturn to zero mark), and the RZ (return to zero) formats. Figure 2–89 shows the relation of the three formats.

In NRZL, a 1 is one signal level and a 0 is another signal level. These levels can be 5 V, 10 V, 0 V, –5 V, or any other selected values, provided that the 1 and 0 levels are entirely different.

In RZ, a 1 bit is represented by a pulse of some definite width (usually a one-half bit width) that returns to zero signal level, while the 0 bit is represented by a zero-level signal.

In NRZM, the level of the pulse has no meaning. A 1 is represented by a change in level, and a 0 is represented by no change in level.

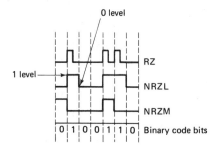

FIGURE 2-89 Typical BCD signal formats.

The 4-Bit System in D/A and A/D Conversion. Although not all digital devices use the 4-bit system it is common and does provide a high degree of accuracy for conversion between analog and digital data. Most conversion systems use the 4-bit format or a multiple of the basic format (8 bits, 16 bits, etc.). The 4-bit system is capable of handling 4 data bits. The number 15 is represented by 1111 and zero is represented by 0000. Any number between 0 and 15 requires only 4 bits. For example, the number 1000 is 8, the number 0111 is 7, and so on.

In practice, a 4-bit A/D converter (also called a binary encoder in some digital literature) samples the voltage level to be converted and compares the voltage to $\frac{1}{2}$-scale, $\frac{1}{4}$-scale, $\frac{1}{8}$-scale, and $\frac{1}{16}$-scale (in that order) of some given full-scale voltage. The A/D converter (or encoder) then produces 4 bits, in sequence, with the decision (or comparison) made on the most significant (or $\frac{1}{2}$-scale) first.

Figure 2–90 shows the relation among three voltage levels to be converted and the corresponding binary code (in NRZL format). Each of the three voltage levels is divided into four equal time increments. The first time increment is used to represent the $\frac{1}{2}$-scale bit, the second increment for the $\frac{1}{4}$-scale bit, the third increment for the $\frac{1}{8}$-scale bit, and the fourth increment for the $\frac{1}{16}$-scale bit.

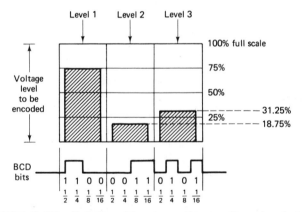

FIGURE 2-90 Relationship among three voltage levels to be encoded and the corresponding BCD code (using the 4-bit system).

In level 1, the first two time increments are at binary 1, with the second two increments at 0. This produces a 1100, or decimal 12. Twelve is three-fourths of 16. Thus, level 1 is 75% of full scale. For example, if full scale is 100 V, level 1 is at 75 V.

In level 2, the first two increments are at 0, while the second two increments are at 1. This represents 0011, or decimal 3. Thus, level 2 is three-sixteenths of full scale (or 18.75 V).

This can be expressed in another way. In the first or $\frac{1}{2}$-scale increment, the converter produces a 0 because the voltage (18.75) is *less than* $\frac{1}{2}$-scale (50). The same is true of the second, or $\frac{1}{4}$-scale increment (18.75 V is less than 25 V). In the third or $\frac{1}{8}$-scale increment, the converter produces a 1, as it does in the fourth or $\frac{1}{16}$-scale increment, because the voltage being compared is *greater than* $\frac{1}{8}$ of full scale (18.75 is greater than 12.5) and greater than $\frac{1}{16}$ of full scale (18.75 is greater than 6.25). Thus, the $\frac{1}{2}$- and $\frac{1}{4}$-scale increments are 0, while the $\frac{1}{8}$- and $\frac{1}{16}$-scale increments are at 1. Also, $\frac{1}{8} + \frac{1}{16} = \frac{3}{16}$, or 18.75%.

A/D Conversion.   One of the most common methods of direct A/D conversion involves the use of a converter that operates on a sequence of *half-split, trial-and-error steps*. This produces digital bits in serial form.

The heart of a converter is a *conversion ladder* such as that shown in Fig. 2–91. The ladder provides a means of implementing a 4-bit binary coding system, and produces an output that is equivalent to switch positions. The switches can be moved to either a 1 or a 0 position, which corresponds to a four-place binary number. The output voltage describes a percentage of the full-scale reference voltage, depending on the switch positions. For example, if all switches are at the 0 position, there is no output voltage. This produces a binary 0000, represented by 0 V at the output.

If switch A is at 1 and the remaining switches are at 0, this produces a binary 1000 (decimal 8). Since the total in a 4-bit system is 16 (0 to 15), 8 represents one-half of full scale. Thus, the output voltage is one-half of the full-scale reference voltage. This is done as follows.

The 2-, 4-, and 8-Ω switch resistors and the 8-Ω output resistor are connected in parallel. This produces a value of 1-Ω across points X and Y. The reference voltage is applied across the 1-Ω switch resistor (across points X and Z) and the 1-Ω combination of resistors (across points X and Y). In effect, this is the same as two 1-Ω resistors in series. Since the full-scale reference voltage is applied across both resistors in series and the output is measured across only one of the resistors, the output voltage is one-half of the reference voltage.

In a practical A/D converter, the same basic ladder is used to supply a comparison voltage to a comparison circuit, which compares the voltage to be converted against the binary-coded voltage from the ladder. The resultant output of the comparison circuit is a binary code representing the voltage to be converted.

The mechanical switches of Fig. 2–91 are replaced by electronic switches, usually FFs (flip-flops). When the switch is "on," the corresponding ladder resistor is connected to the reference voltage. The switches are triggered by four pulses (representing each of the 4 binary bits) from the system clock. An enable pulse is used to turn the comparison circuit (typically a differential amplifier) on and off, so that as each switch is operated, a comparison can be made of the 4 bits.

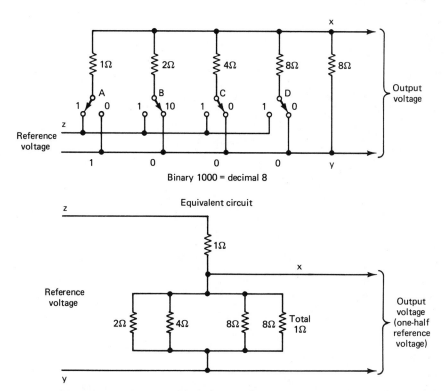

FIGURE 2-91 Binary conversion ladder used in the 4-bit system.

Typical A/D Operating Sequence. Figure 2–92 is a simplified block diagram of an A/D converter that could be used to convert the analog voltage output of a transducer into a 4-bit digital output suitable for a microprocessor-based system. The reference voltage is applied to the ladder through electronic switches. The ladder output (comparison voltage) is controlled by switch positions which, in turn, are controlled by pulses from the system clock. The following paragraphs outline the sequence of events necessary to produce a series of 4 binary bits (digital pulses applied to the microprocessor-based system input) that describe the input voltage (analog output of a transducer) as a percentage of full scale (in $\frac{1}{16}$ increments). Assume that the input voltage from the transducer is three-fourths of full scale (or 75%).

When pulse 1 arrives, switch 1 is turned on and the remaining switches are off. The ladder output is 50% voltage that is applied to the differential amplifier. The balance of this amplifier is set so that its output is sufficient to turn on one AND gate and turn off the other AND gate, if the ladder voltage is greater than the input voltage from the transducer. Similarly, the differential amplifier reverses the AND gates if the ladder voltage is not greater than the

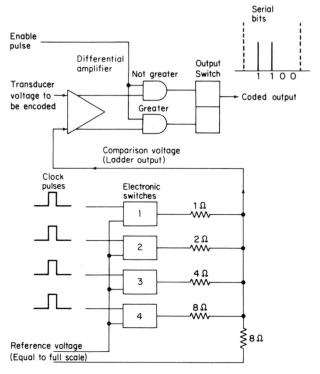

FIGURE 2-92   Simplified A/D converter (binary encoder) using the 4-bit system.

transducer voltage. Both AND gates are enabled by the pulse from the system clock.

In our example (75% of full scale), the ladder output is less than the transducer voltage when pulse 1 is applied to the ladder. As a result, the *not greater* AND gate turns on, and the output FF is set to the 1 position. Thus, for the first of the 4 bits, the FF output is 1.

When pulse 2 arrives, switch 2 is turned on, and switch 1 remains on. Both switches 3 and 4 remain off. The ladder output is now 75% of the full-scale voltage. The ladder voltage equals the transducer voltage. However, the ladder output is still not greater than the transducer voltage. Consequently, when the AND gates are enabled, the AND gates remain in the same condition (the output FF remains at 1).

When pulse 3 arrives, switch 3 is turned on. Switches 1 and 2 remain on, while switch 4 is off. The ladder is now 87.5% of full-scale voltage, and is thus greater than the transducer voltage. As a result, when the AND gates are enabled, they reverse. The not-greater AND gate turns off, and the greater AND gate turns on. The output FF then sets to 0.

When pulse 4 arrives, switch 4 is turned on. All switches are now on. The ladder is at maximum (full scale) and thus is greater than the transducer voltage. When the AND gates are enabled, they remain in the same condition. The output FF remains at a 0.

The 4 binary bits (digital pulses) applied to the microprocessor are 1, 1, 0, and 0, or 1100. This is a binary 12, which is 75% of 16. In a practical A/D converter, when the fourth pulse has passed, all the switches are reset to the off position. This places them in a condition to spell out the next 4-bit binary word (group of four digital pulses).

D/A Conversion. A D/A converter performs the opposite function of the A/D converter just described. The D/A converter produces an output voltage that corresponds to the digital pulses. As shown in Fig. 2–93, a conversion ladder is also used in the D/A converter. The output of the conversion ladder is a voltage that represents a percentage of the full-scale reference voltage. The output percentage depends on switch positions. In turn, the switches are set to on or off by corresponding digital pulses. In a control system, the digital input is taken from the microprocessor-based output, while the d-c output voltage from the ladder is applied to the control device.

The switches in the D/A converter are essentially a form of AND gate. Each gate completes the circuit from the reference voltage to the corresponding ladder resistor when both the enable pulse (from the system clock) and the digital pulses (from the microcomputer output) coincide.

Assume that the digital number from the microprocessor to be converted is 1000 (decimal 8). When the first pulse is applied, switch A is enabled and the

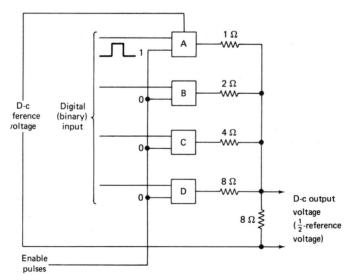

FIGURE 2-93 Digital-to-analog converter using the 4-bit system.

reference voltage is applied to the 1-Ω resistor. When switches B, C, and D receive their enable pulses, there are no digital pulses (or the pulses are in the 0 condition). Thus, switches B, C, and D do not complete the circuits to the 2-, 4-, and 8-Ω ladder resistors. These resistors combine with the 8-Ω output resistor to produce a 1-Ω resistance in series with the 1-Ω ladder resistance. This divides the reference voltage in half to produce 50% of full-scale output. Since 8 is one-half of 16, the 50% output voltage represents 8.

2-13   MEASUREMENTS IN CONTROL AND INSTRUMENTATION SYSTEMS

Transducers convert physical measurements (temperature, rate of flow, acidity, etc.) into electrical quantities of voltage, current, or resistance, and possibly capacitance or inductance. Current, voltage, and resistance are generally measured by means of meters, either analog or digital. Capacitance and inductance are usually measured by some form of bridge circuit. Similarly, many transducers are used in a bridge network, and some meters include a bridge network in their circuits. It is assumed that you are familiar with meter basics, both analog and digital, as well as the operation of basic bridge circuits. If not, you are definitely not ready for microcomputer-based control and instrumentation systems, and your attention is directed to the author's best-selling *Handbook of Electronic Meters* (Englewood Cliffs, N.J.: Prentice-Hall, Inc. 1981).

Many control and instrumentation systems also require a timing or count function as part of their operation. For example, it may be necessary to measure the elapsed time between two events to perform some control function. It may also be necessary to measure the frequency, or to provide a time and frequency reference for another control function. These functions involve the use of *timers* and *counters,* both of which are discussed in this section.

2-13.1   Timers

Time is measured by some form of clock. In modern control and instrumentation systems, time is generally measured by some form of *electronic* clock, although there are systems where the more familiar spring motor or electric clocks are used. The digital wristwatch is a familiar example of an electronic clock.

Timers are widely used in industry to initiate some process and then to stop the process after a predetermined time interval. The duration of such intervals may be seconds, minutes, hours, or even days. For some applications, the timer intervals are measured in microseconds or some other fraction of a second. Clock-driven timers are generally used when the time intervals are about 1 s or longer, although there are exceptions. Figure 2–94 shows some typical clock timers.

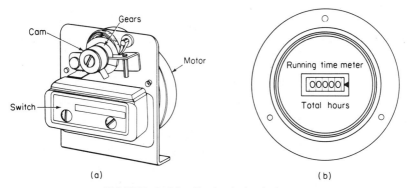

(a)

(b)

FIGURE 2-94 Typical clock timers.

2-13.2 Electronic Timer Basics

Where the time intervals involved are in the order of a few microseconds to a few minutes, electronic timers are generally used. Operation of most electronic timers is based on the *charge and discharge of a capacitor.* If a capacitor is connected to a d-c voltage, the instant the circuit is completed a relatively heavy charging current flows. The current falls off quickly as the capacitor is being charged and stops completely when the capacitor is "fully charged." If a resistor is placed between a voltage source and a capacitor, as shown in Fig. 2–95, the resistor impedes the current flow. The time it takes the capacitor to reach "full-charge" then depends on the values of the capacitor and the resistor. As shown in Fig. 2–95, a capacitor is considered to be "fully charged" when it reaches 63% of the full-charge value. The time that it takes to reach the 63% point is called the *time constant.*

FIGURE 2-95 Relationship among current, CEMF, and time as a capacitor is charged.

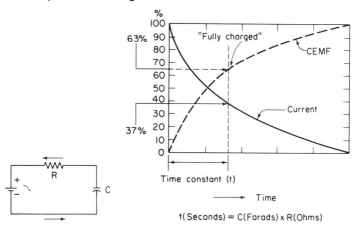

2-13.3   Electronic Time-Delay Relay

The principle of using capacitor charge and discharge through known resistance values can be readily adapted to control the timing function of an electronic timer, also known as an electronic time-delay relay. Such time-delay relays are particularly useful for industrial or other applications that require a time delay of definite duration (typically very short duration) after a switch is opened or closed. For example, in photographic printing, it is necessary to have a carefully controlled exposure time ranging from a fraction of a second to several minutes. An electronic time delay must turn on the exposure or printing lights as a switch is operated, and automatically turn off the lights after a predetermined time interval.

Figure 2-96 shows a basic electronic time-delay relay circuit that uses a capacitor charge to control a time interval. Operation of the circuit is started when pushbutton switch S is closed (pressed), which shorts out capacitor C, effectively removing C from the circuit. Closing switch S also places a negative voltage (from the battery) on the base of transistor Q, turning Q on. With Q on, collector current flows through the coil of relay K, closing the relay contacts. In turn, these contacts control operation of the circuit being timed by the time-delay relay. For example, closure of the relay contacts could turn on photographic exposure lights. When S is released (open), capacitor C starts to charge. When C is charged sufficiently, the forward bias on Q is overcome, and Q stops conducting. This removes current from relay K, and the relay contacts open, removing power to the circuit being controlled or timed (such as turning off photographic exposure lights). Since capacitor C is fixed, resistor R can be adjusted to set the desired time constant of the circuit (the time the relay contacts are closed and opened).

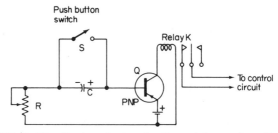

FIGURE 2-96   Basic electronic time-delay relay (for long time intervals).

2-13.4   Counters

Counting is a form of measurement. There are two types of counting found in control and instrumentation systems. One type of counting is used to obtain an *indication of quantity* such as a number of units or of actions performed. An example is counting the number of units passing a given point on a conveyor belt. The other kind of counting is used as a step in control systems where a certain *action is initiated or terminated* after a certain number of units or actions has been counted. An example is the stopping of a conveyor belt after a certain number of units have passed a given point. No matter what the application, there are three basic types of counters used in control and instrumentation systems. These include mechanical, electrical, and electronic counters.

The most common form of mechanical counter is shown in Fig. 2–97. Such counters are also known as *registers*. The counters shown are operated by mechanical force applied to a stroke arm. An electrical counter or register, which often resembles a mechanical register, except that the units wheel is activated by an electromagnet, is able to count electrical pulses. Each pulse or current flowing through the coil of the electromagnet advances the count by one unit. Figure 2–98 shows a typical electrical counter and how it can be used in

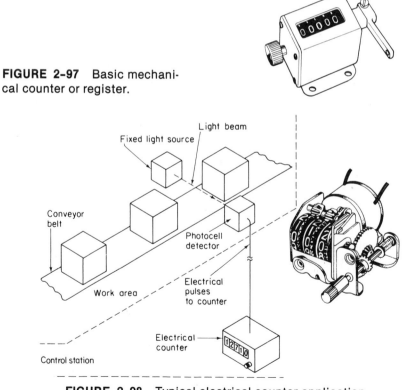

FIGURE 2-97 Basic mechanical counter or register.

FIGURE 2-98 Typical electrical counter application.

conjunction with a light sensor or photocell (Sec. 2–6.1) to count objects passing by on a conveyor belt. The photocell is mounted on one side of a moving conveyor, and a fixed light source is mounted on the other side of the belt. A light beam is interrupted as objects on the belt pass between the photocell and light source. As a result, an electrical pulse is sent from the photocell (or a relay controlled by the photocell) to the electrical counter, advancing the count by one.

2-13.5 Electronic Counters

Mechanical and electrical counters are limited to about 15,000 counts per minute. Beyond that, an electronic counter is generally required for most control applications. An electronic counter operates by comparing an unknown frequency or time interval to a known frequency or known time interval. The counter presents the information in an easy-to-read, unambiguous numerical display or readout. The readout of most electronic counters is similar to that of a digital meter. In fact, a digital meter is essentially an electronic counter, plus a conversion circuit for converting voltage to a series of pulses.

The accuracy of an electronic counter depends primarily on stability of a known frequency, which is usually derived from an internal oscillator. The accuracy of the oscillator can be checked against broadcast standards. Thus, an electronic counter can become a frequency or time standard. Counters are often used with accessories in control systems. For example, there are electronic counters that retain their counts for automatic recording of measurements, digital clocks that control measurement intervals and time information for simultaneous recording, D/A converters for high-resolution analog records of digital measurements, and scanners or multiplexers that can receive the outputs from several electronic counters for entry into a single recording device. Also, there are mechanical and optical tachometers for speed of rotation measurements (Sec. 2–3.3) that are designed to provide inputs to frequency counters.

Although there are many types of electronic counters, there are only five functions related to counters: *totalizing, frequency measurement, period measurement, time-interval measurement,* and *clock operation.*

Figure 2–99 shows the basic counter circuit for *totalizing operation.* With the start–stop switch in the start position (main gate open), the decade readouts (which are some form of digital readout) totalize input pulses until the main gate is closed by the start–stop switch being set to stop. The sensitivity control determines the level of input pulses that are counted (only pulses above a certain amplitude, such as 5 V, are counted). The amplifier and Schmitt trigger shape the input pulses to a suitable form and level that can be accepted by the decade readouts.

Totalizing can be remotely controlled. For example, the input pulses can come from a photocell detector counting objects passing by on a conveyor belt. The manual switch and readouts can be located at a remote control station, or

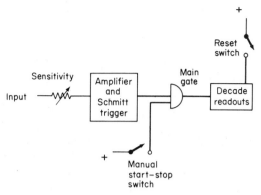

FIGURE 2-99 Basic counter circuit for totalizing operation.

possibly under the control of a microprocessor-based controller. The operator or controller can then start and stop the count by operating the start–stop switch. Counter readout assemblies must be *reset,* either manually or by other electronic control. If not, a new count is added to a previous count each time the gate is opened. Manual reset is done by pushing a reset button, which applies a voltage to all the readouts simultaneously, setting them at a position that produces a numerical zero on each readout. For other modes of operation (such as frequency measurement, time interval, or period measurement), reset is done by a pulse applied to all counters at regular intervals. This pulse is developed by a low-frequency oscillator (usually 2 or 3 Hz). Therefore, two or three counts or "samples" are taken each second. The pulse oscillator (often called the *sample rate* oscillator) is adjustable in frequency on some counters.

Figure 2-100 shows the basic counter circuit for *frequency* measurement.

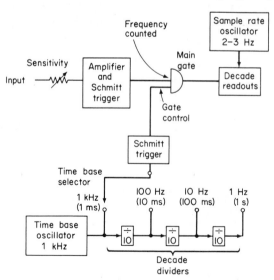

FIGURE 2-100 Basic counter circuit for frequency measurement operation.

The signals to be counted are first converted to uniform pulses by the Schmitt trigger. The pulses are then routed through the main gate and into the counter/readout, where the pulses are totalized. The number of pulses totalized during the "gate-open" interval is a measure of the average input frequency for that interval. For example, assume that a gate is held open for 1 s and the count is 333. This indicates a frequency of 333 Hz. The count obtained, with the correct decimal point, is then displayed and retained until a new sample is ready to be shown. The time-base selector switch selects the gating interval, thus positioning the decimal point and selecting the appropriate measurement units.

Figure 2–101 shows the basic counter circuit for *period* measurement. Period measurements are made with the input and time-base connections reversed from those for frequency measurement. In the period mode, the unknown input signals to be counted control the main gate, and the time base frequency is counted and read out. For example, if the time-base frequency is 1 MHz, the indicated count is in microseconds. A count of 80 indicates that the gate has been held open for 80 μs.

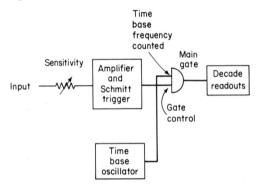

FIGURE 2-101 Basic counter circuit for period measurement operation.

Figure 2–102 shows the basic counter circuit for *time-interval* measurement. Time-interval measurements are essentially the same as period measurements. However, a time-interval mode concerns time between two events, rather than the repetition rate of signals to be counted. Counters vary greatly in the time-interval measuring capability. Some counters measure only

FIGURE 2-102 Basic counter circuit for time-interval measurement operation.

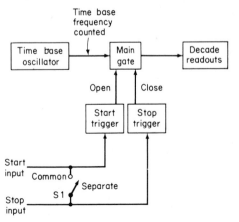

the duration of an electrical event; others measure the interval between the start of two pulses. In the circuit of Fig. 2–102, control of the gate is done by two trigger circuits that receive their inputs from the signals being measured.

Figure 2–103 shows the basic circuit for an *electronic clock*. This circuit is similar to that used for digital watches and clocks. Although all electronic counters do not have a clock function, the same basic circuits are used. As shown, the clock circuit consists essentially of a highly stable crystal oscillator time base (the frequency of which is divided down to produce 1-pulse-per-second pulses) and a digital readout similar to that of an electronic counter.

Once set, the clock operates continuously with the count increasing by 1 second for each pulse. The clock is set by introducing a series of fast pulses (usually from the dividers at some rate much faster than 1 pulse per second) into the counter until the correct time is indicated. Then the counter input is returned to 1 pulse per second. In addition to a visual readout, some clocks used in control systems provide an electrical output that can be applied to other equipment.

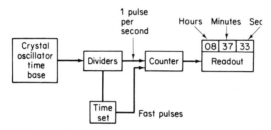

FIGURE 2-103 Basic circuit for electronic clock.

2-14 BASIC CONTROL DEVICES

As discussed in Chapter 1, the final stage of most control systems includes (1) switches which may be opened or closed, (2) valves which may be opened or closed or adjusted to some position between those two extremes, (3) electromagnetic devices (relays, solenoids, actuators) which may be energized by an electric current to perform some mechanical or electrical function, or (4) motors which may be started, stopped, or reversed, or whose speed may be varied while running.

2-14.1 Contactors (Switches and Relays)

Switches and relays are referred to as contactors, since their primary function is to complete an electrical circuit, which is done by opening and closing contacts, manually in the case of switches, electrically in the case of relays. Figures 2–104 through 2–107 show some typical switches used in industrial control systems. Figures 2–108 and 2–109 show typical relays and relay-contact arrangements found in industrial control.

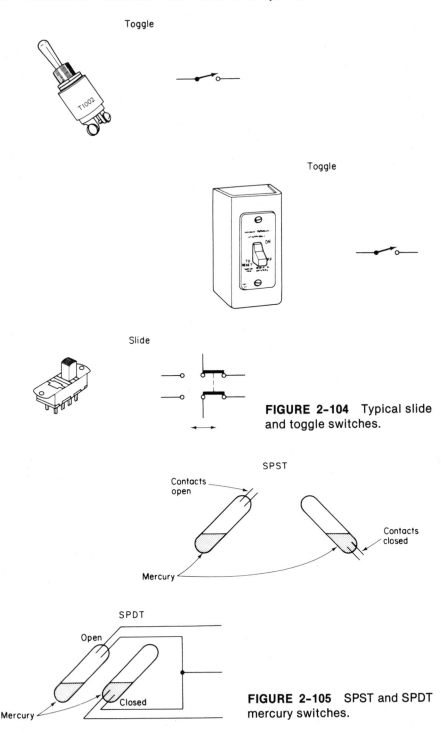

Toggle

Toggle

Slide

FIGURE 2-104   Typical slide and toggle switches.

SPST

Contacts open

Contacts closed

Mercury

SPDT

Open

Closed

Mercury

FIGURE 2-105   SPST and SPDT mercury switches.

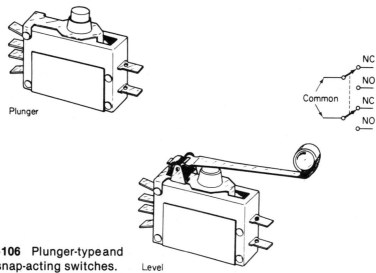

Plunger

Common

NC
NO
NC
NO

FIGURE 2-106 Plunger-type and lever-type snap-acting switches.

Level

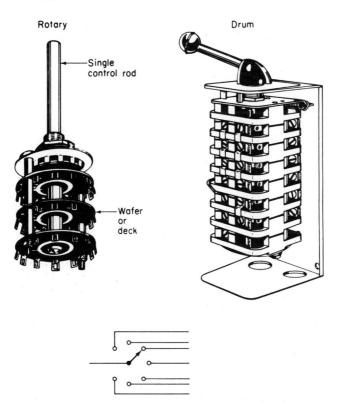

Rotary

Single control rod

Wafer or deck

Drum

FIGURE 2-107 Rotary and drum switches.

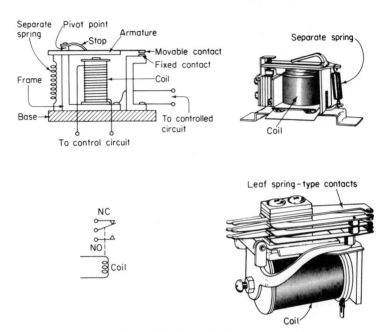

FIGURE 2-108   Typical electromagnetic relays.

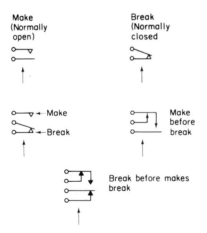

FIGURE 2-109   Typical relay contact arrangements.

Figure 2-110 shows a basic relay control system, and illustrates the two major advantages of a relay: *remote operation* and *control of large currents with small currents*. For example, assume that the load is an electrical device (say a bank of high-wattage lights) that must be operated from a remote location. If the lights are connected directly to a switch, a very heavy duty switch must be used, and the wiring between the switch and lights must also be heavy duty. This results in a considerable power loss in the wiring and the possibility

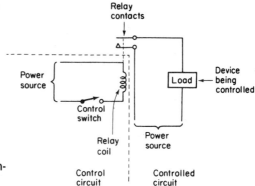

FIGURE 2-110 Basic relay control system.

of early switch contact burnout. With the circuit of Fig. 2–110, the relay can be located as near as possible to the lights, and the switch can be located at any convenient remote location. Thus, the switch and control circuit wiring can be of the low-current type, since the only current they must handle is drawn by the relay coil (typically a few milliamperes or less).

The basic relay application is that of an on–off function. In many cases, a relay must remain energized after a control circuit is turned off. Using the previous example of a relay that controls lights at a remote location, the control switch must be held closed to keep the lights on. Obviously, this is not practical in many applications. Instead, a *latching relay* can be used to keep the lights on after the control switch is released. A latching relay arrangement is shown in Fig. 2–111. The relay has two sets of normally open (NO) contacts. One set of contacts is used for the controlled circuit. The other set of contacts forms part of the control circuit. When the NO switch is pressed, current flows in the coil, and the controlled-circuit relay contacts make, applying power to the lights. The other set of relay contacts also make, completing the electrical circuit between the power source and coil, through the NC (normally closed) switch. The NO switch can then be released, the coil remains energized, and the lights remain on. When the lights are to be turned off, the NC switch is pressed momentarily, power is removed to the relay coil, and both sets of the relay contacts break, removing power from the lights.

FIGURE 2-111 Typical latching relay circuit.

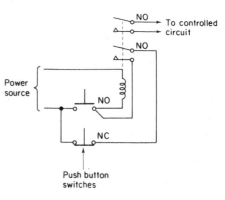

Figure 2–112 shows a rotary stepping relay used in many control systems. Each time the relay coil is energized, the armature actuates a ratchet wheel to advance one position. One or more cams may be attached to the ratchet, as shown. After a predetermined number of energizing pulses have been received by the relay coil, the cam rotates to a point where the spring leaf carrying the movable contact coincides with a notch in the cam. The end of the spring leaf drops into the notch, causing the contacts to make or break, thus closing or opening the controlled circuit. The next energizing pulse brings the leaf out of the notch and restores the contacts to their original position, where they remain until the next notch in the cam is reached. Each cam has its own spring leaf and contact set (and controlled circuit).

Electronic relays are used in control systems where the available control circuit current is not sufficient to operate a relay. A light-operated relay is a typical example. The output current of a photocell is typically a few microamperes, which is not sufficient to operate a heavy-duty relay. Instead, the current is amplified using one or more transistors. Such a combination of relay and amplifier is called an electronic relay. In addition to transistors, electronic relays use various other solid-state devices such as the SCR (silicon-controlled rectifier), unijunction transistors, and light-actuated switches. Such devices are described in Sec. 2–14.4

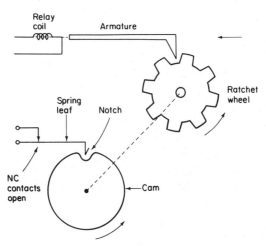

FIGURE 2-112   Rotary stepping relay operation.

2-14.2   Actuators (Solenoids and Motors)

Solenoids and motors are two of the most common actuators used in control systems. An actuator is any device that converts a signal input to a mechanical motion. This is the reverse action of a transducer. The signal may be electrical, pneumatic, hydraulic, or mechanical. The motion, or output from the actuator, may be linear, rotary, reciprocating, and so on. Gears and linkages may be used to change one type of motion to another. In general, solenoids are used to produce linear motion in response to an input signal from a controller, whereas motors are used for rotary motion. However, the reverse can be true in some cases.

Figure 2-113 shows the two basic types (pusher and puller) of solenoid actuators. Both the pusher and puller types consist essentially of a coil, a moving core, and a spring. When the coil is energized by a signal voltage from the controller or other source, the magnetic field around the coil pulls the core into the coil. When the coil is deenergized, the spring pulls the core out of the coil. The device to be actuated is attached to and moves with the core. Thus, the activated device (such as a valve or cylinder) is pulled to one position as the coil is energized and restored to its original position when the coil is deenergized. For example, such a solenoid actuator can be used to open and close a valve. The spring that moves the core back to the deenergized position may be a part of the solenoid or part of the actuated device.

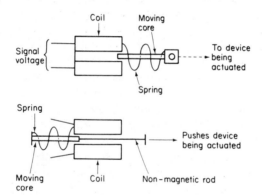

FIGURE 2-113 Basic pusher and puller solenoid actuators.

As shown in Fig. 2-113, a solenoid may also be used as a pusher. When the coil is energized, the core is moved in, and the nonmagnetic rod pushes the device to be actuated. When the coil is deenergized, the spring forces the core and the rod to their original positions. Such pushers frequently are used to remove objects from a moving conveyor belt upon a signal from a controller. Both the pusher and puller described thus far are a form of *linear actuator.* Linear solenoid actuators have many applications, such as the operation of valves, brakes, gates, and door openers, where mechanical force is required to push or pull an object in a straight line.

Figure 2-114 shows operation of a *rotary solenoid* that produces rotary output strokes from about 5 to 90°. Rotary solenoids are often used to operate a ratchet connected to the lever arm of a rotary switch, where each output stroke of the solenoid advances the lever arm of the switch one position.

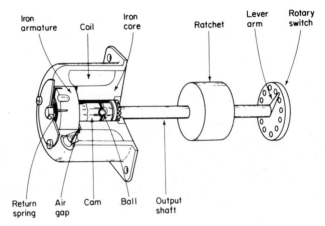

FIGURE 2-114   Rotary solenoid operation.

The *d-c motor* is a common form of actuator. As shown in Fig. 2–115, there are three classes of d-c motors: *series, shunt,* and *compound.* The classification depends on the manner in which the field winding is connected to the armature.

In the *series field motor,* the field winding is connected in series with the armature winding and the power line. Since the two windings are in series, the same current flows through both windings, and the field winding has relatively few turns of wire (of the same size as the armature wire) compared to that of other motor classifications. Series motors have a *high starting torque,* and are often used in control applications where the inertia of a heavy load must be overcome. Typical series motor applications include electric locomotives and cranes. The simplest form of speed control for a series motor is a series variable resistance, as shown in Fig. 2–116. Speed is reduced when resistance is increased, and vice versa. Once adjusted, the speed of a series motor remains fairly constant, provided that the load is constant. However, an increasing load reduces speed, and vice versa.

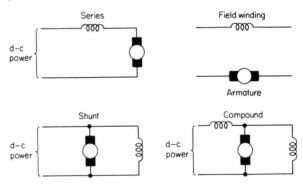

FIGURE 2-115   Classes of d-c motors (series, shunt, and compound).

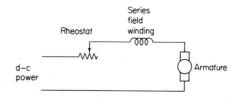

FIGURE 2-116 Basic speed control circuit for series motor.

In the *shunt field motor,* the field winding is connected in parallel or shunt, with the armature winding. The shunt field has fairly high resistance, so as to get maximum current flow through the armature. For this reason, the shunt field winding has many turns of relatively fine wire. Although little current flows through the field winding, proper field strength is maintained because of the many turns of wire. Shunt motors are generally used where *constant speed* is of greater importance than high starting torque. For that reason, shunt motors are used to operate machine tools and blowers. The simplest form of speed control for a shunt motor is a variable resistance in series with the field winding or the armature as shown in Fig. 2–117. In the field winding resistance system, an increase in resistance produces a weaker field and a higher speed. With the armature resistance system, increasing the resistance causes a reduction of armature voltage and a reduction of speed.

In the *compound field motor,* two field windings are used, one series and one shunt. The series winding is wound with a few turns of heavy wire. The shunt winding is wound with many turns of fine wire. A compound motor has the characteristics of both the series and shunt motors. These include the ability to maintain a *fairly constant speed* with variations in load, and the ability to produce a *fairly large torque* (both starting and running). Compound motor speed may be controlled by variable resistances in the armature circuit, the field winding circuit, or both.

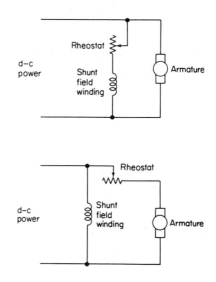

FIGURE 2-117 Basic speed control circuit for shunt motor.

Figure 2–118 shows a simple switch circuit for *reversal of a d-c motor.* A d-c motor rotates because of the repulsion between the magnetic poles of the field and similar poles of the armature. If the polarity of both field and armature windings are reversed, the motor continues to rotate in the same direction. To reverse direction of rotation, the polarity of the field or the armature (but not both) must be reversed. Usually, the armature polarity is reversed.

A-c motors operate by the same basic principle as d-c motors (interaction between magnetic fields). However, the "field winding" or an a-c motor is called the *stator,* since it is stationary (generally in the form of a ring or cylinder). The "armature" of an a-c motor is called a *rotor* and is usually made up of metal segments, although some rotors have windings. There are three basic types of a-c motors: *induction, synchronous,* and *universal.* All three types operate by the principle of a rotating magnetic field. A-c motors can be operated with single-phase a-c power or polyphase (two- or three-phase) power.

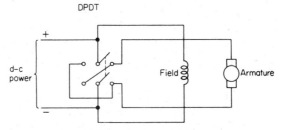

FIGURE 2-118   DPDT switch circuit for reversal of shunt d-c motor.

Figure 2–119 shows the basic elements of an *induction motor,* which is the so-called squirrel-cage motor. When an induction motor is operated from single-phase power, it is necessary to split the power into the equivalent of a two-phase current. There are several methods for doing this. The most common method is to use a *capacitor-start, split-phase induction motor* shown in Fig. 2–120. In this circuit, one stator winding (the *starting winding*) is wound on two opposite poles and has a capacitor in the circuit (to shift the phase of the voltage applied to one stator by 90°). The other stator winding (the *main* or *running winding*) is wound on the other two poles, and has no capacitor in the circuit. Both circuits are connected in parallel across the single-phase power line. Because of the phase difference between the currents in both circuits, the motor starts as a two-phase induction motor. When the rotor reaches about 75% of full running speed, a centrifugal switch mounted on the rotor shaft opens the circuit of the starting winding. The motor then continues to run at normal speed, using the main winding. Induction motors are well suited to *three-phase power.* The effect on the motor is the same as if three generators are used, operating 120° apart electrically. The rotating field is provided by three stator windings wound on three sets of poles, 120° apart. These windings usually are placed in slots along the inner surface of the stator frame.

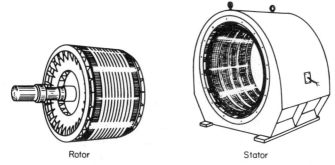

Rotor Stator

FIGURE 2-119 Rotor and stator of squirrel-cage induction motor.

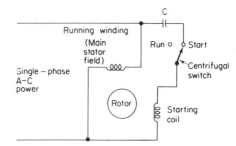

FIGURE 2-120 Capacitor-start, split-phase induction motor.

The stator of a *synchronous motor* is essentially the same as that of an induction motor. However, the rotor of synchronous motor does not depend on induced current from the stator for a magnetic field. In large synchronous motors, the rotor contains a winding (somewhat similar to that of the d-c motor) which is excited by a separate source of direct current supplied by means of slip rings and brushes. In small synchronous motors, the rotor winding may be replaced by permanent magnets, eliminating the need for an external d-c source. Because the rotor has its own magnetic field, there is no need for the rotor to slip behind the rotating stator field. As a result, the rotor rotates in *exact step,* or *synchronization,* with the revolution of the field.

If alternating current is applied to a series d-c motor, the polarity of the magnetic fields around both the stator and rotor (field and armature) windings change in step with alternations of the current. Such an arrangement is known as a *universal motor.* Since like magnetic poles repel, regardless of whether they are two north poles or two south poles, a series d-c motor can be operated with a-c power (in addition to d-c power).

Even the simplest motors must have a means of starting and stopping, as well as overcurrent protection. The subject of motor control is quite complex, and is not described here due to space limitations. For a full discussion of motor control, the reader's attention is invited to the author's best-selling *Handbook of Simplified Electrical Wiring* (Englewood Cliffs, N.J.: Prentice-Hall, Inc., 1975).

Motors may be coupled to the device they actuate directly on the same shaft or through a train of gears. When gear trains are used, the actuated device may rotate faster or slower than the speed of the motor, depending on the *gear ratios* used. Also, the gear train can provide *torque amplification,* if required, since torque is increased in proportion to a decrease in speed. In some cases, it is necessary to quickly engage and disengage a motor from the device being actuated, which is the function of a *clutch.* The most common type of motor clutch is the *friction disk clutch.* There are several methods for actuating clutch disks. In industrial control, the most common clutch actuator is an electromagnet or solenoid shown in Fig. 2–121. Current flowing through the solenoid coil windings produces a magnetic field that forces one of the clutch disks toward (or away from) the other clutch disk. The same principles used for

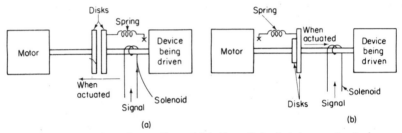

FIGURE 2-121   Operation of friction disk clutches actuated by an electromagnet or solenoid.

clutches can also be used to brake a motor, as shown in Fig. 2–122. Here, only one friction disk is mounted on the shaft between the motor and the actuated device. The other friction surface is supplied by the housing which encloses the brake. In Fig. 2–122a, a spring holds the disk against the housing, preventing the shaft from rotating. When a *brake release* signal is applied to the coil, the disk is forced away from the housing, and the shaft is free to rotate. When the signal is removed, the spring pulls the disk back against the housing, and the rotation is stopped. The functions of clutch and brake can also be incorporated in a single device.

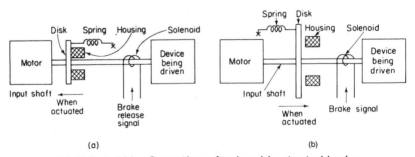

FIGURE 2-122   Operation of solenoid-actuated brakes.

2-14.3 Valves and Fluid Actuators

A *valve* is a variable opening or orifice used to control the flow of a fluid or semifluid (such as powered material). There are two basic types of valves: the *shutoff* type, where the opening is either completely open or completely closed, and the *throttling* type, where the opening may be adjusted to any size between the two extremes. Of course, a throttling valve does provide shutoff when completely closed. There is an infinite variety of valve used in modern control systems. Only the most commonly used are described here.

The *globe valve* shown in Fig. 2–123 is the most common type of *plug-and-seat* valve, and is generally used to provide complete shutoff. The flow of fluid through the valve is controlled by a movable plug. As the plug is brought closer to the seat by action of the stem, the opening in the valve is reduced, as is flow through the valve. The position of the plug is determined by the position of the stem. In turn, the stem position is set by the solenoid-operated actuator.

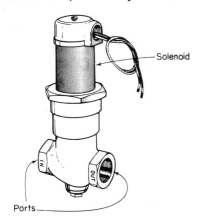

Solenoid

Ports

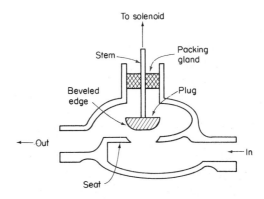

FIGURE 2-123 Solenoid-operated plug-and-seat (globe) valve.

The *butterfly valve* shown in Fig. 2–124 is useful if the line size is large and the line pressure low. Butterfly valves are generally used to provide throttling action, particularly to control the flow of gas or air (for example, at the intake of an automobile carburetor). The valve consists of a circular vane pivoted within the valve body. The position of the vane, and thus the effective size of the passageway through the valve, is controlled by means of a rotary actuator or linear actuator (Sec. 2–14.2) with a suitable mechanical linkage which converts the linear motion to rotary motion. A butterfly valve is especially suited for controlling the flow of pulpy or semisolid materials, which can foul other types of valves.

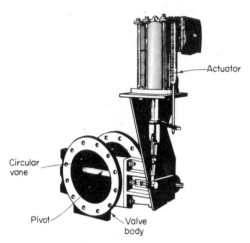

FIGURE 2–124   Butterfly valve.

2–14.4 Electronic Control Devices

The use of electronic devices in control and instrumentation systems is constantly increasing. Solid-state control devices such as the *controlled rectifier* or *thyristor* are now in common use, and have generally replaced the hydraulic and pneumatic systems. Even the electrical control devices such as the thyratron and ignatron have been replaced by solid-state electronic control devices. The controlled rectifier is similar to a basic diode, but must be triggered or turned on by an external voltage source. Technically, a thyristor is defined as any solid-state switch or control device whose operations depend on regenerative feedback.

One of the most commonly used electronic control devices is the SCR shown in Fig. 2–125. With some manufacturers, the letters SCR refer to *semiconductor-controlled rectifier* and can mean any type of solid-state controlled rectifier. However, SCR usually refers to *silicon-controlled rectifiers*. Either a-c or d-c voltage can be used as the gate signal to turn the SCR on, provided that the gate voltage is large enough to trigger the SCR into the ON condition. However, an SCR is used to best advantage when both the load and trigger are alternating current. With a-c power, control of the power applied to the

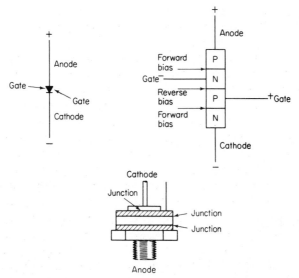

FIGURE 2-125   Symbol, block diagram, and basic operation of a typical SCR.

load is determined by the *relative phase* of the trigger signal versus the load voltage. Because the trigger control is lost once the SCR is conducting, an a-c voltage at the load permits the trigger to regain control. Each alternation of alternating current through the load causes conduction to be interrupted (when the a-c voltage drops to zero between cycles), regardless of the polarity of the trigger signal.

Figure 2-126 shows some basic forms of *a-c phase control.* Phase control is the process of rapid ON–OFF switching that connects an a-c power supply to a load for a controlled fraction of each cycle. This is a highly efficient means of controlling average power to loads such as lamps, heaters, and motors. Control is done by governing the *phase angle* of the a-c waveform at which the control device is triggered. The control device then conducts for the remainder of the half-cycle.

The simplest form of phase control is the half-wave control, shown in Fig. 2-126a. This circuit uses one SCR for control of current flow in one direction only and is used for loads that require power control from zero to one-half of full-wave maximum. The circuit is also useful where direct current is required (or permitted) for the load.

The addition of one rectifier, as shown in Fig. 2-126b, provides a fixed half-cycle of power which shifts the power control range to half-power minimum and full-power maximum. The use of two SCRs, as shown in Fig. 2-126c, controls from zero to full power but requires two gate signals. A single gate or trigger signal is required for the zero to full-power control circuit of Fig. 2-126d. The most flexible circuit, Fig. 2-126e, uses one SCR inside a bridge rec-

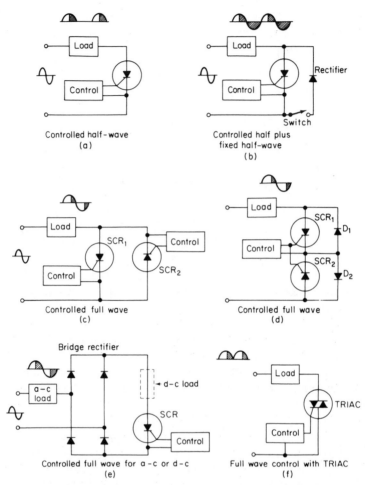

FIGURE 2-126 Basic forms of a-c phase control.

tifier and may be used for control of either a-c power or full-wave rectified d-c power.

Generally, the simplest, most efficient, and most reliable method for controlling a-c power is by the use of a *Triac,* shown in Fig. 2–126f. This circuit provides full-wave control in both directions, using only one gate or trigger (often a *Diac*). For that reason, the Triac–Diac combination is, by far, the most popular a-c power control circuit. Figure 2–127 shows the symbol, outer shell, and controls of a typical Triac (*tri*ode *a-c* semiconductor, as coined by General Electric). Unlike the SCR, the Triac conducts in *both directions* and is, therefore, useful for controlling devices operated by a-c power (such as a-c motors). The Triac is made to conduct when a "breakdown" or "breakover"

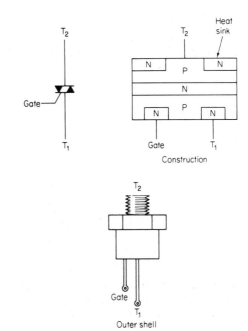

FIGURE 2-127 Symbol, outer shell, and construction of a typical Triac.

voltage is applied across terminals T1 and T2, and when a trigger voltage is applied. Triacs can be triggered from many sources. One of the most common trigger sources is the Diac (*di*ode *a-c* semiconductor device, as coined by General Electric) shown in Fig. 2–128. The diodes in a Diac do not conduct until a certain "breakover" voltage is reached. For example, if a Diac is designed for a breakover voltage of 3 V, and the Diac is used in a circuit with less than 3 V, the diodes appear as a high resistance (no current flow). Both diodes conduct when the voltage is raised to any value over 3 V.

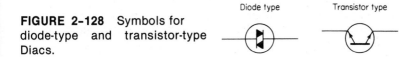

FIGURE 2-128 Symbols for diode-type and transistor-type Diacs.

Another popular electronic control device is the SCS (or *silicon-controlled switch*) shown in Fig. 2–129. The SCS is similar to the SCR, except that the SCS has two gates, thus permitting various combinations of positive and negative gate signals and load voltages. For example, if a negative load voltage is applied to terminal 4, with a positive voltage at terminal 1, the SCS does not turn on, no matter what trigger signals are applied. However, with a positive voltage at terminal 4 and a negative voltage at terminal 1, the SCS is turned on by either a positive voltage at terminal 2 or a negative voltage at terminal 3.

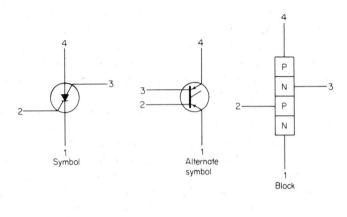

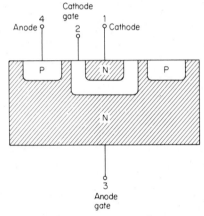

FIGURE 2-129   Circuit symbols, block diagram, and basic physical construction of a typical SCS.

Figure 2–130 shows the symbols and equivalent circuits of the SUS and SBS. The SUS (*silicon unilateral switch*) is essentially a miniature SCR with an anode gate (instead of the usual cathode gate) and a built-in low-voltage zener diode between the gate and cathode. The SUS switches, or turns on, at a given voltage. The SBS (*silicon bilateral switch*) is essentially two identical SUS structures arranged in an inverse-parallel circuit. Since the SBS operates as a switch with both polarities of applied voltage, the SBS is particularly useful for triggering Triacs with alternate positive and negative gate pulses.

Figure 2–131 shows the UJT (*unijunction transistor*), which is another commonly used trigger source control rectifier. Figure 2–131 shows the UJT connected in a basic trigger circuit, known as a *relaxation oscillator,* that produces trigger pulses at a regular frequency or interval. The frequency or timing of a relaxation oscillator is controlled by the resistor–capacitor (*RC*) factor or time constant discussed in Sec. 2–13.2.

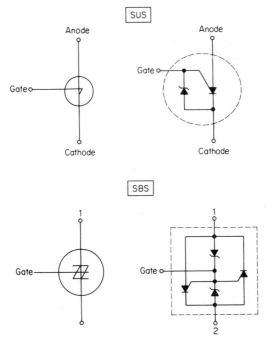

FIGURE 2-130 Symbols and equivalent circuits for SUS and SBS.

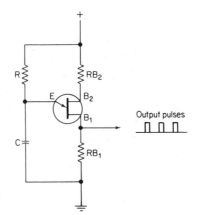

FIGURE 2-131 Basic UJT relaxation oscillator.

There are many ways of connecting the various versions of a basic relaxation oscillator circuit by using different trigger devices, control devices, and supply and load circuits. Figure 2-131 shows the basic half-wave and full-wave phase control circuits. With either circuit, the load, control device, and trigger device are all operated from the a-c power supply. Capacitor C is charged through adjustable resistor R on alternations of the a-c supply. In the half-wave circuit (SUS-SCR combination), C is charged once for each half-alternation or half-cycle. In the full-wave circuit (Diac–Triac combination), C is charged on both alternations of each cycle. When C is charged to a certain voltage, the trigger device turns on and provides a trigger signal to the control device. This switches the control device on for the remainder of the half-cycle, and power is applied to the load. If R is set to minimum resistance, C charges quickly, both the trigger and control devices go on early in the half-cycle, and maximum power is applied to the load. The opposite occurs when R is set to maximum resistance (minimum power to the load).

When the light-activated principle discussed in Sec. 2–6 is applied to electronic control devices, they are generally referred to as *light-activated semiconductors* (LAS). When light strikes silicon, there is an increase in current flow. In devices such as the SCR or SCS, the current increase acts as a trigger to turn on the device. The most common LAS devices are the LASCR (light-activated SCR), LASCS (light-activated SCS), and the opto-coupler (or light-activated switch).

Figure 2–132 shows the symbols and construction for the LASCR and LASCS. Note that the arrows indicate light or radiant energy striking the silicon chip. Both devices are similar in operation and characteristics to their corresponding SCR or SCS, except for the glass window on top of the can or enclosure. In a typical application the gate or trigger terminal is connected to a fixed voltage in the circuit. The LASCS is then triggered by light passing through the window onto the silicon chip area.

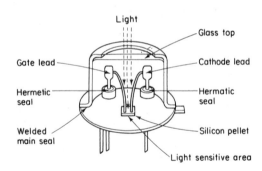

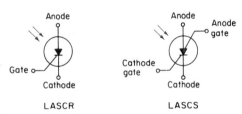

FIGURE 2-132 Symbols and construction for LASCR and LASCS.

Figure 2–133 shows a typical light-activated switch or opto-coupler where both the photocell and light source are sealed in a lightproof enclosure. When the light source is off, the photocell resistance is very high, and the ''switch'' is ''open.'' When the light source is on, the light strikes the photocell and causes its resistance to drop to zero. This ''closes'' the ''switch.'' Such a switch is completely noise-free and spark-free, which are important factors for many control applications. The light source can be an incandescent lamp. However, most modern opto-couplers use a light-emitting diode (LED).

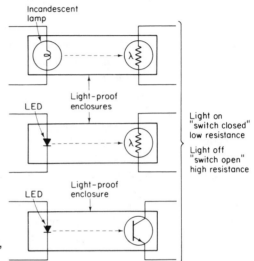

FIGURE 2-133 Typical opto-couplers (light-activated switches, LASS).

Electronic control devices are not limited to phase control. Almost any static switching function performed by various mechanical and electromechanical switches can be done with electronic controls. The *electronic proximity switch* shown in Fig. 2–134 is an example. This circuit is ideally suited to conveyor belt counting systems, flow switch actuators, door control, bank-

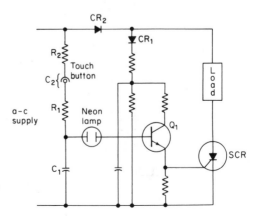

FIGURE 2-134 Electronic proximity switch.

safe monitors, and so on. Capacitor C_1, resistors R_1/R_2, and the sensor plate "capacitor" C_2 form a voltage divider across the a-c supply. The voltage across C_1 depends on the ratio of C/C_2 and the supply voltage. The capacitance of C_2, in turn, depends on the proximity to the sensor plate of any reasonably conductive and grounded object (metals passing on a conveyor belt, human body, etc.). As soon as the voltage across C_1 exceeds the breakdown voltage of the neon lamp, capacitors C_1 and C_2 discharge through the base and emitter of transistor Q_1. This discharge current is amplified by Q_1 and turns the SCR on to energize the load. The load remains energized as long as the sensor plate or "button" is touched.

One of the most comon electronic control applications is phase control of *electric motor speed*. There are many motor control systems, so we discuss only the basic ones here. The main problem of motor speed control is *sensing motor speed* to provide *feedback* to offset changes in speed. If motor speed increases (due to a change in load or supply voltage) the feedback signal decreases motor speed, and vice versa.

Figure 2–135 shows the basic circuit for speed control of a-c motors, using a tachometer generator geared to the motor. The output of the tachometer generator (or feedback signal) is rectified by diodes D_1 through D_4, and applied through resistor R_1 to amplifier transistor Q_1. This feedback signal is inverted by Q_1 and is used to charge capacitor C_1 through Q_2. The charge on C_1 determines the SCR on time. If the motor speed increases, the tachometer generator produces a greater output, which is rectified into a positive d-c voltage by the diodes. The positive voltage output is inverted by Q_1 to a negative voltage which charges C_1 to a lower value. The SCR then triggers at a later point, and the motor slows down. The charge on C_1 (and thus the motor speed) can also be set by adjustment of R_1.

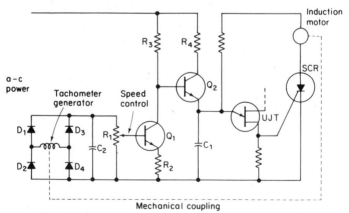

FIGURE 2-135   Induction motor speed control.

3

ELEMENTS OF MICROCOMPUTER AND MICROPROCESSOR-BASED SYSTEMS

In this chapter we review and summarize microcomputers and microprocessor-based digital equipment. The number systems, circuits, and elements discussed here are generally limited to those necessary to understand the digital control and instrumentation equipment described in Chapters 4 and 5. For a more thorough coverage of digital electronics, your attention is directed to the author's books referenced in Chapter 1 (Sec. 1-1.4)

3-1 DIGITAL NUMBER SYSTEMS AND ALPHANUMERIC CODES

Although the outside world generally uses the familiar decimal number system, the circuits found in microcomputers most often use some form of the *binary* number system. This is because binary numbers are compatible with *electrical pulses* used in digital equipment. Binary numbers use only two digits, 0 or 1, instead of the 10 digits found in the decimal system. In binary, the 0 can be represented by the absence of a pulse, with the 1 being represented by the presence of a pulse (or vice versa in some systems). The pulses, typically about 5 V in amplitude and a few microseconds (μs) or nanoseconds (ns) in duration, can be positive or negative without affecting the binary number system, as long as *only two states exist.*

When the binary number system is used in microcomputer systems, electrical pulses arranged in binary form are often referred to as *machine language.* This language, although quite compatible with electronic circuits, is cumbersome when the values are beyond a few digits. For that reason, most computer systems use some other form of number system for assembly of computer programs. Such systems (sometimes referred to as *assembly language*) are essentially shorthand versions of the binary system. The most common shorthand number systems used to enter and read out programs in computers and other digital electronic devices are the *octal, hexadecimal* (or *hex*), *binary-coded decimal* (or BCD), and *alphanumeric* systems or codes. It is assumed that you are already familiar with all of the number systems and codes noted above. If not, you are definitely not ready for microcomputer-based control systems!

3-1.1   Binary-Based Codes

There are a number of codes based on the binary number system. The simplest form of such coding is where decimal numbers (0 to 9) are converted into binary form using 4 binary digits or bits. This *4-bit system* is one of the original codes used in early digital computers, and is still used by some systems. With this system, generally known as *binary-coded decimal* or BCD, decimal 1 is represented by 0001, decimal 2 by 0010, and so on. When the decimal number has more than one digit, 4 binary bits are used for each decimal digit. For example, the decimal number 38 is represented by 8 binary bits, in groups of two, as follows:

$$3 \qquad 8 \quad \text{(decimal)}$$

$$0011 \quad 1000 \quad \text{(BCD)}$$

Note that this combination of eight binary digits is commonly used in microcomputers to form a binary *word.* In digital work, binary digits are referred to as *bits* (a contraction of *bi*nary digi*ts*). When eight binary digits are used to form words, the arrangement is known as an *8-bit system.* When all 8 bits are used at once, the combination is referred to as a *byte.* Any number less than 8 bits is called a *nibble,* although in an 8-bit system, a nibble is generally considered to be 4 bits. Similarly, some digital systems use 4-bit or 16-bit binary words or bytes. In fact, many of the newer microcomputer systems are designed for 16-bit words but also accept 8-bit words so as to be compatible with older systems.

There are also many other codes using the binary system, including the 2421, 5421, XS3, reflected Gray, 2 out of 5, and biquinary. Such codes are summarized in Fig. 3-1.

Decimal	Binary	Octal	Hexadecimal	BCD	Reflected gray	2 out of 5	Biquinary 5043210	2421	5421	XS3
0	0000	0	0	0000	0000	00011	0100001	0000	0000	0011–0011
1	0001	1	1	0001	0001	00101	0100010	0001	0001	0011–0100
2	0010	2	2	0010	0011	00110	0100100	0010	0010	0011–0101
3	0011	3	3	0011	0010	01001	0101000	0011	0011	0011–0110
4	0100	4	4	0100	0110	01010	0110000	0100	0100	0011–0111
5	0101	5	5	0101	0111	01100	1000001	1011	1000	0011–1000
6	0110	6	6	0110	0101	10001	1000010	1100	1001	0011–1001
7	0111	7	7	0111	0100	10010	1000100	1101	1010	0011–1010
8	1000	10	8	1000	1100	10100	1001000	1110	1011	0011–1011
9	1001	11	9	1001	1101	11000	1010000	1111	1100	0011–1100
10	1010	12	A	0001–0000	1111			0001–0000	0001–0000	0100–0011
11	1011	13	B	0001–0001	1110			0001–0001	0001–0001	0100–0100
12	1100	14	C	0001–0010	1010			0001–0010	0001–0010	0100–0101
13	1101	15	D	0001–0011	1011			0001–0011	0001–0011	0100–0110
14	1110	16	E	0001–0100	1001			0001–0100	0001–0100	0100–0111
15	1111	17	F	0001–0101	1000			0001–1011	0001–1000	0100–1000

FIGURE 3-1 Summary of codes used in digital electronics.

3-1.2 Alphanumeric Codes

While the 4-bit system is adequate to represent any decimal digit from 0 to 9, additional bits are necessary to represent letters of the alphabet and special characters (such as dollar signs, percent symbols, etc.) that are often required for digital applications (particularly computers). Most digital equipment manufacturers have settled on the United States of America Standard Code for Information Interchange, or USASCII, which is now generally written as ASCII (pronounced "askey"). ASCII is an 8-bit code and is thus ideally suited for hex representation. Also, since hex–binary conversion is relatively simple, both on paper and in the digital circuits, ASCII can be adapted to any digital system (and to microprocessor-based systems in particular).

Figure 3–2 shows the conversion between ASCII and hex. To convert from ASCII to hex, select the desired letter, symbol, or number, then move up vertically to find the hex MSD (most significant digit, also called the MSB or most significant bit). Then move horizontally to the left and find the hex LSD (least significant digit). For example, to find the hex code for the letter I, note that I appears in the "4" column of the hex MSD and in the "9" column of the hex LSD. Thus, hex 49 equals the letter I in ASCII. Going further, the hex 49 can be converted to 0100 1001 in binary, as is generally done inside digital circuits. The process can be reversed to convert from binary to ASCII. For example, binary 0010 0100 is 24 in hex, and $ in ASCII. As an exercise, find the ASCII letters for binary 0100-1100 0100-0101 0100-1110 0100-1011.

Most-significant hex digit

		0	1	2	3	4	5	6	7
	0	NUL	DLE	SP	0	@	P	\	p
	1	SOH	DC1	!	1	A	Q	a	q
	2	STX	DC2	"	2	B	R	b	r
	3	ETX	DC3	#	3	C	S	c	s
	4	EOT	DC4	$	4	D	T	d	t
	5	ENQ	NAK	%	5	E	U	e	u
Least-significant hex digit	6	ACK	SYN	&	6	F	V	f	v
	7	BEL	ETB	/	7	G	W	g	w
	8	BS	CAN	(	8	H	X	h	x
	9	HT	EM	)	9	I	Y	i	y
	A	LF	SUB	*	:	J	Z	j	z
	B	VT	ESC	+	;	K	[	k	{
	C	FF	FS	,	<	L	\	l	¦
	D	CR	GS	−	=	M	]	m	}
	E	SO	RS	.	>	N	↑	n	~
	F	SI	US	/	?	O	←	o	DEL

Notes:

(1) Parity bit in most-significant hex digit not included.
(2) Characters in columns 0 and 1 (as well as SP and DEL) are non printing.
(3) Model 33 teletype prints codes in columns 6 and 7 as if they were column 4 and 5 codes.

FIGURE 3-2 ASCII–hexadecimal conversion table.

3-1.3 Relationship between Binary Number Systems and Digital Pulses

Thus far we have discussed how binary numbers and words are used "on paper." Microcomputers operate with electrical signals (generally pulses) arranged in binary form. For example, a microprocessor performs its functions (program counting, addition, subtraction, etc.) in response to *instructions*. Usually, these instructions come from a *memory* within the system, but they can also come from the outside world via a terminal. A typical microprocessor can perform from 70 to 100 functions (or possibly many more), with each function being determined by a specific instruction.

The instructions are applied to the microprocessor as electrical pulses, arranged to form a binary word. Each pulse is applied on a separate electrical line (or wire) as shown in Fig. 3-3, where a basic microprocessor has eight lines to accommodate an 8-bit binary word or *data byte* (or 8 *data bits*). In this system, which is typical for the great majority or microprocessors, the pulses are + 5 V in amplitude and a few nanosecond or microseconds in duration. The presence

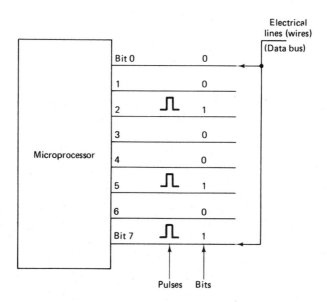

FIGURE 3-3 Relationship between binary numbers and electrical signals.

of a pulse indicates a binary 1; the absence of a pulse (or zero volts) indicates a binary 0. Thus, in Fig. 3–3, the microprocessory is receiving a binary 1010 0100, which can be converted to hex A4 for convenience.

As is discussed further in this chapter, hex A4 may be an instruction to perform addition for one particular microprocessor. For another microprocessor, the same words may mean "perform subtraction." For still another microprocessor, the word may be meaningless.

3-2 BASIC DIGITAL LOGIC

It is assumed that you are familiar with basic digital logic, including such subjects as logical algebra, truth tables, digital functions and operations, digital circuit symbols, and digital mapping, so we will not discuss these subjects here. However, we will summarize and review a few elements in digital logic so that you will be able to understand the functions described in the remaining sections of this chapter and in Chapters 4 and 5.

3-2.1 Digital Operations

Figure 3–4 shows the six basic operations found in digital circuits. These six operations include the AND, OR, NAND, NOR, EXCLUSIVE OR, and EXCLUSIVE NOR functions, as performed by the six basic *logic gates* shown in Fig. 3–4. For example, the AND operation is true when all of the ANDed quantities are true, and is false when one or more of the ANDed quantities are false. In the case of a digital AND gate, the output is true, or 1, when all of the inputs are 1, and is 0 (or false) when one or more of the inputs are 0.

Note that Fig. 3–4 illustrates both *positive* and *negative logic*. Positive logic defines the 1 or true state as the most positive voltage level, whereas negative logic defines the most negative voltage level as the 1 or true state. Because of the difference in definition of states, it is possible for some digital elements to have two equivalent outputs, depending on definition. For example, a positive-logic AND gate produces the same outputs as a negative-logic OR gate, and vice versa.

When gate outputs are connected in parallel, an AND function or an OR function can result. These functions are often referred to as "wired-OR" and "wired-AND." If the true condition is represented by zero volts (or ground), the parallel outputs of gates produce an OR function. If the true condition is represented by a voltage of any value or polarity, then the function is AND. The reason is that if gate output is zero volts (ground), all the other outputs are, in effect, shorted to ground.

Inputs		Positive logic					
		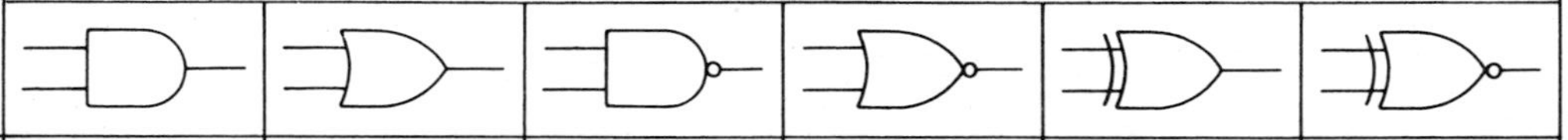					
A	B	AND	OR	NAND	NOR	EXCLUSIVE OR	EXCLUSIVE NOR
0	0	0	0	1	1	0	1
0	1	0	1	1	0	1	0
1	0	0	1	1	0	1	0
1	1	1	1	0	0	0	1
A	B	OR	AND	NOR	NAND	EXCLUSIVE NOR	EXCLUSIVE OR
Inputs		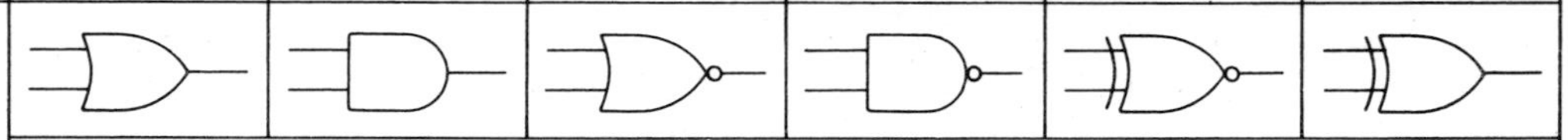					
		Negative logic					

FIGURE 3-4 Comparison of positive and negative logic functions.

3-2.2 Some Typical Combinational Circuits

There are many types of combinational circuits used in digital electronics. Similarly, an infinite variety of combinational circuits are available in IC form. The following paragraphs describe some typical examples.

Decoder Circuits. The basic functional of a combinational circuit is to produce an output (or outputs) only when certain inputs are present. Thus, combinational circuits indicate the presence of a given set of inputs by producing the corresponding output. Decoders are classic examples of combinational circuits. In effect, all combinational circuits are decoders of a sort.

Variable Input Decoders: These produce an output that indicates the state of input variables. The circuit of Fig. 3–5 is a gated two-variable decoder. As the truth table shows, one and only one output is true for each of the four possible input states. Such circuits are often found in IC form. The outputs are available only when an "enable," "strobe," "gate," or "clock" signal is present. Such "turn-on" signals can be in pulse form or can be a fixed d-c voltage controlled by a switch. Note that the enable signal can be either true or complemented.

Code Converters: These are a very common type of decoder found in IC form. Such decoders convert one type of digital code to another. For example,

A	B	True output
0	0	1
0	1	3
1	0	2
1	1	4

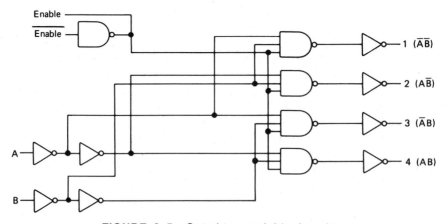

FIGURE 3-5 Gated two-variable decoder.

a binary-to-decimal decoder converts a 4-bit binary number into a decimal equivalent. The circuit of Fig. 3–6 is a BCD-to-decimal decoder. A typical line of digital IC code converters could include binary or BCD-to-octal, BCD-to-hex, binary-to-ASCII, and so on.

The term "encoder" is often used to indicate any combinational circuit

Decimal	BCD			
	D	C	B	A
0	0	0	0	0
1	0	0	0	1
2	0	0	1	0
3	0	0	1	1
4	0	1	0	0
5	0	1	0	1
6	0	1	1	0
7	0	1	1	1
8	1	0	0	0
9	1	0	0	1

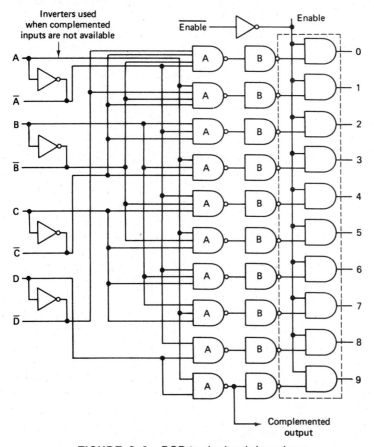

FIGURE 3-6   BCD-to-decimal decoder.

that provides the opposite function of a decoder. For example, the decoder of Fig. 3–6 converts a 4-bit BCD number to a 10-bit decimal number. An encoder, in this context, converts a 10-bit decimal number to the BCD equivalent. However, both encoders and decoders are forms of combinational circuits in that they both produce an output (or outputs) only when certain inputs are present. The circuit of Fig. 3–7 is a decimal-to-BCD encoder.

Data Distributor and Selector Circuits. Also known as *demultiplexers,* and *multiplexers* these are very similar to decoders. The data selector or multiplexer (also called a *multiplex switch*) selects data on one or more input lines and applies the data to a single output channel, in accordance with a binary code applied to the control line. A four-input data selector circuit is shown in Fig. 3–8. Data selection from more than four locations (or inputs) can be implemented using several basic data selector circuits. Such arrangements are often used in control and instrumentation systems to sample the outputs of many transducers at regular intervals, and apply the outputs to a common measurement circuit. This function is sometimes referred to as *scanning,* and the circuits are called *scanners.* A *data distributor* performs the opposite function, and distributes a single channel of input data to any number of output

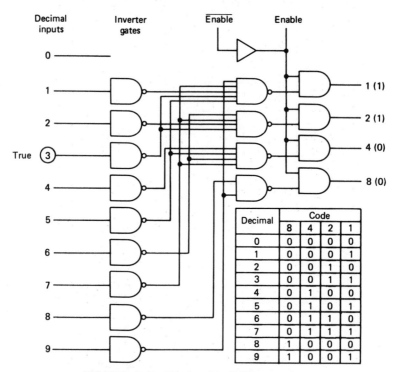

FIGURE 3-7 Decimal-to-BCD encoder.

Symbol

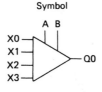

A	B	Input
0	0	X0
0	1	X1
1	0	X2
1	1	X3

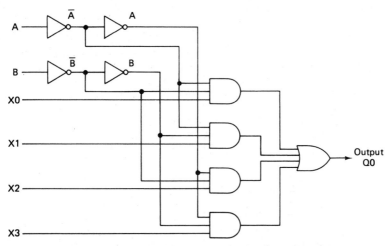

FIGURE 3-8   Four-channel data selector or multiplexer.

lines, in accordance with a binary code applied to control lines. Both two-channel and four-channel data distributors are shown in Fig. 3-9.

3-2.3 Some Typical Sequential Circuits

There are many types and forms of sequential circuits used in digital electronics, and there is an infinite variety of sequential circuits available in integrated circuit (IC) form. The following paragraphs describe some typical examples.

Flip-Flops and Latches.   Sequential circuits are based on the use of flip-flops (FFs) and latches. (A latch is essentially a flip-flop that can be latched in one state or the other.) The simplest FF (the basic *reset–set* or RS) is shown in Fig. 3-10. The presence of a pulse at either the SET or RESET inputs causes the cross-coupled gates to assume the corresponding state, as shown in the truth table. The gates remain latched in the state until a pulse is applied at the correct input to change states. The cascaded or JK FF is shown in Fig. 3-11. As shown, the JK is essentially two FFs, with the common inputs of the two FFs separated.

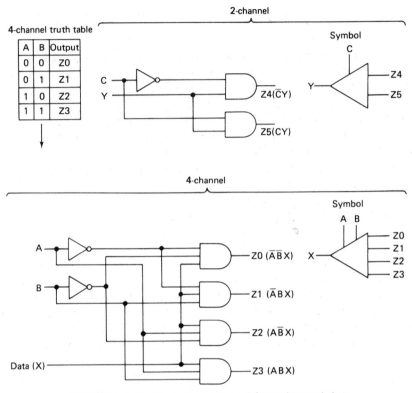

FIGURE 3-9   Two-channel and four-channel data distributors.

This requires two timing or clock pulses, with one pulse delayed from the other. The *master–slave* FF shown in Fig. 3–12 is similar to the cascaded FF with two major exceptions. The outputs of the slave FF in Fig. 3–12 are not tied back to the input, but the common inputs are tied together. The master–slave FF provides greater flexibility and does not need two clock or timing pulses. The FF of Fig. 3–13 is capable of being *preset* by d-c voltages. Thus, the circuit may be set or reset asynchronously (may be preset, without regard to the clock or any other input) with the PJ and PK inputs. The FF may also be switched synchronously using the J and K inputs together with a clock pulse. These features make the FF well suited for use in the counters and registers described in the following paragraphs.

Counters.   There are three basic types of counters used in digital electronics: *serial* or *ripple, synchronous,* and *shift.*

Serial counters (also known as *ripple counters*) use the output of a counting element (generally an FF) to drive the input of the following counting

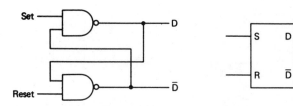

Previous state		Input condition		Result	
D	D̄	Set	Reset	D	D̄
0	1	0	1	1	0
1	0	1	0	0	1
0	1	1	1	No change	
1	0	1	1	No change	
1	0	0	1	No change	
0	1	1	0	No change	
0	1	0	0	1	XXX
1	0	0	0	1	XXX

XXX = unknown.

FIGURE 3-10 Basic RS FF using cross-coupled NAND gates.

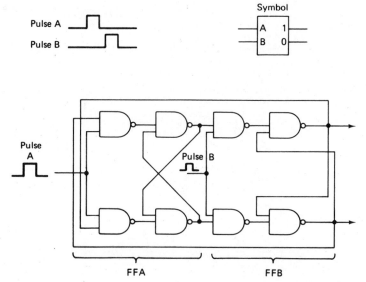

FIGURE 3-11 Cascaded or JK FF.

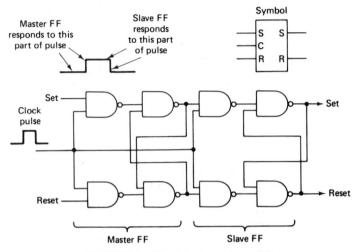

FIGURE 3-12 Master–slave FF.

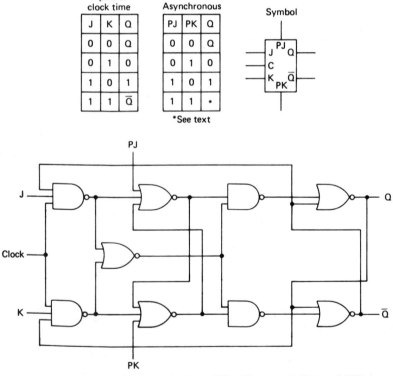

FIGURE 3-13 JK master–slave FF with preset (PJ and PK).

elements, as shown in Fig. 3–14. In serial counters, the FFs operate in a *toggle* mode (that is, they change state with each clock pulse), with the output of each FF driving the clock input of the following stage. Serial counters fall into two groups: *straight binary* and *feedback*. Straight binary counters divide the input by 2^N, where N is the number of counting elements. As shown in Fig. 3–14, straight binary counters count in a binary code, with the first counting element (FF) containing the least significant bit (LSB). Feedback serial counters also count in a binary code, but a number of higher-value states are eliminated by the feedback, as shown in Fig. 3–15. The count sequence table for this counter shows the state of each FF for all counts from decimal 0 through 9 in a BCD format.

A *synchronous* (or *clocked*) counter is one in which the next state depends on the present state (through gating action), and all state changes occur simultaneously with a clock pulse, as shown in Fig. 3–16. Since all FFs change simultaneously, the output (or count) can be taken from synchronous counters in *parallel* form (as opposed to serial form for ripple counters). Synchronous counters can be designed to count up, count down, or do both, in which case they are often called *bidirectional* counters.

Shift counters are a specialized form of clocked counter. The name is

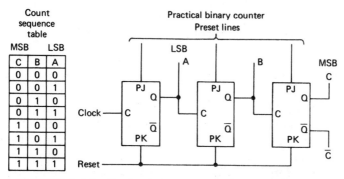

FIGURE 3-14   Basic and practical binary serial counters.

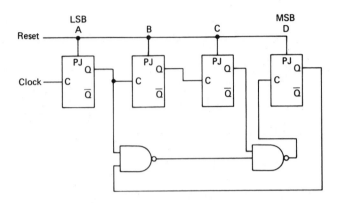

Count sequence table

D	C	B	A	Decimal
0	0	0	0	0
0	0	0	1	1
0	0	1	0	2
0	0	1	1	3
0	1	0	0	4
0	1	0	1	5
0	1	1	0	6
0	1	1	1	7
1	0	0	0	8
1	0	0	1	9

BCD format

FIGURE 3-15   Feedback ripple counter with BCD format count.

derived from the fact that the operation is similar to a *shift register*. In general, the shift counter produces outputs that may easily be decoded, and normally requires no gating between stages (thus permitting high-speed operation). Figure 3-17 shows a typical decade shift counter (also called a Johnson counter or switch-tail counter).

Shift Registers and Shift Elements.   The term "register" can be applied to any digital circuit that stores information on temporary basis. Permanent or long-term storage is generally done with magnetic cores, tapes, disks, drums, and other memories. The term "register" is usually applied to a digital circuit consisting of FFs and gates that can store binary or other coded information.

A *storage register* is an example of such a digital circuit. The various counter circuits discussed thus far are, in effect, a form of storage register. Counters accept information in serial form (the clock or count input) and parallel form (by presetting the FFs to a given count), and hold this information

Decimal	Up n				Up n+1				Decimal	Down n				Down n+1			
	D	C	B	A	D	C	B	A		D	C	B	A	D	C	B	A
0	0	0	1	1	0	1	0	0	9	1	1	0	0	1	0	1	1
1	0	1	0	0	0	1	0	1	8	1	0	1	1	1	0	1	0
2	0	1	0	1	0	1	1	0	7	1	0	1	0	1	0	0	1
3	0	1	1	0	0	1	1	1	6	1	0	0	1	1	0	0	0
4	0	1	1	1	1	0	0	0	5	1	0	0	0	0	1	1	1
5	1	0	0	0	1	0	0	1	4	0	1	1	1	0	1	1	0
6	1	0	0	1	1	0	1	0	3	0	1	1	0	0	1	0	1
7	1	0	1	0	1	0	1	1	2	0	1	0	1	0	1	0	0
8	1	0	1	1	1	1	0	0	1	0	1	0	0	0	0	1	1
9	1	1	0	0	0	0	1	1	0	0	0	1	1	1	1	0	0

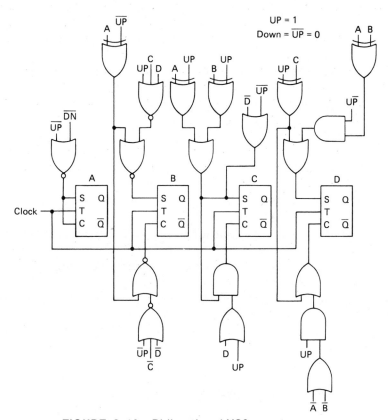

FIGURE 3-16 Bidirectional XS3 counter.

(the count) as long as power is applied and provided that no other information
(serial or parallel) is added. With proper gating, the information can be read in
or read out. Figure 3–18 shows the circuit of a typical binary storage register
available in IC form.

Truth table

	A	B	C	D	E
0	0	0	0	0	0
1	1	0	0	0	0
2	1	1	0	0	0
3	1	1	1	0	0
4	1	1	1	1	0
5	1	1	1	1	1
6	0	1	1	1	1
7	0	0	1	1	1
8	0	0	0	1	1
9	0	0	0	0	1

Output decoding table

0	$\overline{A}\,\overline{E}$
1	$A\overline{B}$
2	$B\overline{C}$
3	$C\overline{D}$
4	$D\overline{E}$
5	AE
6	$\overline{A}B$
7	$\overline{B}C$
8	$\overline{C}D$
9	$\overline{D}E$

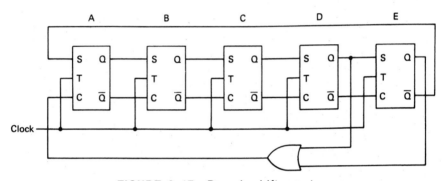

FIGURE 3-17   Decade shift counter.

A shift register is a circuit for storing and shifting (or manipulating) a number of binary or decimal digits (rather than the simple storage function of a storage register). In addition to their use in arithmetic operation, shift registers are used for such functions as conversion between parallel and serial data. Figure 3-19 shows the circuit of a basic shift register. This circuit may be preset by parallel data input if desired, or may be cleared of all data simultaneously. The serial data input shifts the contents of the register one position to the right for each occurrence of the clock pulse.

3-2.4   Digital Readouts (Numerical Displays)

There are many types of digital readouts (also called numerical displays), including LCDs (liquid crystal displays), LEDs (light-emitting diodes), gas discharge, and fluorescent and incandescent displays. Most present-day readouts or displays use some form of the *seven-segment* format in either *direct drive* or *multiplex* systems.

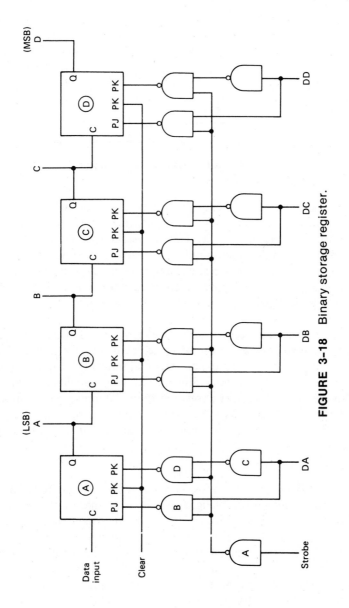

FIGURE 3-18 Binary storage register.

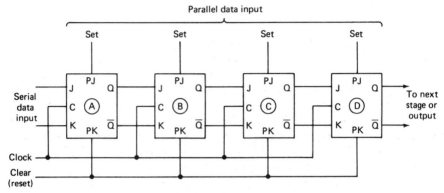

FIGURE 3-19   Basic shift register.

Direct-Drive Displays.   The simplest type of display system, shown in Fig. 3–20, consists of four lines of BCD information feeding the display through a decoder/driver. This direct-drive system does not have information storage capability and thus reads out in *real time.* Another display system, also shown in Fig. 3–20, contains a decade counter, a quad or four-line latch (FFs), a decoder/driver, and the display, one such channel for every digit. This alternate system has storage capability (the FF latches) which allows the counter to re-count during the storage.

Both systems have decoder/drivers which convert the BCD count into voltages suitable for operating the seven-segment displays. Figure 3–20 also shows the relationship between the decoder and numerical display, as well as a truth table. As shown by the truth table, the segments are illuminated in accordance with the decimal number applied at the BCD input. For example, for a decimal 3, the BCD signal is 0011, and segments *a, b, c, d,* and *g* are illuminated. Segments *e* and *f* are not illuminated, and the display forms a numerical 3.

Multiplex Displays.   The most commonly used system for multiplexing displays is the system shown in Fig. 3–21. By time sharing the one decoder/driver, the parts count, interconnections, and power can be saved. The N-stage data register (one stage for each digit) feeds a scanned multiplexer. In turn, the sequenced BCD output of the multiplexer drives like segments of the display. The digit-select elements are sequentially driven by the scan circuit, which also synchronously drives the multiplexer. Thus, each display is scanned or strobed in synchronism, with the BCD data presented to the decoder at a sufficiently high rate, usually greater than 50 scans per second, to appear as a continuously energized multidigit display.

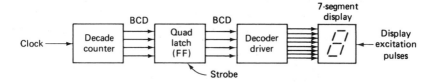

Simple direct drive display (real time)

Direct drive with storage

Relationship between decoder and numerical display

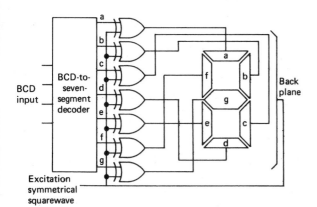

Digit	Segments						
	a	b	c	d	e	f	g
0	1	1	1	1	1	1	0
1	0	1	1	0	0	0	0
2	1	1	0	1	1	0	1
3	1	1	1	1	0	0	1
4	0	1	1	0	0	1	1
5	1	0	1	1	0	1	1
6	0	0	1	1	1	1	1
7	1	1	1	0	0	0	0
8	1	1	1	1	1	1	1
9	1	1	1	0	0	1	1

Truth table

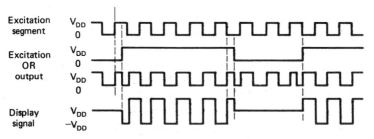

FIGURE 3-20 Basic direct-drive displays.

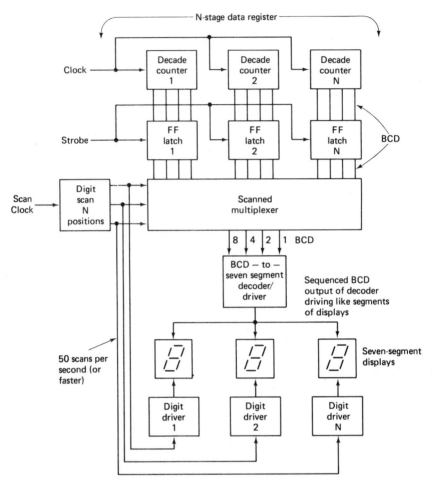

FIGURE 3-21 Basic multiplexed (time-shared) display.

3-3 MICROCOMPUTER TERMS

Now that we have reviewed the basics of digital electronics, let us define some terms used in microcomputers. The heart of most microcomputers is the microprocessor, which is an IC that performs many of the functions found in a digital computer. A single microprocessor IC is capable of performing all the arithmetic and control functions of a computer. By itself, a typical microprocessor IC does not contain the memories and input/output (I/O) functions of a computer. However, when these functions are provided by additional ICs, a *microcomputer* is formed.

Typically, a basic microcomputer requires a ROM (read-only memory) to store the computer program or instructions, a RAM (random-access memory) to store temporary data (the information to be acted upon by the computer program), and an I/O IC to make the system compatible with outside (or *peripheral*) equipment such as an interactive video terminal, electric typewriter, line printer, keyboard/digital readout, or calculator.

3-4 ELEMENTS OF A MICROCOMPUTER

As discussed in Sec. 3-1.1 (and illustrated in Fig. 3-3), a microprocessor performs its function (program counting, addition, subtraction, etc.) in response to instructions in the form of electrical pulses (arranged to form a binary word). For one microprocessor, this word may be an instruction to perform addition. For another microprocessor, the same word may be meaningless. Thus, one of the first things you must do to understand and use a microprocessor is to learn all its instructions (known as the *instruction set*), including the corresponding binary code, hex code, and what is done by the microprocessor when the instruction is received. Microprocessor manufacturers provide information on the instruction set in their manuals. This is fortunate, since it is nearly an impossible task to remember the entire instruction set of even a simple microprocessor.

3-4.1 Microprocessor Memories and Addresses

Microprocessors also use electrical signals arranged in binary form to communicate with other elements in the system. Most microprocessors are used with memories (RAMS or ROMs, typically both) which hold *data bytes* to be manipulated by the microprocessor, and *instruction bytes* to be followed by the microprocessor, during the program. (Data bytes are usually stored or held in the RAM; instructions are usually stored in the ROM.)

Memories are divided into locations called *addresses*. Each address is identified by a number (usually decimal). During a typical microcomputer program, the microprocessor selects each address in a certain order (determined by the program) and reads the contents of the address. Such contents can be an instruction, data, or a combination of both. Similarly, it is possible to write information into memory using electrical signals arranged in binary form.

3-4.2 Buses and Ports

A typical microprocessor/memory arrangement is shown in Fig. 3-22, where a microprocessor is connected to a RAM and a ROM by data and address *buses*. The term *bus* is applied when several electrical lines are used for a common purpose. In our example, the data bus has eight lines (which is typical) and the address bus has eight lines (which is not typical). Generally, the address bus will have as many as 16 lines. The eight-line system is used here for simplicity. The

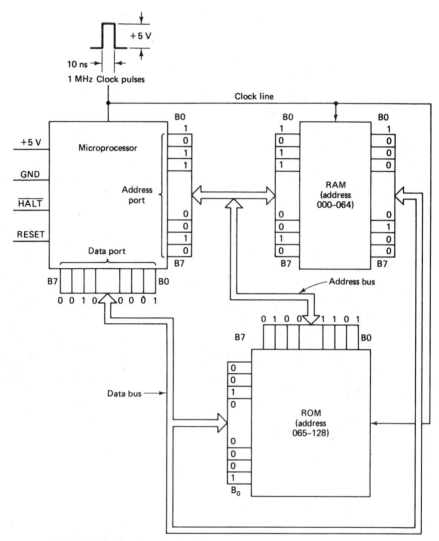

FIGURE 3-22 Typical microprocessor memory arrangement, including data and address buses.

term *highway* is sometimes used when a bus is used to interconnect many system components. Also, the term *handshake* bus is sometimes used to indicate a bus that interconnects a microprocessor system with the outside world. Although there is little standardization within components, industry has generally standardized on formats or arrangements of buses that interconnect components of a microcomputer system. For example, there is a General Purpose Interface Bus (GP-IB) in common use, as well as a Hewlett-Packard Interface Bus

(HP–IB) used to interconnect Hewlett-Packard equipment (which is discussed in chapters 4 and 5).

The term *port* is often applied to the point or terminals at which the bus enters the microprocessor or other IC element. Thus, in the microprocessor of Fig. 3–22, there is an address port and a data port. Buses are generally bidirectional. That is, the electrical pulses (representing data bytes, addresses, etc.) can pass in either direction along the bus lines. For example, data bytes can be written into memory from the microprocessor, or read from memory into the microprocessor on the same data bus. Ports may or may not be bidirectional, depending on the design.

3-4.3 Address and Data Buses

Note that in Fig. 3–22 the electrical pulses appearing on the address bus are arranged to produce binary 01001101, or decimal 77. Thus, address number 77 is being selected by the microprocessor. Both the ROM and RAM receive the same set of electrical pulses (or binary word), since these pulses appear on the address bus. However, since address 77 is located in ROM, the contents of the ROM at that address are read back to the microprocessor via the data bus. The pulses on the address bus have no effect on the RAM, and no information is obtained from the RAM. Similarly, the address pulses have no effect on other addresses in the ROM. Only the information at the selected address is read back on the data bus. In Fig. 3–22, the electrical pulses on the data bus are arranged to form the binary word 00100001, which can be converted to hex 21. In our particular microprocessor, hex 21 is an instruction to add the contents of a register within the microprocessor to the contents at some address in the RAM (read out during a previous step in the program).

3-4.4 Clock and Timer Pulses

The electrical pulses used by the microprocessor, ROM, and RAM are generated by a *clock* or *timer,* which may be part of the microprocessor or can be external. In Fig. 3–22, the clock is external and is a + 5-V pulse of 10-ns duration, at a frequency of 1 MHz. The clock circuit is an oscillator that produces pulses of fixed amplitude and duration at regular intervals (typically 1 to 3 MHz).

The microprocessor, ROM, and RAM do not actually generate the binary pulses but produce their binary word pulses on the address and data lines when they receive clock pulses. It may take many clock pulses to form a binary word. In some cases, the microprocessor, ROM, and RAM must also receive other signals before they produce the binary word pulses or data byte. For example, an RAM usually requires a "read" signal, plus the clock signal, before the contents of an address are read into the data bus from the RAM. Such control signals are discussed later in the chapter.

3–4.5   *Power Supply and Other Signals*

Not all electrical voltages and signals applied to a microprocessor, ROM, or RAM are in pulse form. For example, referring to Fig. 3–22, note that there are two lines into the microprocessor, labeled + 5 V and GND. These are the power supply lines connected to an external 5-V power supply.

There are also two lines, labeled $\overline{\text{HALT}}$ and RESET, respectively. The RESET and $\overline{\text{HALT}}$ lines receive a + 5-V signal from various circuits in the system. This signal may be a momentary pulse identical to those on the address and data buses, or may be a fixed + 5 V which remains on the line for some time. When a fixed signal (sometimes called a *level*) is applied, the line is said to be "high" and the function is "turned on."

For example, if + 5 V is applied to the RESET line, the RESET line is high and all circuits within the microprocessor are reset to zero, regardless of their condition before the line goes high. When the fixed voltage is removed, the RESET line goes low (is at zero volts) and the RESET function is no longer in effect. In most microprocessors, when a reset signal is received, all circuits return to zero and then resume their normal function (counting, etc.).

An overbar is used on the word $\overline{\text{HALT}}$. This indicates that the $\overline{\text{HALT}}$ function operates on the reverse of all other lines. That is, the $\overline{\text{HALT}}$ function is in effect when the line is at 0 V (the normal low condition for other functions). When the line is at + 5 V (normal high), the $\overline{\text{HALT}}$ function is removed. In our microprocessor, when the $\overline{\text{HALT}}$ line is at 0 V, all functions within the microprocessor (counting, etc.) stop and remain stopped as long as the $\overline{\text{HALT}}$ line remains low. All functions resume normal operation when the $\overline{\text{HALT}}$ line is made high by a + 5-V level. If the microprocessor is in the middle of some operation when $\overline{\text{HALT}}$ is applied (by 0 V on the line), the operation stops, but will continue from the same point when the + 5 V is reapplied.

3–5   MICROCOMPUTER CIRCUIT FUNCTIONS

The circuit elements of a microcomputer are primarily in IC form, so you do not have access to them, nor do you know exactly how they are interconnected. However, there are some circuit elements in common use, and we review operation of these elements here.

3–5.1   *Counters, Registers, Accumulators, and Pointers*

For our purposes, counters, registers, accumulators, and pointers are all circuits used to hold and manipulate binary numbers in electrical (level or pulse) form. As such, these circuits have one stage for each binary bit to be held or manipulated. Thus, an 8-bit counter/register has eight stages. As discussed in

Secs. 3-1 and 3-2, FF stages are used in counter/registers, and an FF can be in only one of two electrical states, 1 or 0.

In a microprocessor, the purpose of a counter is to count events (such as steps in a program, a sequence of addresses selected, etc.). This is usually done by counting pulses. Counters are sometimes used as *pointers*, in that they point to another event or location. For example, a typical *program counter* counts each step of the program, and then advances to the next address to be used in the program. Thus, the counter "points" to the next step of the program. Note that when a counter, register, or another circuit is a microprocomputer system and is used solely or primarily for one purpose, it is said to be *dedicated*. For example, a microprocessor counter used only to count program steps is referred to as a *dedicated counter*.

A microprocessor register is similar to a counter except that the primary function of a register is to hold the binary numbers (or words) so that they can be manipulated. Registers are often used to hold some binary number taken from a particular address in memory so that numbers may be added to another number in memory. Similarly, one register can hold a binary number that is to be added to another binary number in another register. When a register is used primarily for arithmetic operations, the word *accumulator* is often applied.

Serial Operation of Counters/Registers.   Figure 3-23 shows operation of a typical counter or register used to count serial pulses. Assume that the circuit is used as a program counter and that it receives one pulse for each step of the program. That is, the counter is to be *incremented* (or advanced) for each pulse representing a step. (When each step or pulse removes one count, the counter is said to be *decremented*.)

Initially, all stages are *reset* or *cleared* to low, binary 0, or 0 V, by a reset signal. In serial operation, the first or LSB stage operates on the pulses to be counted. All other stages receive a pulse from the stage ahead. As each pulse to be counted is applied, the stage representing the LSB is changed from a 0 to 1 (0 V to + 5 V). When the next pulse arrives, the first stage returns to 0 V (binary 0) and sends a signal to the next stage, which moves to binary 1. This process continues until all pulses are counted. If there are four pulses, as shown in Fig. 3-23, the third stage moves to 1 and the first two stages are at 0. All remaining stages are at 0. The counter indicates a binary 00000100 (decimal 4) and corresponds to the number of pulses applied and, in turn, to the number of steps in the program accomplished thus far. In this way, the instantaneous count corresponds to the program step just done, or to be done next, depending on the design.

When all stages are moved by sufficient pulses to 1 (the binary count is 11111111, decimal 127), the counter is full. Generally, the counter sends a *flag* or signal to other circuits, indicating the full count. This flag can be used to halt or reset operation of the microprocessor if the program has only 127 steps. Or, the flag can be used as the first pulse to the LSB of another counter (to accom-

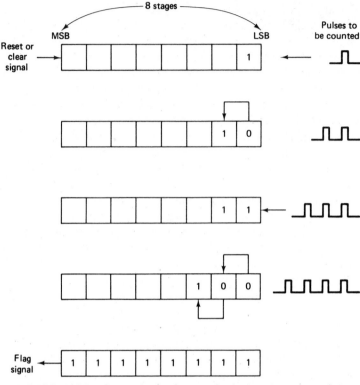

FIGURE 3-23   Operation of a typical counter or register used to count serial pulses.

modate a 16-bit word). It should be noted that flag signals do not always indicate a full count in microcomputers. The term "flag" can be applied to any signal which indicates that a particular condition has occurred (full count, error, request for further information, etc.).

Parallel Operation.   Counters and registers can also be designed to receive information in parallel form, as shown in Fig. 3–24. Here, all the stages are set simultaneously by pulses in the binary word 01100100 (decimal 100). That is, bits 2, 5, and 6 receive + 5-V pulses, and all other bits remain at 0 V. Sometimes, the terms *load* or *dump* are used when data bytes are so applied to a register. Typically, a register holds the data byte (all stages remain in this selected state) until the register is cleared (reset to zero) or until another set of pulses that form a data byte is applied (or the power is removed).

Initializing.   This ability to be set by both serial and parallel pulses makes it possible to *initialize* counters and registers. It is not always desired to start all counts from zero, or that all counts go through every step in the count.

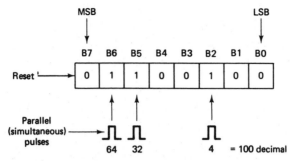

FIGURE 3-24 Operation of a typical counter or register used to count (or receive) parallel pulses.

For example, assume that the count is to start at the seventh step of a program. This can be done by applying + 5-V pulses to bits 1, 2, and 3 simultaneously, as shown in Fig. 3–25. Then the first serial pulse to be counted moves bit 1 to 0, which in turn moves bit 2 to 0, bit 3 to 0, and bit 4 to 1.

Shifting. The contents of counters and registers can also be shifted by an appropriate shift signal. That is, the contents of each stage in the counter or register are shifted by one position to the right or left by a shift signal applied to all stages simultaneously. The effects of a left shift are shown in Fig. 3–26, where a register is holding the binary word 00001000 (decimal 8). Bit 3 is at binary 1, and all remaining bits are at 0. During the shift, the contents of bit 0 move to bit 1, bit 1 to bit 2, and so on. After the shift, bit 0 remains at binary 0, since there is no new pulse entering bit 0. Bit 4 is at binary 1, since that was the

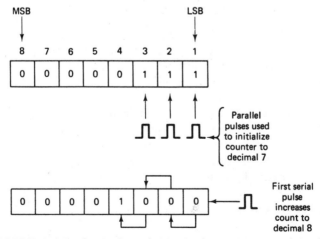

FIGURE 3-25 Operation of a typical counter or register initialized to decimal 7 by parallel pulses, and increased to decimal 8 by first serial pulse.

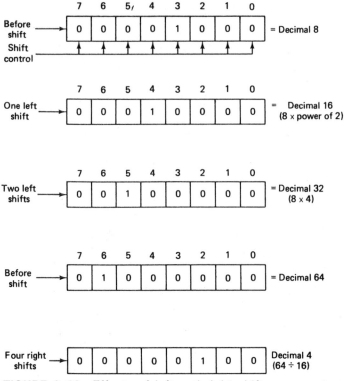

FIGURE 3-26 Effects of left and right shifts on counters and registers.

state of bit 3 before the shift. All other bits are at 0, since 0 was the state of corresponding stages to the right (before the shift).

As a result of the shift, the binary number is changed from 00001000 to 00010000 or from decimal 8 to decimal 16. Thus, one left shift multiplies the number by the power of 2. If there are two left shifts, the binary number is changed to 00100000, decimal 32 (or the same as multiplying by 4). Three left shifts produce 01000000, decimal 64 (multiplication by 8). Registers can also be shifted to the right, which results in division by the power of 2. This is also shown in Fig. 3–26, where a register is shifted four places to the right for a division by 16. That is, binary 01000000 (decimal 64) is shifted to binary 00000100 (decimal 4); 64 divided by 16 is 4.

3-5.2 Decoders and Multiplexers

The terms "decoder" and "multiplexer" are often interchanged in microprocessor literature. As discussed in Sec. 3–2.2, in a strict sense, a decoder converts from one code numbering system to another, such as from BCD to seven-segment, and so on. Equally strict, a multiplexer (or MUX) is a data selector and/or distributor. However, in microprocessor literature, the terms are generally applied to any circuit that converts data from one form to another. For example, one microprocessor contains a circuit (designated by the manufacturer as a multiplexer) that converts 16 lines of information from a register into eight lines suitable from an eight-line address bus. Another microcomputer system contains a decoder in each ROM which makes it possible to select one of 128 memory addressess with an 8-bit word supplied on an 8-bit address bus. The symbol for such decoders and multiplexers is usually a box with the appropriate number of lines in and out, as shown in Fig. 3–27.

FIGURE 3-27 Basic decoder/ multiplexer symbol.

3-5.3 Buffers, Drivers, and Latches

Buffers, drivers, and latches are also terms often interchanged in microprocessor literature. A buffer can be considered as any circuit between two other circuits that serves to isolate the circuits under certain conditions and to connect the circuits under other conditions. A buffer circuit between an internal register and the data bus (at the data port) is a classic example, as shown in Fig. 3–28. Here, the buffer can be switches on or off by a *bus enable* signal or pulse. (This same signal can also be known as an *enable, select,* or *strobe* signal.)

When the enable signal is present, the buffer passes data, instructions, or whatever combination is on the data bus to the register within the microprocessor. When the enable signal is removed, the buffer prevents passage of data. This feature is necessary, for example, when the register is holding old data bytes not yet processed, but there are new data bytes on the bus. The buffer closes the data port until the register is ready to accept new data. This raises the obvious problem of what happens when the new data byte is momentary. In such cases, the buffer has a "latch" function (usually an FF for each bit, as discussed in Sec. 3–2.3), which permits each bit in the buffer to be latched to a 1 or a 0 by the data pulses.

Three-State Buffers. Typically, buffers are three-state devices, with one stage for each bit to be handled. The stages can be in one of three stages: *in, out,* or at a *high-impedance* level. The high-impedance level or state makes it appear that the circuit is closed to the passage of data. Some buffers also include a driver function, particularly where the buffer is going to feed many devices simultaneously via a bus. The output of a register or counter may be sufficient to drive one other register, but not many registers or devices. Thus, the buffer includes a driver function which amplifies the drive capability.

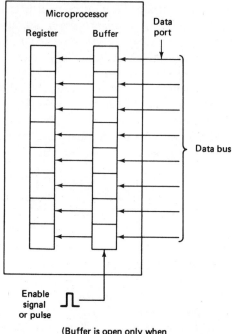

(Buffer is open only when
enable signal is present)

FIGURE 3-28 Buffer circuit between an internal register and the data bus.

3-5.4 Matrix

The term "matrix" is generally applied to the circuits within the RAM, ROM, or ferrite core memory, but is also applied by some manufacturers to a group of registers in the microprocessor. A typical memory matrix is divided into sections or locations, with each section identified by an address as shown in Fig. 3–29. In turn, the addresses are divided into a number of stages, with one stage for each bit to be held in memory. Thus, each address in an 8-bit memory has 8 bits. The number of addresses in a memory matrix depends on use. Generally, the number is based on the powers of 2, since the addresses are selected by a number system based on binary (such as hex or octal).

A typical ROM matrix has 128 addresses, each with 8 bits, and is described as a 128 × 8 matrix. A typical RAM matrix can have 512, 1024, or 4096 addresses (or possibly more). A 1024 × 8 memory is typically described as 1K memory since there are approximately 1000 (actually, 1024) addresses available. Similarly, a 4096 × 8 memory is called a 4K memory.

Matrix Vectors. The addresses within a matrix are selected by some form of *vector* or *intersect* system, such as shown in Fig. 3–30. The memory ad-

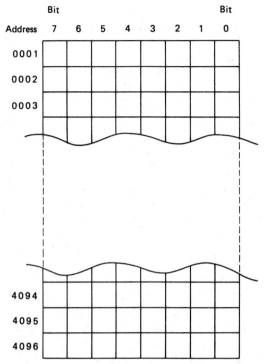

FIGURE 3-29 Typical 4096 / 8 memory matrix.

dress to be read in or read out is selected when a combination of two appropriate bit lines have a + 5-V pulse present (are at binary 1). Only one of the X lines and one of the Y lines can be binary 1 at any given time. All other lines are at binary 0. This action is controlled by some form of decoder or multiplexer. As an example, assume that address 8 is to be selected. This causes bits B1 and B5 to receive pulses (+ 5-V or binary 1). All remaining lines are at binary 0 (zero volts). Thus, the address (number 8) at the intersection or vector of the two lines is selected. Keep in mind that there are 8 bits in each address, and that each of the 8 bits is fed back to the microprocessor or other destination on a bus (usually the data bus).

3-5.5 Arithmetic Logic Unit

Virtually all microprocessors have an arithmetic logic unit or ALU (although it may not be called an ALU). The ALU performs the arithmetic and logic operation on the data bytes. In microprocessor literature, the symbol for an ALU is usually a simple box with lines or arrows leading in or out. Sometimes, the box contains some hint as to the functions capable of being performed by the ALU.

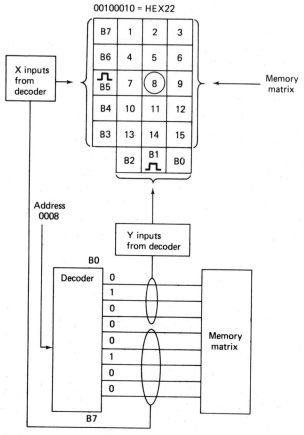

FIGURE 3-30   Vector system for selecting one address in a 15-address memory matrix.

However, these functions (addition, subtraction, multiplication, etc.) are usually described only in the instruction set of the microprocessor.

3-5.6   Control Circuitry or Logic

All microprocessors have some form of control or logic circuit (or circuits). As in the case of the ALU, the symbol for the control circuit is usually a simple box with lines and arrows leading in and out. Generally, the halt, reset, interrupt, initialize, start, and similar lines are shown going into the control logic box symbol. This is because the control logic is the primary functional circuit or unit within the microprocessor. Using clock inputs, the control logic maintains the proper sequence of events required for any processing task.

For example, after a microprocessor instruction is taken from memory (or "fetched") and decoded, the control logic issues the appropriate signals (to the microprocessor, and to such external units as the ROM, RAM, and I/O) for initiating the proper processing action (such as a "write" signal to write data into memory, a "read" signal to read data from memory, and so on).

One function found in most microprocessor control logic circuits is the capability of responding to an *interrupt* signal or *service request* (say from an external video terminal or keyboard). An interrupt request causes the control logic to interrupt the program execution temporarily, *jump* to a special routine to service the interrupting device, and then return automatically to the main program.

3-6 MICROCOMPUTER HARDWARE

The term *hardware* applied to a microcomputer system refers to the physical components, wiring, and so on. This contrasts with the term *software,* which applies to programs, instructions, and the like. Some microprocessor manufacturers also use the term *firmware* to describe something between hardware and software. For example, when instructions (software) are permanently programmed into a ROM (hardware), the result is firmware.

The microprocessor of one manufacturer has little in common with the microprocessor of another manufacturer, with the possible exception of outward physical appearance. Compare the two microprocessors shown in Fig. 3–31. Both are 40-lead, dual-in-line (DIP) IC packages. Both are about 2 in. long and ½ in. wide. Now compare this to the terminal assignment diagrams of Fig. 3–32. Although both have 40 leads (also known as *pins* or *terminals*), the leads are used for entirely different purposes.

For example, the RCA microprocessor has 8 data lines to a data bus and 8 memory lines to an address bus, whereas the Motorola unit has 8 data lines (D) and 16 address lines (PA and PB). From this it can be seen that you must have all available data on a particularly microprocessor to use the unit effectively.

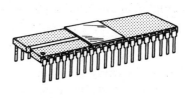

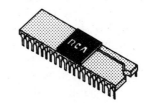

FIGURE 3-31 RCA and Motorola microprocessors in 40-lead dual-in-line packages (DIPs).

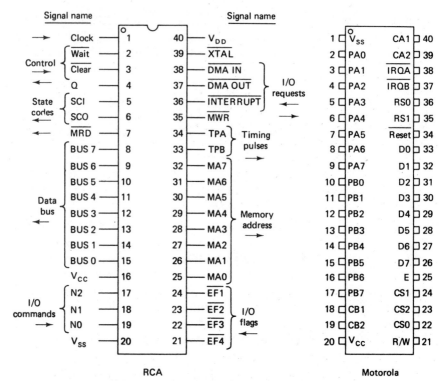

Typical microprocessor terminal assignment diagrams.

Fortunately, such information is available, although the format used to show the interval arrangement of microprocessors varies from manufacturer to manufacturer.

3-6.1 Microprocessor Architecture

The term *architecture* is most accurately applied to the arrangement of counters, registers, ALUs, and so on, within the microprocessor. However, some manufacturers apply the term "architecture" to the entire system arrangement. There are two commonly used methods to show architecture. The block diagram of Fig. 3–33 shows the internal registers, counters, and so on, of the Motorola M6800 microprocessor of Figs. 3–31 and 3–32. Compare this to the *program model* of Fig. 3–34, which shows only accumulator, register, counter, and pointers. Obviously, the information shown in Fig. 3–34 is suitable for programming only. The information in Fig. 3–33 is required for design and service, since each line to and from the microprocessor is identified as to function (or destination) and pin number. For example, line or pin 2 is the

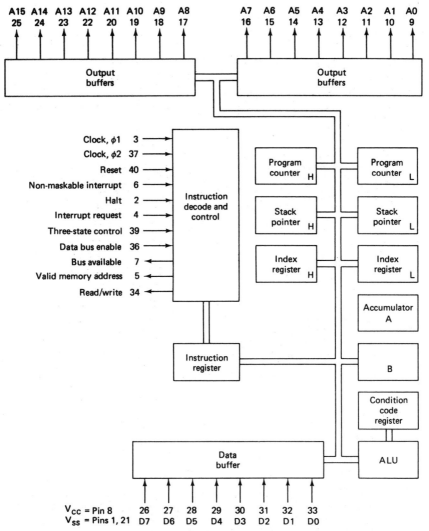

FIGURE 3-33 Motorola M6800 microprocessor, block diagram.

HALT line into the microprocessor, and pin 7 is the "bus available" signal from the microprocessor. Compare this to the block diagram of Fig. 3-35, which shows the architecture of the RCA CDP1802 microprocessor (also shown in Figs. 3-31 and 3-32).

Note that none of these diagrams show how a microprocessor does its job (in the same sense that a TV set block diagram shows the functions of the circuits in a set). This is typical for microprocessor design and user literature. You must consult the instruction set to find out what the microprocessor does in

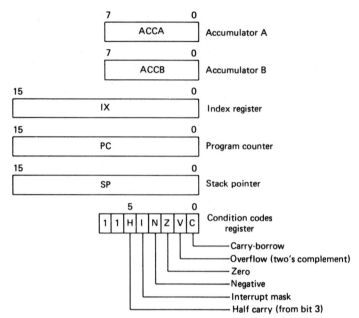

FIGURE 3-34 Motorola M6800 microprocessor, programming model.

response to commands. You will probably never know how the microprocessor accomplishes this response.

3-7 MEMORY HARDWARE

There are two types of memory units used in microprocessor-based systems; the RAM and ROM. Generally, each of these memories is contained in a separate IC package. However, there are systems where one of the memories, or both, are contained in the same IC package as the microprocessor (such as the Intel MCS-48 microprocessor, known as a "computer on a chip").

3-7.1 RAM Circuits

Figure 3-36 shows the package, pin assignment diagram, and functional block diagram of a typical RAM. This unit is described by the manufacturer as a 128 × 8 static RAM, meaning that the matrix has 128 addresses, each with 8 bits. Thus, 8-bit bytes can be read into, or out of, 128 locations. The data bytes appear on data lines D0 through D7, usually connected to a data bus. The data byte is read into the matrix if the buffer is in the "in" state, and is read out when the buffer is in the "out" state. The data lines are disconnected from the matrix if the buffer is in the "high-impedance" state.

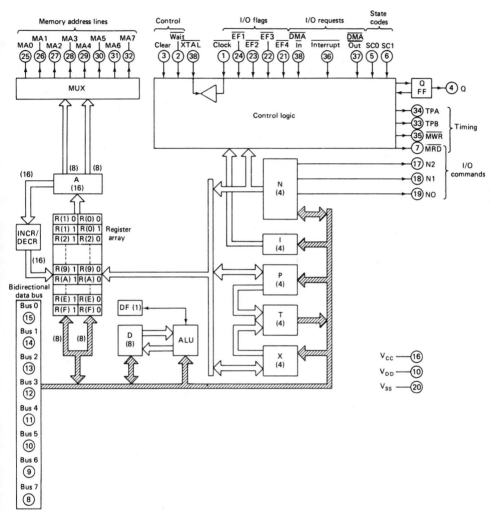

FIGURE 3-35 RCA CDP1802 microprocessor block diagram.

Buffer-State Control. The buffer state is controlled by two factors; the read/write signal at pin 16, and the control signals at pins 10 through 15. If any one of the control signals (called "chip select inputs") is absent, the buffer remains in the high-impedance state, and no data bytes pass between the matrix and the data lines. Thus, it is possible to shut off the memory from the microprocessor system by controlling only one of six lines or inputs.

Note that some of the chip select inputs are *active high* (turned on when the line is at binary 1), whereas others are *active low* (turned on when the line is at binary 0). Active lows are indicated by the overbars. This arrangement per-

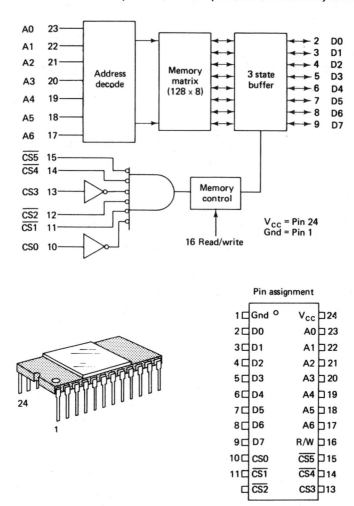

FIGURE 3-36   Motorola 128 / 8 static RAM.

mits one memory IC to be turned on, with other memories to be turned off, by the same signal on the address line. When all the chip select inputs are present (all active highs are at 1, all active lows are at 0), the buffer can be placed in the write (data into the matrix) or read (data from the matrix to the data line) conditions by a signal on the read/write line.

Address Selection.   The address to be read in or out is selected by an address decoder, which, in turn, is controlled by the binary word on the address bus (lines A0 through A6). In certain systems, part of the address lines are connected to some of the chip select inputs. This is done where there may be several memories, all connected to the address and data buses. For example, assume

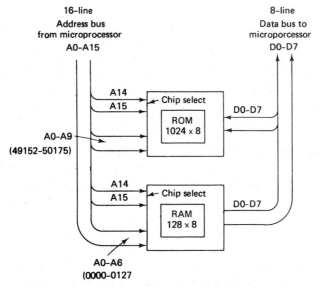

FIGURE 3-37 Typical address and data bus arrangement, where one address line (A15) is used for chip select.

that a 128 × 8 RAM is used on the same data and address buses with a 1024 × 8 ROM, as shown in Fig. 3-37. Usually, the RAM is assigned to lower number addresses (say from 0000 to 0127, in decimal) with the ROM containing the higher-number addresses (say from 49152 to 50175, in decimal). When the highest address line A15 is at 1, the ROM is made active, when A15 is at 0, the RAM is active. Keep in mind that the use of address line signals to control memory ICs is not used in all systems. There are many other arrangements.

3-7.2 Static Versus Dynamic RAMs

In a typical dynamic RAM, information is stored as an electrical charge on the gate capacitance of a MOS transistor. Since MOS transistors have some leakage, the charge is removed in time, even with the power applied. Thus, the information (binary 0 for 1 for each bit at each address) is lost in time if the charge is not periodically *refreshed*. There are many ways to refresh a dynamic RAM. The circuitry is complex and usually involves circuits outside the RAM IC. The main advantages of a dynamic RAM are high-speed operation and low power consumption.

In a typical static RAM, each bit of information is stored on a flip-flop or latch. Static RAMs do not require refreshing and are thus far less complex than dynamic RAMs of the same capacity. However, static RAMs are slower and consume more power.

3-7.3   Volatile RAMs

Most present-day semiconductor RAMs are *volatile*. That is, all information is lost when the power is removed. This problem can be avoided by using a battery-maintained power supply during standby operation. Dynamic RAMs are often used for battery operation, since they draw less power than static RAMs. CMOS RAMs are particularly well suited for battery operation because of their low power consumption.

3-7.4   ROM Circuits

The term "ROM" is applied to a wide range of devices in which fixed two-state information is stored for later use. Usually, the ROM is housed in a separate IC package containing a matrix of addressed locations. In a ROM, each bit in each address is *permanently set* to binary 1 or 0. ROMs are generally used to hold the program of microprocessor instructions and possibly other data constants, such as routines, tables, and so on. Unlike the RAM, the ROM is nonvolatile (the memory remains after power is removed), and the write function does not exist for a ROM.

Figure 3-38 shows the functional block diagram of a typical ROM. This unit is described by the manufacturer as a 1024 × 8 ROM. This means that the matrix has 1024 addresses, each with 8 bits. Thus, 8-bit binary words or bytes can be read out of 1024 locations. The bytes appear on the data lines D0 through D7, connected to the data bus. Although the buffer is three-state, only the high-impedance and output states are used. When chip select (CS) inputs are available, the permanent information stored at the selected address is passed to the data bus. When one or more of the chip select inputs are absent, the buffer remains in the high-impedance state and no data bytes pass from the matrix to the data bus. Thus, it is possible to shut off the ROM from the system by controlling only one of the lines or inputs.

Note that the user can define whether the chip select inputs are active high or active low. Also, note that the user must define the binary word to be stored at each address. Generally, the user defines the desired contents of the ROM by means of IBM cards or punched paper tape. The manufacturer then programs the ROMs (sets in the binary bit pattern at each address), usually by means of a mask for the final metallization step in IC manufacture. This process is generally used where a large number of ROMs are required (typically 300 or more), but can be used for smaller numbers. As in the case of a RAM, the address to be read in or out of the ROM is selected by an address decoder which, in turn, is controlled by the binary word on the address bus (lines A0 through A9).

There are two obvious problems for this method of custom ROM manufacture. First, the cost of the metallization mask (used for all the ROMs of a given program) is quite high. Thus, if only a few ROMs are needed, the cost per ROM is quite high. More important, the user rarely (if ever) knows the exact

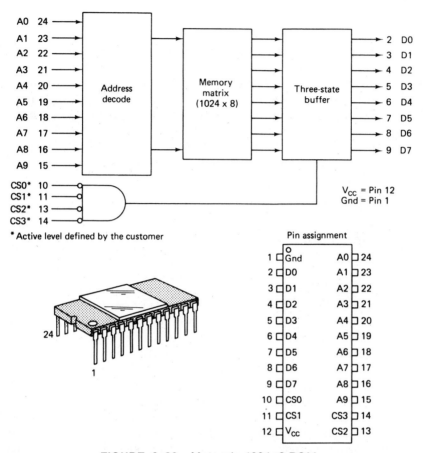

FIGURE 3-38 Motorola 1024/8 ROM.

programming required for a ROM until after the program has been tested and debugged. That is, you do not know what binary word is to be found at which address until you have written the program, tested it, and found that the program works under all circumstances. There are several ways to overcome this problem, including the use of PROMs (programmable ROMs), EPROMs (erasable, ultraviolet PROMs), EAROMs (electrically alterable ROMs), and RMMs (read-mostly memories), all of which are described in the following paragraphs.

3-7.5 PROM Circuit

A PROM is shipped by the manufacturer with all bits at each address blank (or at binary 0, in most cases). The user then programs each bit at each address by means of an electrical current. Typically, when current is applied to a bit, a

Nichrome wire is "fused" or opened by the current, making that bit assume the electrical characteristics of a binary 1. Bits to be at binary 0 are left untouched. The program in the PROM is then permanent and irreversible.

The programming can be done with simple switches and a voltage source, as shown in Fig. 3–39. In this circuit, the address switches are set to produce the binary word at the address terminals of the PROM (switches closed to provide 5 V for each binary 1, switches open for a 0). With the proper address selected, the rotary programming switch is set to each bit requiring a binary 1, in turn, and the fusing switch is pressed for about 1 s to fuse the Nichrome wire within the PROM. This process is very time consuming and tedious. Also, if a mistake is made on even one bit in one address, the entire PROM is made useless for that program. There are automatic and semiautomatic PROM programming devices available to overcome this problem.

3–7.6   EPROM Circuit

Even though it is possible to program a large number of PROMs with automatic equipment rather quickly, there is still the problem of testing de-bugging before a final program is obtained for the ROM. This problem is over-come by means of an EPROM in which information is stored as a charge in a MOSFET transistor. Such EPROMs can be erased by flooding the IC with ul-traviolet radiation. Once erased, new information can be programmed into the PROM in the normal manner. The erasure and programming process can be repeated as many times as required. As shown in Fig. 3–40, an EPROM package is provided with a transparent lid that allows the memory content to be erased with ultraviolet (UV) light. For proper erasure, the semiconductor chip within the IC package must be exposed to strong UV light for a few minutes. Exposure to ordinary room light takes years to produce erasure. Thus, there is

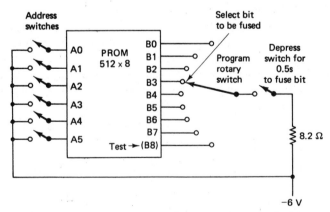

FIGURE 3–39   Basic PROM programming circuit.

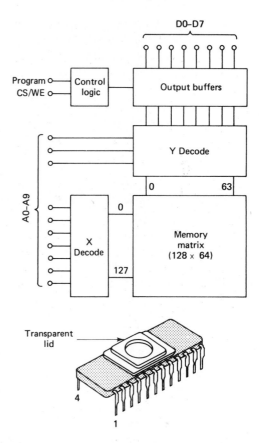

FIGURE 3-40 Motorola 1024 / 8 alterable (ultraviolet) ROM.

no danger of the program's being erased accidentally. Even exposure to direct sunlight does not produce erasure for several days.

Except for the erasure feature, a typical EPROM is similar to a ROM in function, as shown by the block diagram of Fig. 3-40. In addition to the usual address inputs, data outputs, decoders, and buffers, an EPROM usually has a ''program'' input line. An appropriate signal on the program line permits information to be programmed into the selected address.

3-7.7 EAROM and RMM

These devices are a form of erasable PROM, but use electrical currents instead of UV light for erasure. The programming is similar to that of the EPROM, but the erasure is a slow process and requires special circuits. For that reason, EPROMs are generally used for microprocessor-based systems, rather than EAROMs and RMMs.

3-8 INPUT/OUTPUT HARDWARE

The microprocessor and memories described in Secs. 3-6 and 3-7 can be connected to form a simple and almost complete microcomputer system. The missing element is an input/output device between the microcomputer hardware and the outside world. Without some I/O hardware, the transfer of data between the outside world and the microcomputer is impossible.

Assume, for example, that a basic microcomputer (microprocessor, ROM, and RAM) is used with a video terminal (keyboard and video display), and that the data lines of the video terminal are connected to the microcomputer data buses. Information to be processed is typed on the keyboard and transmitted directly to the microcomputer data lines. After processing, the data bytes are returned directly to the video display. There are three basic problems with such an arrangement.

First, data bytes from the keyboard can easily appear simultaneously with data from the selected memory. Second, the video terminal and microcomputer would have no way of telling each other than they are ready to transmit or receive data. Third, there is no synchronization of timing between the microcomputer and the video terminal. That is, the microcomputer and video terminal clocks may be operating at different frequencies, phase relationships, and so on.

A further problem is created if the terminal operates with serial data rather than the parallel data required for the microcomputer. Also, there is always the problem of *interfacing* between electronic devices of any kind (different operating voltage levels, impedances, etc.). These and other problems are overcome by means of an input/output IC. Most microprocessor manufacturers supply one or more I/O ICs for their systems. Typically, there is one I/O device for interfacing with parallel peripherals (terminals, keyboards, etc.), and another for serial peripherals.

3-8.1 *Typical Parallel I/O IC*

Figure 3-41 is the block diagram of a basic parallel I/O IC. The circuit is described as an *8-bit input/output port* by the manufacturer, and consists essentially of an 8-bit register and 8-bit buffers, together with the control elements. The MODE control is used to program the device as an input port or output port. The MODE control is 0 for input and 1 for output.

Input Port.   When used as an input port, information is passed into the 8-bit register when pulses on the clock line are high. The clock also sets the service request (SR/SE) circuit and latches data in the register. The SR output can be used to signal or flag the microprocessor that the data bytes from the peripheral are ready for processing. The CS1 and CS2 inputs are used to control the three-state buffers. The buffers are enabled when the CS1 and CS2 lines are

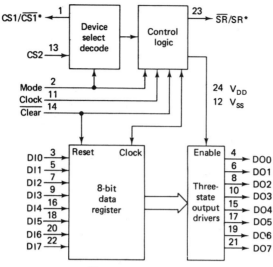

CS1/$\overline{\text{CS1}}$* ← 1

Device select decode

CS2 → 13

Control logic

23 → $\overline{\text{SR}}$/SR*

Mode → 2
Clock → 11
$\overline{\text{Clear}}$ → 14

24 V_{DD}
12 V_{SS}

DI0 → 3
DI1 → 5
DI2 → 7
DI3 → 9
DI4 → 16
DI5 → 18
DI6 → 20
DI7 → 22

Reset   Clock

8-bit data register

Enable

Three-state output drivers

4 → DO0
6 → DO1
8 → DO2
10 → DO3
15 → DO4
17 → DO5
19 → DO6
21 → DO7

*Polarity depends on mode.

FIGURE 3-41   RCA COSMAC 8-bit I/O port.

high. This also resets the SR circuits (to flag the microprocessor that the data bytes have been passed).

Output Port.   When used as an output port, the buffers are enabled at all times, and information is passed into the 8-bit register (if CS1, CS2, and the clock are all high). The service request SR signal is generated when CS1 and CS2 are swinging low, and remains until the clock swings low. Stated another way, SR is generated during the time that CS1 and CS2 go from 1 to 0, and remain until the clock line goes to 0.

CLEAR Signal.   A CLEAR signal is provided for resetting the register and the service request circuit. The CLEAR function operates in both the input and output port modes.

From these descriptions, it can be seen that the circuit of Fig. 3-41 provides the basic I/O functions. Using the video terminal example, a data byte from the keyboard can be held in the register until the microprocessor is ready to accept new data. This condition is signaled or flagged to the microprocessor by the SR line. Then the buffers are enabled by the microprocessor and the data byte is passed to the microcomputer system. The buffers are set to the high-impedance state and the registers are reset. After processing in the microcomputer system, the data byte is placed in the registers, and this condition is flagged to the video terminal by the SR line. When the video terminal is ready to accept data for display on the CRT, the buffers are enabled by the video terminal, the byte is passed to the CRT display, the buffers are again returned to the high-impedance state, and the registers and SR line are reset.

3-8.2   Serial I/O IC

Operation of a serial I/O circuit is generally far more complex than that of the basic parallel I/O circuit just described. In addition to all the control, timing, and data-transfer functions, a serial I/O must also convert from parallel to serial, and vice versa, for each exchange of information between the peripheral and microcomputer system. Because of this complexity, and because each manufacturer uses a somewhat different system for the I/O devices, we will not go into the details of serial interface here.

3-9   BASIC MICROCOMPUTER SYSTEM

Now that we have covered basic microcomputer hardware (microprocessor, ROM, RAM, and I/O ICs) and the circuits within these ICs, we are now ready to describe a simple, yet complete microcomputer system. Figure 3–42 is the block diagram of such an elementary microcomputer. One difficulty with understanding microcomputers is that there are many different types of microprocessors, and even more microcomputer system arrangements. As you will discover, there is no real standardization in hardware, software, or microcomputer system configurations.

Since it is difficult for anyone (even experienced technicians and engineers) not already familiar with computers of some type (standard, mini, or micro) to immediately grasp the operation of any microcomputer, we shall con-

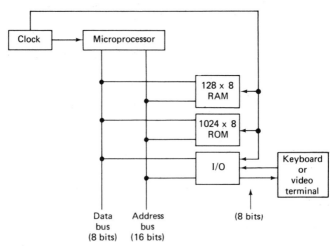

FIGURE 3-42   Block diagram of LENKMICROCOMP.

sider a generalized and simplified microcomputer that does not exist. Nevertheless, this microcomputer contains the basic principles upon which all microprocessor-based systems operate. Once you understand how this simplified microcomputer operates, you should have no difficulty in understanding any microprocessor-based system. Borrowing a technique used by microcomputer manufacturers, we shall call our system the LENKMICROCOMP (LENK MICROCOMPuter).

3-9.1 Microcomputer System Hardware

Our microcomputer consists of a microprocessor, a 128 × 8 RAM, a 1024 × 8 ROM, and an I/O device. The microprocessor is of special design but contains the usual registers, accumulators, counters, pointers, decoders, multiplexers, buffers, drivers, latches, ALU, and control circuitry. As is typical, the registers are used as temporary storage locations for data bytes or words, such as the accumulators in the ALU section, where the mechanical operations are performed. The counters are used to tally various items of information, such as commands (instructions) and locations (addresses) in memory where the information can be found. Decoders translate the instructions into electrical signals (pulses) for executing these commands and translate addresses into pulses. This permits the microprocessor to locate the required information and transfer it to the appropriate destinations. Interconnecting all these elements are electronic and logic circuits (buffers, drivers, latches, flip-flops, etc.) that direct the signals along the right paths.

3-9.2 Peripheral Equipment

In most microcomputers there is a means of direct human-to-machine communication. Even where the microcomputer system is used for control or processing of information to and from other electronic devices (such as when a microcomputer is used in industrial control, and provides communications between sensors and actuators) there must be some human-to-machine communications. Such communications is the job of peripheral equipment.

For simplicity, we have chosen a manually operated keyboard device. This keyboard permits the operator to enter information into any location in the memory or to insert extra instructions. Our keyboard is in the form of an electronic typewriter. With this arrangement, the typewriter can both insert and print out information. As an alternative, we can use a video terminal, where information is inserted by the keyboard, and read out by the video display. However, the video terminal does not provide a permanent record, as does the typewriter. In Chapters 4 and 5 we describe a system where the human-to-machine communication is done by the keyboard and paper printout of a desktop calculator.

The information fed to the microcomputer from the peripheral keyboard falls into two general classes. There are the *data bytes* (consisting of numbers, alphabetic letters, symbols, or combinations of all three that are to be processed), and the *instruction bytes* (the commands indicating how the data bytes are to be processed). Since the microcomputer language is composed of binary numbers (in the form of electrical pulses), all information to be used is first converted to numbers (or combinations of letters and numbers) and then the numbers are converted to binary.

In the LENKMICROCOMP keyboard, the conversion is done by means of a decoder. The keyboard decoder converts letters, numbers, and symbols from the keyboard into an ASCII code which appears at the keyboard output in the form of an 8-bit binary word or byte. This byte is in parallel form, and is applied to the 8-bit I/O IC of the microcomputer. As an example, assume that the letter A on the keyboard is pressed. This is converted to a hex 41 by the keyboard decoder, and appears as binary 01000001 at the I/O terminals.

3-9.3 Microcomputer Program

Microcomputers solve problems in a step-by-step manner. Since the microcomputer cannot think by itself (contrary to popular opinion), a *program* must be written that breaks the problem down into a series of sequential, logical, and simple steps. This is the task of the programmer. While an extended discussion on the art of programming (and it is an art, not a science) is not intended for this book, you must have some understanding (preferably a very detailed understanding) of the program if you are to learn how a microcomputer operates. For example, the first step in troubleshooting a microcomputer is to operate the system through its normal program and note any abnormalities in operation, sequence, or failure to perform a given step.

Since there are many variations among microprocessors, programs must be specifically developed for a particular microprocessor. The programmer must know the microprocessor language and the manner in which the microprocessor operates. In short, you must know the instruction set! The program that we shall consider here is for our hypothetical general-purpose microcomputer, the LENKMICROCOMP.

3-9.4 The Basic Program

As an example of how a program may be prepared for the microcomputer, let us consider how the microcomputer might solve a simple problem in industrial control. Assume that there are two tanks used to hold a liquid under pressure in an industrial process. The *ratio* or relationship between the pressures in the two tanks must be maintained according to a specific equation $A = (BC^2)/2$, where A is the pressure ratio, B the pressure in tank 1, and C the pressure in tank 2. The pressures in each tank are monitored by pressure transducers (Chapter 2) and converted to electrical signals, as shown in Fig. 3-43. In turn, the electrical

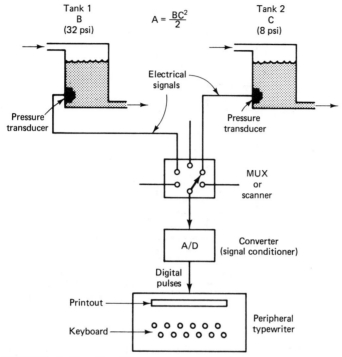

FIGURE 3-43 Simplified application of a microcomputer used to solve a basic application in industrial control.

signals are converted to digital pulses (analog-to-digital conversion, Chapter 2) in an 8-bit format, and applied to the peripheral typewriter where they are printed out.

The printout from the transducers shows the actual pressure in each tank, but not the ratio. The microprocessor can be programmed to print out the ratio, in addition to the pressures. Keep in mind that the problem described here is extremely simple for even the most elementary microcomputer. In the real world, the microcomputer would probably also be programmed to provide control of the pressures, not just monitoring and printout. However, for simplicity, we concentrate here on how the microprocessor is programmed to print out the ratio. In Chapters 4 and 5 we discuss how various functions are monitored and converted to data bytes suitable for a calculator (which has a keyboard and paper printout similar to that of a typewriter).

As a first step, the programmer analyzes the problem and breaks it down into a sequential series of logic steps. The programmer then draws up a *flowchart,* which diagrams the sequence of steps to be taken in solving the problem. Such a flowchart is shown in Fig. 3-44. Although the flowchart helps the programmer analyze the problem, the microcomputer cannot use the flowchart as is. The microprocessor has its own language (machine language), which is

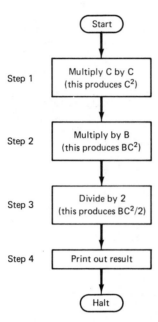

FIGURE 3-44 Basic flowchart for industrial control problem.

based on binary numbers, not alphabetic letters or words. Accordingly, the flowchart must be converted to a program or sequential set of instructions (in machine language) which the microprocessor can follow. The conversion process is known as *assembly,* and is discussed in Sec. 3–11. Some microprocessor manufacturers provide software programs, known as assemblers, that aid in the conversion process.

There are many ways in which manufacturers identify their instructions. First, some manufacturers call their instructions *operation codes* (or simply *op codes*). In some cases, each op code or instruction is identified by a binary number. This is the same binary number applied to the data inputs of the microprocessor to initiate an instruction or function. However, as discussed in Sec. 3–11, machine-language programming (using binary numbers) is very laborious and subject to error, except for very simple, short programs.

Most microprocessor manufacturers identify the instructions by an alphabetic abbreviation or *mnemonic,* by a numeric abbreviation (usually in hex), and by an assembly code or statement. Examples of such identification for our LENKMICROCOMP are shown in Fig. 3–45. Note that the assembly code or statement is used for the convenience of the programmer when writing a program. However, only the numerical portion is used by the microprocessor (in binary form). The hex representation is used as a shorthand for the binary number.

Both the numbers representing the instructions and the numbers that constitute data are stored in the memory at particular addresses. Each instruction or data byte is stored at a separate address. The programmer must keep a record

Alphabetic representation (mnemonic)	Numberical representation Hex	Binary	Meaning of instruction
CAD	3A	0011 1010	Clear accumulator and add
ADD	3B	0011 1011	Perform addition
SUB	3C	0011 1100	Perform subtraction
MUL	3D	0011 1101	Perform multiplication
DIV	3E	0011 1110	Perform division
STO	3F	0011 1111	Store number in accumulator
PRT	7A	0111 1010	Print out data
HLT	00	0000 0000	Halt microcomputer operation

FIGURE 3-45 Examples of typical op codes for the LENKMICROCOMP.

of the address of each instruction or data byte. Then, if the programmer wishes to obtain any specific instruction or data byte, the address is put on the address bus by the program, and the instruction or data byte stored at that address appears on the data bus.

Arrangement of Instruction Addresses. There are several methods for arranging the instruction addresses in memory. Since the instructions follow in sequence, the address of the instructions may also be in sequential order. Thus, instruction 1 may be stored at address 0001, instruction 2 at address 0002, and so on. Before the start of operations, the address of instruction 1 (0001) is placed in a *program counter* register within the microprocessor. Then, as the microprocessor executes instruction 1, a signal is sent to the program counter, advancing the count by 1. The number in the program counter is now 0002, which is the address of instruction 2. The microprocessor gets the address of the second instruction from the program counter (that is, the number in the program counter appears on the address bus). As the microprocessor executes instruction 2, the program counter advances to 0003, which is the address of instruction 3. This process continues as long as there are instructions to be carried out. The final instruction directs the microprocessor to stop.

Keep in mind that the instructions are *permanently programmed* into the ROM at the addresses indicated. Neither the instructions nor the order in which they appear can be altered (unless the ROM is erasable). An erasable or alterable ROM is used during development of the program. When the program is "debugged" and the desired order of instructions is determined, a ROM is permanently programmed to that order. (The term "debugging" applies to finding any fault in a program, particularly when the program is new and untried. This is not to be confused with "troubleshooting," which is the term used to find electrical or mechanical faults in a microprocessor system, particularly in the hardware. Troubleshooting imples that the system once performed the program properly.)

Arrangement of Data Addresses.   There are several methods for arranging the data bytes in memory. One method is to store both the instruction and data bytes in each address. Then, when the microprocessor is directed to that address (that is, when the address word appears on the address bus), the microprocessor finds both the op code indicating an instruction and the data to be acted upon. Another method is to store each data byte at any address that is unoccupied and available. Using this system, each step of the program requires two *machine cycles,* one for instructions and one for data. Some microprocessors require three machine cycles for each program step. (As discussed in Sec. 3–10, a machine cycle usually consists of 8 consecutive bits of data.) Typically, the first machine cycle is for the op code or instruction, with the remaining two cycles for data. Keep in mind that data bytes are temporarily programmed into the RAM at the desired addresses. In our case, the data bytes are entered at the peripheral typewriter keyboard.

Note that with any of the systems for instruction and data addressing, the program does not contain the actual data but the address at which the data bytes are stored. For example, if the programmer wishes the microprocessor to add a certain number, the programmer indicates to the microprocessor the op code for addition (the addition instruction word appears on the data bus) and gives the address of the data byte number to be added (the data byte address appears on the address bus). The microprocessor then obtains the data byte at the selected address, and adds the data byte number to whatever number appears in the microprocessor arithmetic register or accumulator.

Example of Programming.   As an example, let us program the industrial control application (finding the ratio or relationship between pressures in two tanks, using the flowchart of Fig. 3–44 and the instructions or op codes of Fig. 3–45). Assume that the data values are as follows:

1. B, the pressure in tank 1, is 32 psi (pounds per square inch).

2. C, the pressure in tank 2, is 8 psi.

3. 2, the number by which BC^2 is divided.

These data bytes may be stored at unoccupied address in memory. For example, the data byte for C (8) can be stored at address 1003, data byte B (32) address 1007, and data byte 2 at address 1008. The program listing then appears as shown in Fig. 3–46.

This method of listing the program is often called an *assembly listing* since it shows the program in assembly language (hex op codes, mnemonics, explanations, etc.) rather than in machine language. The differences in program listing methods are discussed further in Sec. 3–11.

Initially, the program counter is set to instruction address 0001 by a signal from the peripheral typewriter (via the keyboard decoder, I/O IC, and the data

Instruction address	Operation code	Data address	Explanation
0001	3A	1003	CAD (clear and add). Erase any number remaining in the accumulator from a previous operation. Bring the contents of address 1003 (C, or 8) to the accumulator.
0002	3D	1003	MUL (multiply). Multiply the number in the accumulator by the number at data address 1003 (C, or 8), (the result is C^2, or 64).
0003	3D	1007	MUL (multiply). Multiply the number in the accumulator by the number at data address 1007 (B, or 32) (the result is BC^2, or 2048).
0004	3E	1008	DIV (divide). Divide the number in the accumulator by the number at data address 1008 (2) (the result is $BC^2/2$, or 1024).
0005	3F	1138	STO (store). Store the number in the accumulator (1024) at data address 1138.
0006	7A	1138	PRT (print). Print out data stored at data address 1138 (1024).
0007	00		HLT. Halt operation of microprocessor.

FIGURE 3-46 LENKMICROCOMP program listing for industrial control problem.

bus and/or control lines). The instruction at that address (which happens to be op code 3A) tells the microprocessor to clear the accumulator to zero, and then add the number found at data address 1003 (which is decimal 8, or C). In some microprocessors, this operation can be done in one machine cycle, since part of the byte at address 0001 is the op code (3A) and part is the address (1003) at which the data byte to be addressed resides. This second part of the byte is described as the *operand* in some microprocessor literature (since the second part is to be operated on by the instruction or op code).

In our microcomputer, the operation is done in two machine cycles (one for the op code, one for the data or operand address). However, the program counter in our microprocessor advances only one step (to instruction address 0002), even though two machine cycles are required. The instruction at address 0002 (which is op code 3D) tells the microcomputer to multiply the number in the accumulator by the number found at data address 1003. This is the same data address used in the previous step and contains a data byte equal to decimal 8. The result in the accumulator is now 8×8, or 64, or C^2. Again, two machine cycles are used (one for the instruction and one for the data), and the program counter advances to instruction address 0003.

The instruction at address 0003 (again op code 3D) tells the microprocessor to multiply the number in the accumulator by the number found at data address 1007 (which is decimal 32, or B). The result in the accumulator is now 64×32, or decimal 2048, or BC^2, and the program counter advances to instruction address 0004. The instruction at address 0004 (now op code 3E) tells the microcomputer to divide the number in the accumulator by the number found at data address 1008 (which is decimal 2). The result is now $(BC^2)/2$, or decimal 1024, which is the answer to our problem (the ratio or relationship between pressures in the two tanks is a factor of 1024). The program counter advances to instruction address 0005.

The instruction at address 0005 (now op code 3F) tells the microprocessor to store the number appearing in the accumulator at address 1038. The program counter advances to instruction address 0006, which tells the microprocessor to print out the result at address 1038 on the peripheral typewriter (via the data bus, I/O IC, and keyboard decoder). The operator thus has a permanent record of the answer. In the case of a video terminal, the answer appears on the display, but there is no record. After the printout, the program counter advances to instruction address 0007, which directs the microprocessor to halt.

3-9.5   Special Program Instructions

In addition to the routine instructions for our LENKMICROCOMP system, typical examples of which are shown in Fig. 3-45, there are a number of instructions that help make the microcomputer such a flexible, decision-making machine. These are the *branch* instructions (also known as *jump, skip,* or *transfer* instructions) shown in Fig. 3-47. These instructions direct the microcomputer to leave the main program at some other designated point in the program. This is sometimes known as a branch or subroutine *call.*

For example, assume that op code 20 and address 0033 appear at a certain point of the program, say at instruction address 0011. The instruction (op code 20) tells the microprocessor to leave the main program at this point and branch or jump to address 0033. However, the program counter first increments by 1 to the address 0012. The contents of the program counter (0012) are then put into an address in an unoccupied area of memory, usually called the *stack.* The stack thus saves the address of the instruction to be executed after the branch routine is completed.

With the address of the next step in the main program safely stored in memory, the program counter goes to the address specified by the branch instruction (0033 in our case). After the instruction at 0033 is performed, the mi-

Alphabetic (Mnemonic) Representation	Numerical Representation		Meaning of Instruction
	Hex	Binary	
BRA	20	0010 0000	Branch, unconditionally
BRN	21	0010 0001	Branch, on negative
BRP	22	0010 0010	Branch, on positive

FIGURE 3-47   Examples of branch op codes for the LENKMICROCOMP.

croprocessor follows, in sequence, instructions at addresses 0034, 0035, and so on, until the last address of the branch instruction is reached. This last address usually contains an instruction to return to the main program. Such an instruction need specify no address. When the microprocessor receives a return instruction, the microprocessor replaces the current contents of the program counter with the address stored in the stack (0012). This causes the microprocessor to resume execution of the original program at the point immediately following the original branch instruction.

Conditional and Unconditional Branches. We have just described an *unconditional branch* instruction. The other two branch instructions shown in Fig. 3–47, BRN (op code 21) and BRP (op code 22), are examples of *conditional branch* instructions. If, for example, op code 21 and address 0033 appear in the program, it means that if the number in a certain counter or register is negative, the microprocessor must branch to address 0033, perform the instruction, and proceed (in sequence) from there. If the number is not negative, the microprocessor is to ignore the branch instruction and proceed with the original program. The BRP instruction is the same as the BRN except branching occurs if the number is positive. Otherwise, the branch instruction is ignored.

3-9.6 Microcomputer Operation Cycle

Once the program has been entered (or *loaded*) into memory (that is, with instructions permanently programmed into the ROM, and data bytes temporarily entered into the RAM via the peripheral typewriter), the microcomputer is ready to go automatically through the program cycle. Each cycle has two alternate phases: the *instruction* phase (or instruction *fetch* as it may be called) and the *execution* phase. After these two phases have been completed, the cycle is repeated. The duration of each phase is determined by a fixed number of clock pulses. Typically, there are eight clock pulses per machine cycle. Each phase may require one or more machine cycles.

The combination of fetch and execution of a signal instruction is referred to as an *instruction cycle*. The portion of a cycle identified with a clearly defined activity is called a *state*. The interval between clock pulses is referred to as a *clock period,* as discussed in Sec. 3–10. Typically, one or more clock periods are necessary to complete a state, and there are several states in a cycle. The flow diagram of the LENKMICROCOMP operation cycle is shown in Fig. 3–48.

Instruction or Fetch Phase. The first instruction fetch is initiated by a start command. In our case, this command is initiated by the peripheral typewriter. The start command sets the first instruction address (0001) into the program counter. The instruction phase of the operation cycle starts when this address is transferred to the address register.

Note that as information is transferred from one storage location to

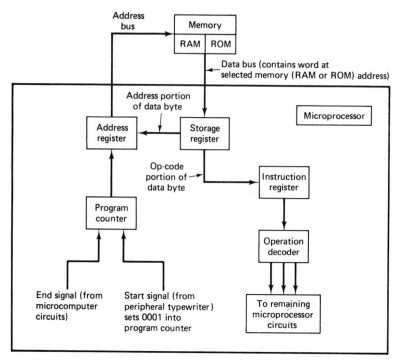

FIGURE 3-48   Flow diagram of LENKMICROCOMP operation cycle.

another, the information is not erased from the original location unless specifically so ordered. Thus, in our example, the address of the first instruction word appears in both the program counter and the address register. On the other hand, when new information is placed in a storage location, any previous information stored at that location is first erased.

The output of the address register is applied to memory via the address bus, as shown in Fig. 3–48. The word at the selected address in memory is transferred to the storage register via the data bus. From the storage register, the op-code portion of the word is transferred to the instruction register. Here, the word is decoded by the operation decoder, and the microprocessor circuits (ALU, etc.) perform the indicated instruction. Also from the storage register, the address portion of the word is transferred to the address register, first erasing the information previously stored there. This completes the instruction phase of the cycle.

Execution Phase.   The execution phase starts when the data address placed in the address register during the instruction phase is applied to memory via the address bus. The data word at the selected address in memory is transferred to the storage register via the data bus. The data byte is then processed in accordance with the instruction (still in the instruction register). When the processing is finished, an *end signal* or *processing complete* signal advances the program counter by 1 (to 0002 in our case). The program counter now contains the address of the next instruction, and the instruction fetch or phase can start.

This completes the execution phase of the operation cycle. The cycle is repeated over and over again, the instruction phase alternating with the execution phase for each cycle, until the entire program is complete. In the case of a branch operation the op-code portion of the instruction word is that of the branch instruction, and the operand portion is the address of the *next instruction to be followed* if branching is to take place. Under such conditions, this address is placed in the program counter, replacing the address already there, as described in Sec. 3-9.5. The microcomputer then follows the branch program until a return to the original program is instructed.

We have just described the complete operation cycle of the LENKMI-CROCOMP. Different microcomputers may have different methods for going through the full cycle, but the basic principles of operation are essentially the same for all microcomputers.

3-9.7   Subroutines, Libraries, and Nesting

Practically every instruction to the microprocessor involves a routine series of steps. For example, to add two 8-bit numbers, the LSD must be added first. If there is a carry, the carry must be added to the next-significant bits. Then these bits must be added. If there is another carry, this carry must also be added to the MSD, and then they must be added. Although the series of calculations is complete within itself, the series may only be part of a larger program.

Since the microprocessor can only follow instructions, this routine series of steps must be included in the program. However, to save time, this series of steps is listed in the microprocessor literature. Such listings or general-purpose set of instructions are called *libraries, routines,* or *subroutines.* Often, the term "libraries" is given to a group of routines.

A typical subroutine might include all the steps necessary to find square root, sines, cosines, logarithms, and so on. If these types of calculations are repeated throughout the program, the programmer may prepare a special program for each of them and store the program in memory. Usually, subroutines are handled as a branch or jump. Then, when the programmer calls for a routine, the microprocessor is given the branch op code and the address of the first branch instruction, as discussed in Sec. 3-9.5.

Subroutines are often *nested.* That is, one subroutine calls a second subroutine. The second may call a third, and so on. This is acceptable as long as the microcomputer has enough capacity to store the necessary return addresses, and the microprocessor is capable of doing so. The maximum depth of nesting is determined by the depth of the stack (or reserve memory). If the stack has a space for storing three return addresses, three levels of subroutines may be accommodated.

3-9.8   Interrupts

Most microprocessors have some provision for interrupts. Generally, interrupts are used for communications with peripheral equipment. For example, assume that the LENKMICROCOMP is processing a large volume of data, portions of which are to be printed on the peripheral typewriter. The microcomputer can produce one 8-bit data byte output (or one alphabet character) for each machine cycle, but it may take the typewriter the equivalent of several machine cycles (or several dozen) to actually print out the character specified by the data byte. The microprocessor could then remain idle, waiting until the typewriter can accept the next data byte.

If the microprocessor is capable of interrupts, the microprocessor can output a data byte, then return to data processing. When the typewriter is again ready to accept the next data byte, the typewriter can request an *interrupt* or *service request*. When the microprocessor acknowledges the interrupt, the main program is suspended, and the microprocessor automatically branches to a routine that outputs the next data byte. (This is known as *servicing* the peripheral device, or servicing the interrupt.) After the data byte is delivered to the typewriter and the corresponding character is printed, the microprocessor continues with main program execution. Note that this is, in effect, quite similar to a branch or subroutine call (Sec. 3-9.5), except that the jump is initiated externally (by the typewriter) rather than by the program.

There are more complex interrupt schemes, particularly where several peripherals must share the same microprocessor. Usually, such interrupts involve assigning priority levels (prioritizing) the peripherals. One approach (called the *polled* method, or *polling*) is for the microprocessor to check each peripheral, in turn, on a given priority basis, for a service request. The polled method is generally wasteful, since part of the main program is used up whether the peripherals need service or not. It is generally more effective for the microprocessor to stop only when the peripheral sends an interrupt. The peripheral can still be assigned priorities. For example, if peripheral A is first priority and B is second priority, A is serviced before B if both peripherals make a service request simultaneously. B is serviced first only if A is not making a request.

3-10   MICROCOMPUTER TIMING
AND SYNCHRONIZATION

It is obvious that all the system functions described in Sec. 3-9 and shown in Fig. 3-48 must by synchronized as to time. For example, if a data byte is to be entered into memory at a particular address, that (and only that) data byte must be on the data bus when the desired address byte is on the address bus. If the two bytes (data and address) are not synchronized exactly, the data byte is entered at the wrong address (or at no address). This problem is overcome by timing within the microprocessor. Registers are opened and closed at exact time intervals (by the clock pulses) to produce the desired results.

System timing is primarily an internal function of the microprocessor. As in the case of microprocessor instructions, you cannot change the time relationships or operating cycles of the microprocessor. However, you can change system speed or operating frequency (which is determined by the clock pulse frequency). Clock frequency, internal or external, is generally controlled by a quartz crystal, identical to those used to control frequency in communications transmitters. If a 1-MHz crystal is used, the clock pulses are approximately 1 μs; with a 3–MHz crystal, the clock pulses are about one-third of this, or about 333 ns. However, if it takes eight clock pulses to complete a certain function or instruction at one speed, it takes eight clock pulses to complete the same function at any other speed.

The time relationships and synchronization are shown by timing diagrams such as that shown in Fig. 3–49. The clock pulses are shown at the top and bottom of the diagram. There are two sets of eight clock pulses. Thus, each clock pulse represents 1 bit in an 8-bit byte. Some functions are done with the first

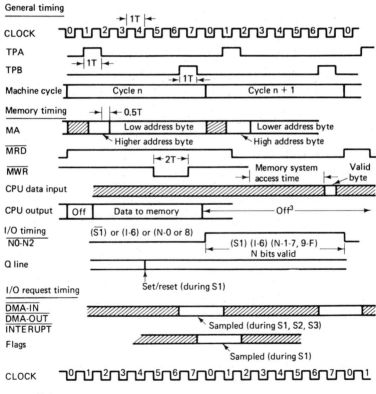

FIGURE 3-49 Timing diagram for basic RCA COSMAC microcomputer system.

byte; other functions require two bytes. Note that there is no reference to operating speed on the clock pulse, but that one clock cycle is shown as a time interval 1T (at clock pulse 3 on the top line). This is known as a *clock period.* If the clock frequency (set by the crystal or other external clock pulse source) is 1 MHz, the time interval or clock period 1T is approximately 1 μs.

From a programming standpoint, the timing intervals and relationships are not that critical. It is generally more important that the programmer know that it takes one or two bytes to perform a given function or instruction. However, from a design or troubleshooting standpoint, timing synchronization is critical.

3-11   MACHINE LANGUAGE VERSUS ASSEMBLY LANGUAGE

A microprocessor may be programmed by writing a sequence of instructions in binary code which the microprocessor can interpret directly. For example, referring back to the instructions of the LENKMICROCOMP shown in Fig. 3-45, the instruction for addition is binary 00111011. If this byte is programmed into memory and then appears on the data bus when the microprocessor data port is open, the microprocessor adds (probably the contents of one register to another). This is *machine language programming* and is useful only where the program to be written is small.

At best, writing a program in machine language is a tedious task, subject to many errors. The task of writing a program can be speeded up and error minimized when hex is used instead of binary (both hex and binary are shown in Fig. 3-45). However, hex coding has two major limitations. First, hex is not self-documenting. That is, the code itself does not give any hint in human terms of the operation to be performed. The user must learn each code, or constantly use a *program reference card* or *sheet* to convert. Second, and more important, hex coding is *absolute.* That is, the program works only when stored at a specific location in memory. This because branch or jump instructions in the program make reference to specific addresses elsewhere in the program.

Consider the example shown in Fig. 3-50, which is a listing of an eight-step program written in machine code (but with the digits grouped in hex format). Steps 0007 and 0008 make reference to step (or instruction address) 0004. If the program is moved, step 0008 must be changed to refer to the new address of step 0004.

3-11.1   Assembly Language

The problems just discussed can be overcome by writing the program in *assembly language,* where alphanumeric symbols are used to represent machine-language codes, branch addresses, and so on. (Chapter 5 describes

Step Number	Machine Code	Explanation
0	1011 1000	Load decimal 32 in
1	0010 0000	register R0
2	1011 1010	Load decimal 5 in
3	0000 0101	register R2
4	0000 1001	Load port 1 to accumulator
5	1111 0000	Transfer contents of accumulator to register addressed by register 0
6	0001 1000	Increment R0 by 1
7	1110 1010	Decrement register 2
8	0000 0100	by 1; if result is zero, continue to step 9; if not, go to step 4
9	—	
10	—	

FIGURE 3-50 Basic eight-step program written in machine code arranged in hex format.

assembly-language programming of multiprogrammer used for industrial control systems.) As an example of assembly-language programming, the instruction to increment the contents of register 0 becomes INC R0, instead of hex 18, giving the user the meaning of the instruction at a glance. Our example program of Fig. 3-50 can then be written in assembly language as shown in Fig. 3-51.

The use of assembly language makes it much easier to write a program, but it results in a program that is useless to the microprocessor (which operates only with binary numbers). One way to overcome this problem is to write the program in assembly language but to include the hex codes (as shown in Fig. 3-51). Then, when you enter the program into the microcomputer, it is relatively easy to convert from hex to binary. Of course, this requires that you remember both the hex code and the assembly code for each instruction of the microprocessor. Although it is not a bad idea for you to learn all of the hex codes, it does require more remembering (or looking up) on your part, and thus increases the chance for error.

Step Number	Hex Code		Assembly Code
0	B8		MOV R0, #32
1	20		
2	BA		MOV R2, #05
3	05		
4	09	INP:	IN A, P1
5	F0		MOV @R0, A
6	18		INC R0
7	EA		DJNZ R2, INP
8	04		

FIGURE 3-51 Basic eight-step program written in assembly language, but including hex code.

A more convenient method is to assemble programs using an *assembler,* which is a program that converts from one code to another. In our case, the assembler converts from a verbal-type assembly code to binary numbers. In practice, the assembler program is entered into another computer, you write the program for your microcomputer on paper (known as the *source program*), and you enter your microcomputer program into the other computer (known as the *host computer*), which prints out a program (usually on paper tape or disks or possibly on cassette tapes) in binary form. This program is known as the *object program,* and can be entered directly into your microcomputer from the paper tape, disk, or cassette.

When a different computer is used for assembly, the program is known as a *cross-assembler.* It is also possible to use *time-sharing* services for assembly, and there are special devices and equipment developed by manufacturers for assembly of their microcomputer programs.

3-12   PERIPHERALS FOR MICROCOMPUTER CONTROL SYSTEMS

In a microcomputer, the primary function of peripheral equipment is to translate human instructions and data into microprocessor language (binary data bytes) and from microprocessor language into a form suitable for a readout. In effect, the peripheral equipment (in conjunction with the microcomputer I/O IC) reconciles the "outer world" with the microcomputer. There are two major reasons for this reconciliation or translation. First, the outer world rarely expresses anything in binary data bytes. Generally, the outer world uses numbers, letters, words etc. However, the microprocessor always uses binary data bytes. Second, the microprocessor operates at extremely high speeds when compared to the outer world. For example, in the fraction of a second that it takes to strike the key of terminal keyboard, a microprocessor can perform hundreds or thousands of operations.

When a microcomputer is used for such functions as data processing, there are *on-line* and *off-line* peripherals used to provide *direct* and *indirect* connection to the microcomputer. For example, a paper-type punch that is operated by an electric typewriter is an off-line device for indirect input. The paper-tape reader that converts holes in the paper type into pulses applied to the microcomputer is an on-line device for direct input.

Microcomputer systems used in control and instrumentation applications receive continuously changing inputs and produce corresponding readouts. There are generally no off-line devices with such systems. Instead, these microcomputer systems receive inputs from transducers which convert such factors as process temperature, flow rate, and volume into electrical voltages. The voltage, which are analogs of the temperature, flow, and volume, are converted into data bytes by A/D circuits. The automatic readout from the microprocessor system, in addition to supplying a permanent record on a typewriter or printer, is also used to control the industrial process. At the microcomputer output, the data bytes are converted to a corresponding electrical voltage by D/A circuits. The output electrical voltages are then applied as control voltages to switches, motors, valves, and so on, as needed to control the industrial process.

Most control and instrumentation microcomputers operate on a real-time basis, where the microcomputer stands ready to solve problems presented by the human operator. Where human operators must command a microcomputer, a manual keyboard (as found on an electric typewriter, teletype, or calculator) is the simplest and most common form of input/output device. The commands are typed and applied directly to the microcomputer (in the form of data bytes). The processed output signals from the microcomputer then "type out" the answers on the same keyboard. In Chapters 4 and 5 we discuss a system where the keyboard and paper printout of a desk-top calculator are used to provide both control and a permanent record for control and instrumentation systems.

3-12.1 Keyboard Terminals

Not all keyboards operate in exactly the same manner. However, all terminals using a keyboard (such as an electric typewriter, teletype, video terminal, and calculator) have many functions in common, including keyboard decoders and parallel/serial I/O ICs that operate in response to service request flag signals. We conclude this chapter with a brief discussion of these terminal functions.

3-12.2 Basic Input Circuit

Figure 3–52 shows the input relationship between a peripheral typewriter keyboard and a microcomputer for both serial and parallel operation. With any such input system there must be circuits between the keyboard and the microcomputer input that (1) convert the data instructions into bytes compatible with the microcomputer circuits, and (2) store the bytes until they can be entered into the microcomputer circuits without disrupting normal operation. This procedure is sometimes referred to as a *service routine*. The conversion is done by a decoder circuit, while the storage and timing is done by registers and buffers. The present design trend is to include the register and buffer function in the I/O IC of the microcomputer, with the decoder function in the typewriter.

Note that the data bytes are transmitted in both parallel and serial form between the keyboard and microcomputer. The parallel method is the fastest and requires the simplest I/O circuit in the microcomputer. However, many systems require that the data bytes be transmitted over a single telephone line (or pair of lines). Eight lines, plus any control flag, service request, or interrupt

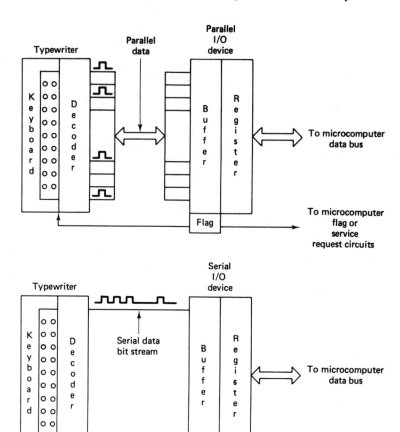

FIGURE 3-52 Input relationship between a peripheral typewriter and a microcomputer for both serial and parallel operation.

lines are required for an 8-bit parallel system. Thus, many systems require a special serial I/O IC (often called an *asynchronous* or *universal* I/O). Most major microprocessor manufacturers produce at least one serial I/O.

Serial Data Transmission.   It is conventional to transmit serial data in a fixed format similar to that shown in Fig. 3-53. When a user strikes a key on the keyboard (an "M," for example), the information denoting that character is converted to its ASCII code (4D in hex) and appears at the output as a *serial data bit stream*. Note that each of the character data bits (B0 through B6) is identified on Fig. 3-53. The character (the letter M in this case) is framed by a start bit B and two stop bits FF. By convention (or serial data transmission *pro-*

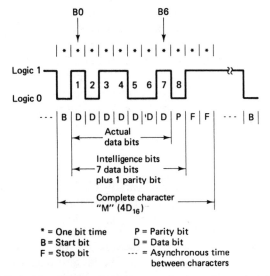

FIGURE 3-53 Serial data transmission format (showing character "M").

tocol), two stop bits are used for data transmitted at 10 characters per second, and one stop bit for higher data transmission rates.

Input Timing Sequence. With either serial or parallel transmission, the data/instructions must pass from the keyboard to the microcomputer circuits in a precisely timed sequence. As shown in Fig. 3-52, the decoder output is applied to a register/buffer combination. The buffer is opened and closed by pulses or control signals from the microcomputer, in response to *service requests* (also called flags, interrupts, etc.) from the keyboard. This reconciles the high speed of the microcomputer with the slow speed of the keyboard. For example, assume that the buffer can be opened and closed 10,000 times per second, and it takes 1 s for the typewriter key to be pressed and released. No matter what time the data byte from the keyboard starts and stops, the buffer/register has thousands of times to read in, store, and read out the data byte to the microcomputer.

This combination of service request signals and timing signals is necessary to prevent undesired conflict between the keyboard and microcomputer circuits. Assume, for example, that the microcomputer is performing a series of mathematical calculations on data bytes previously entered by the keyboard and that the operator starts to enter more data. In the normal sequence, a service request is sent by the typewriter. Generally, a service request is sent by the keyboard. Generally, a service request is sent for each data byte, or each time the key is struck. The service request indicates to the microcomputer that there are new data bytes to be entered into the buffer. If old information in the buffer has been read out to the microcomputer, the buffer is reset to zero, and the new data bytes are entered and read out in the microcomputer.

Now assume that the microcomputer is not ready to accept new information (previous data bytes are still being processed). Then the buffer accepts the new data bytes, but does not pass them to the microcomputer until the circuits are ready. Keep in mind that since the microcomputer operates at such a high speed, the operator does not have to "wait" until the microcomputer is finished before striking the next key.

3-12.3 Basic Output Circuit

Microcomputer output circuits are essentially the reverse of input circuits. The output circuits to a keyboard must (1) convert the processed data bytes to a form (usually numbers, letters, words, etc.) that is compatible with the

FIGURE 3-54 Output relationship between a peripheral typewriter and a microcomputer for both serial and parallel operation.

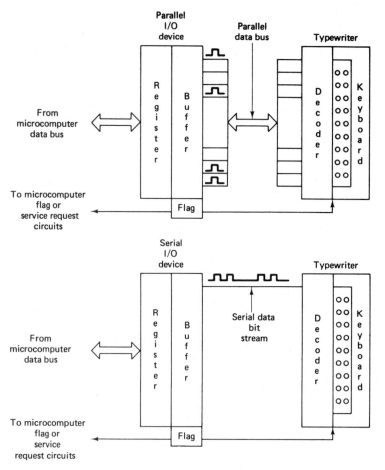

typewriter keys, and (2) synchronize the high-speed microprocessor output with that of the lower-speed typewriter. As in the case of input, the conversion is done by a decoder circuit (usually within the terminal), whereas the synchronization is done by the I/O buffer/register, which operates in response to a combination of microcomputer and keyboard signals.

Figure 3-54 shows the output relationship between a keyboard and a typical microcomputer. In the readout mode, the keys are operated by electrical voltages from the decoder. When the buffer/register is opened, the data byte is applied to the decoder, which, in turn, applies the operating voltage to the appropriate key. This causes the key to strike and print out the corresponding character (number, letter, symbol, etc.). In the normal sequence, a service request is sent by the keyboard. This indicates to the microcomputer that the keyboard is ready to receive data from the buffer. The register is set to zero, the new data byte is entered from the microcomputer, the buffer is opened, and the data byte is passed to the decoder. In turn, the decoder operates the corresponding key.

It is obvious that the microcomputer can solve problems faster than the keyboard can type them out. The means that two conditions must occur. First, the output buffer must be held in the existing state long enough for the key to be struck. Second, the normal routine of the microcomputer must be interrupted so that the answers to several problems are not computed while the output buffer is held open. In actual practice, the interruption occurs at some convenient point in the microcomputer operation (usually at the end of a timing cycle).

4

INTRODUCTION TO
THE MULTIPROGRAMMER

Now that we have reviewed the basics of control and instrumentation (Chapter 2) and microcomputer control (Chapter 3), let us discuss an actual system that combines the two basic functions. As established in Chapter 1, such a system must accept a variety of inputs from various sensors, then process the information under the control of a microcomputer and finally produce outputs that control or stimulate the test or process being sensed.

4-1 HEWLETT-PACKARD 6940B/6941B MULTIPROGRAMMER

The system selected for discussion is the Hewlett-Packard HP 6940B/6941B Multiprogrammer shown in Fig. 4-1. Although designed to be controlled by Hewlett-Packard minicomputers, desktop computers, and calculators, the multiprogrammer can be operated by a number of other 16-bit controllers to provide complete automatic test and process control functions. The multiprogrammer provides the link between the controller and the test or process. This relationship is shown in Fig. 4-2. In simple terms, the multiprogrammer is the interface between the controller and the physical world. Thousands of multiprogrammers are in use now as part of user-defined and assembled systems for

FIGURE 4-1 HP 6940B/6941B Multiprogrammer. (Courtesy Hewlett-Packard Company.)

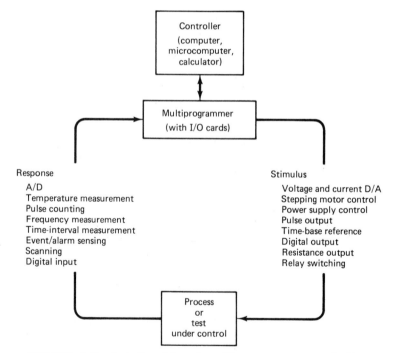

FIGURE 4-2 Relationship of multiprogrammer, controller, and process or test under control of the system.

production testing and control, data acquisition for industrial systems, process monitoring, life testing, quality control, and component evaluation.

The multiprogrammer consists essentially of a mainframe with internal microprocessor-based control circuits and front-panel pushbutton switches, as well as slots and connectors for up to 15 *plug-in input/output (I/O) cards.* This arrangement is illustrated in Fig. 4–3, which shows a few of the I/O cards, as well as the mainframe connected to a Hewlett-Packard HP 9825A calculator. These cards provide the circuits necessary for programmable I/O functions. We discuss card functions further in Sec. 4–2 and in Chapter 5.

The most unique feature of the multiprogrammer is that the user need install *only those cards necessary* to accomplish their particular control or instrumentation function. Thus, the multiprogrammer can be adapted to very simple or very complex systems, and can be changed (by the user) if the system requirements change. Take the very simple case of the closed-loop system, described in Sec. 1–2.4, where temperature of a liquid in a tank must be kept constant by means of steam in a jacket surrounding the tank. Temperature control is provided by operating a steam-control valve using one of the acuators described in Chapter 2 (probably a solenoid or possibly a motor). This makes it necessary to install an *output card* that is capable of controlling a solenoid (probably a *relay control card* to apply a fixed voltage to the solenoid, or possibly a *stepper motor card* to apply opening and closing pulses to a motor-actuated valve). A *temperature measurement input card* is needed to convert the output of a thermocouple (immersed in the liquid) to a value that can be recognized by the multiprogrammer.

In this oversimplified example, only two cards (one temperature-sensing input and one valve-actuating output) need be installed in the mainframe. Of

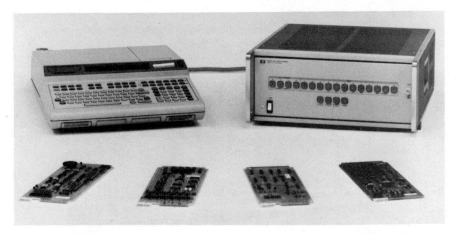

FIGURE 4-3 HP 6940B Multiprogrammer with I/O cards and HP 9825A Calculator. (Courtesy Hewlett-Packard Company.)

course, the complete system must be operated by a controller. Also, a controller-multiprogrammer program must be written so that the output actuator signals to the valve are given only when the tank temperature deviates from the desired set point, and so that the output signals to the valve are of a polarity to open and close the valve properly to correct any temperature deviations. (If the temperature goes up, the valve is closed to reduce the steam heat, and vice versa.) Several I/O cards are needed in any real-world control and instrumentation system. Figure 4–4 shows I/O cards installed in the mainframe for a typical system.

In addition to the mainframe (Model 6940B), there is an *extender* (Model 6941B) available for larger systems. The extenders are similar in appearance to the mainframe unit, except that the extender does not have front-panel switches. Each extender accommodates up to 15 I/O cards. Up to 15 extenders can be chain-cabled together with a mainframe to get up to 240 individual addressable I/O channels (one card per channel). The extenders can be separated from one another, and from the mainframe, by up to 100 feet.

Interface kits are required between the mainframe and the controller. These interface kits include hardware and software for operating the multiprogrammer from various Hewlett-Packard controllers. For example, the HP 59500A interface is for computers using the HP–IB (Hewlett-Packard Interface Bus). This interface is necessary since the HP–IB uses serial ASCII

FIGURE 4-4 I/O cards installed in a multiprogrammer mainframe. (Courtesy Hewlett-Packard Company.)

alphanumerics, whereas the multiprogrammer uses a 16-bit parallel format. The HP 14550B interface is a 16-bit parallel interface for use with Hewlett-Packard minicomputers such as the HP 1000, while the HP 98032A is for desktop computers with 16-bit I/O capability, such as the HP 9800 series. The Model 9825A calculator shown in Figs. 4–3 and 4–4 uses either the HP–IB interface or a GPIO (General Purpose I/O) requiring the HP 98032A-Option 040 interface. Operation of the multiprogrammer with the calculator is described in Chapter 5.

4-2 INPUT/OUTPUT CARD FUNCTIONS

The I/O cards available for use with the multiprogrammer can be grouped into six types: analog output, analog input, functional, digital output, digital input, interrupt, and breadboard. The following paragraphs summarize the functions of the various I/O cards. Chapter 5 describes the cards in greater detail, particularly in regard to programming and operation with a controller (the calculator).

4-2.1 Analog Output Cards

These cards produce a voltage, current, or resistance as programmed by the controller. The cards include a D/A voltage converter, a quad D/A voltage converter, a D/A current converter, a resistance output card, and a voltage regulator card.

69321B D/A Voltage Converter Card. This card provides a high-speed, bipolar output voltage in the range of ± 10 V at 5 mA that is the analog of the 12-bit digital input data (from the controller). The card can control analog instruments, drive analog recorders, simulate units under test, and generate user-defined waveforms under software control. The card features emergency shutdown and dual-rank storage for simultaneous outputs. Dual-rank storage is a feature that allows all D/A cards in a system to change the outputs simultaneously, and is discussed further in Sec. 4–5. If more than ± 10 V at 5 mA is required, the output can be boosted with an HP 6827A power supply/amplifier.

69322A Quad D/A Voltage Converter Card. This card provides four individually programmable bipolar output voltages in the range of ± 10 V at 5mA that are the analog of the digital data input. Two of the 12-input data bits specify which output is programmed and the remaining 10 bits represent the desired output voltage. The four outputs share a common-ground connection which is isolated from the data input ground. The card is a lower-cost alternative to the 69321B, where multiple outputs of only 10-bit resolution are required. The dual-rank storage feature is not available on this card.

Figure 4–5 is a block diagram of the quad D/A card. Each of the four individually programmable output circuits consists of a 10-bit storage latch and a 10-bit digital-to-analog converter (DAC). When the card is addressed and data strobed (DST), bits 0 to 9, representing the desired bipolar output voltage, are transferred into the storage latch specified by bits 10 and 11. The latch retains the data bits until they are selected again and reprogrammed with new data. The associated DAC converts bits 0 to 9 into the equivalent output (-10.24 to $+10.22$ V).

The -10- to $+10$-V programmable output voltages available at each of the four outputs on the card can be used to control or test a variety of analog devices. Quad D/A cards are often used in control applications that require voltage signals to change at programmed intervals of time. Up to 160 quad D/A cards (up to 10 per mainframe) provide up to 640 D/A channels (4 per card)

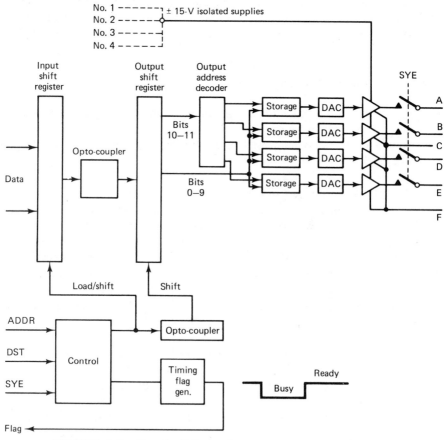

FIGURE 4-5 Quad D/A voltage-converter card block diagram.

which can be individually controlled from a single chain of multiprogrammer mainframes. The time interval between programmed changes can be as short as 100 μs or as long as desired. The time intervals can be established by using the timer, pulse counter, and frequency reference cards discussed in Sec. 4-2.3.

Figure 4-6 shows some typical applications for the D/A cards. As shown, the cards can be used to control flow valves and analog displays. The D/A function is also often used to control other process control equipment such as func-

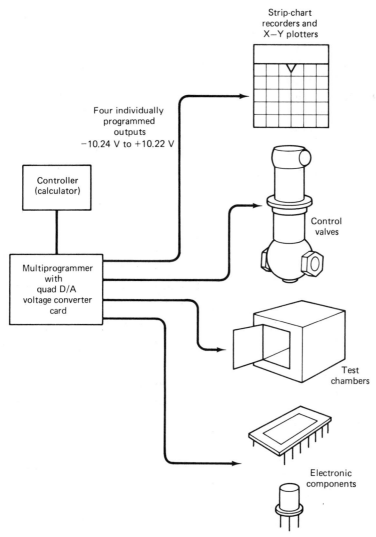

FIGURE 4-6 Typical applications for quad D/A voltage converter cards.

tion generators. Special waveforms necessary in some processes may be created by calculator software and the quad D/A cards. In the lab, environmental chambers and shake tables can be controlled with the help of D/A-supplied synthesized waveforms. The analog outputs from the D/A are also used in margin testing and component evaluation. The D/A outputs can also be used to drive the analog inputs of strip-chart recorders and X–Y plotters. D/A card functions are discussed further in Secs. 4–3 and 4–4.

69500A–69513A Resistance Output Cards. These cards provide a programmed value of resistance as their output. Figure 4–7 is a simplified block diagram. Twelve magnetically shielded, mercury-wetted, reed relays select the resistance values by modifying the value of a series string of high-accuracy, binary-weight resistors. A maximum of 15 resistance cards may be used in any one mainframe. Typically, the resistance cards control a variety of unipolar d-c power supplies with output up to 100 V and 1000 A. The outputs of all power supplies are isolated from ground and from each other by the relay/resistor networks on these cards.

69370A D/A Current Converter Card. This card provides a high-speed, constant-current output that is the analog of the binary digital input data

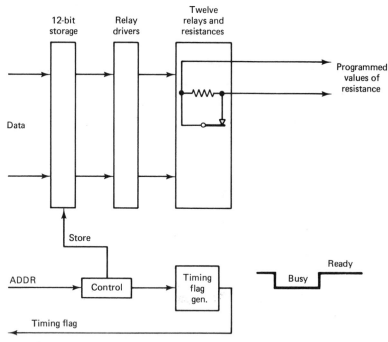

FIGURE 4-7 Simplified block diagram of resistance output cards.

from the controller (calculator). Figure 4–8 is a simplified block diagram. The card provides dual-rank storage (Sec. 4–5), a feature that allows all D/A cards in a system to change their outputs simultaneously. The 0 to 20 mA current output of this card can be used for test or control of devices with input impedances of up to 500 Ω. Many types of electrical-to-mechanical, hydraulic, or pneumatic converters using 1- to 5- or 4- to 20-mA inputs can be controlled by the card.

The current D/A card is often used with a voltage D/A card in control applications that require voltage or current signals to change at programmed intervals of time. In automatic test systems, the application is frequently called *arbitrary waveform generation*. The waveforms can be used to control instruments, operate the unit under test, or act as supervisory signals that control stresses during a life test. Up to 240 independently controlled D/A channels (up to 15 per mainframe) can be controlled from a single chain of multiprogrammer mainframes. The time intervals between programmed changes can be as short at $50\mu s$ or as long as desired. The time intervals can be established by using the timer, pulse counter, and frequency reference cards discussed in Sec. 4–2.3.

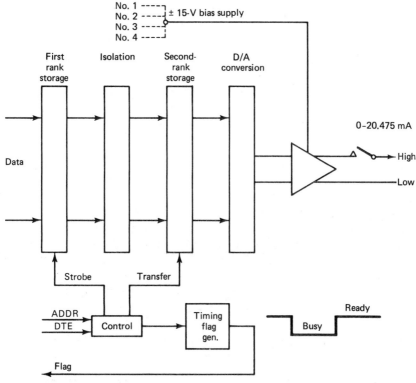

FIGURE 4-8 Simplified block diagram of D/A current-converter cards.

69351B Voltage Regulator Card. This card provides four regulated, isolated bias supplies for the various analog cards. One voltage regulator must be used in each mainframe in which one or more of the analog cards are used. The regulator card is inserted in a slot reserved for this purpose in each mainframe and does not take up an I/O card slot.

4–2.2 Analog Input Cards

These cards provide for temperature, voltage, current, and resistance measurement, as well as A/D conversion and waveform analysis or measurement. The cards include a high-speed A/D voltage converter card and a low-level A/D and scanner card.

69422A High-Speed A/D Voltage Converter Card. This card monitors bipolar d-c voltages in one of four ranges, ± 100 mV, ± 1 V, ± 10 V, or ± 100 V, and returns a 12-bit digital word to the controller to indicate the magnitude and sign of the measured voltage. The card uses a high-performance sample/hold amplifier and successive approximation A/D converter which provide a high conversion speed with accuracy. The d-c input voltage is guarded to maintain high input impedance. Up to 20,000 voltage readings per second can be transferred from the card to the controller through the mainframe circuits. The readings can be initiated by program commands or by an external trigger signal applied to the card. Data bits are also available at the card for transfer to external data receivers at up to 33,000 readings per second. The card can interrupt the computer when the data bits are ready for transfer.

69423A Low-Level A/D and Scanner. Figure 4–9 is the block diagram for the card. Six channels of thermocouples or other low-level d-c sources in the range of ± 20 mV can be monitored with this card. The card returns a 12-bit digital word to the controller to indicate the sign and magnitude of the measured voltage on the selected channel. The selection of either the unipolar or bipolar range and the desired channel are programmable from the controller.

As shown in Fig. 4–9, the signal being measured passes through an amplifier into a multiple-slope integrating A/D. Low thermal reed relays are used to select one of the six input channels. A seventh channel is used to read back the temperature of the isothermal input terminal block (which functions as a reference junction, Sec. 2–7.4). Use of this seventh channel eliminates the need for an ice bath in thermocouple applications. Instead of using the ice bath, the reference junction temperature is automatically compensated for in software. Although designed for thermocouple applications, the card can also be used in general low-level d-c input applications.

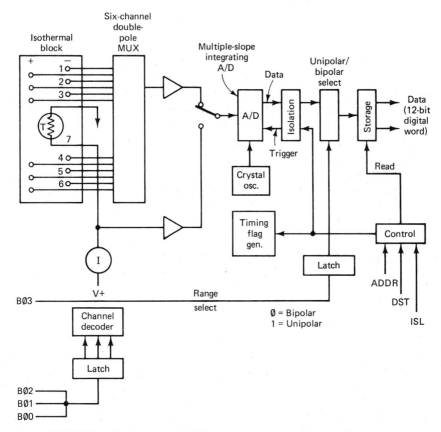

FIGURE 4-9 Low-level A/D and scanner card block diagram.

4-2.3 Functional Cards

These cards provide for frequency and time measurements, as well as counting and motor control functions. The cards include a programmable timer, a frequency reference, a pulse counter, and a stepping motor control card.

69600B Programmable Timer Card. This card can be used to hold off controller operation for a programmable period of time when making periodic readings or generating outputs at specific intervals. The card can also be used to supply a one-shot output or to interrupt the controller at programmable times. The card generates a crystal-controlled one-shot output and end-of-output pulse each time it is commanded by the program. Both pulses are available in both positive-true and ground-true form. One or more (up to 15) timers may be used in a mainframe to hold off or interrupt the controller program for the purpose of pacing input or output operation with other plug-in cards or instruments. Known-interval outputs generated by this card can be connected to the count-enable input of a pulse counter card as a period-reference for frequency measurements. The output of this card can be used to turn off a normally on relay or circuit that is connected to an audible alarm, safety interlock switch, or other "fail-safe" circuit. At regular intervals, the controller reprograms the card to disable the fail-safe circuit. If, for any reason, the controller does not reprogram the card as scheduled, the fail-safe circuit is activated at the end of the previously programmed timer interval. This is commonly known as a *watchdog timer* or *stall alarm*.

69601B Frequency Reference Card. The output from this card is a crystal-controlled square wave which is used to pace A/D measurements. The square-wave outputs are available for external use. This card provides six square-wave outputs at fixed frequencies from 1 Hz to 100 kHz, derived from a 1–MHz crystal. The outputs may be turned off with the low state of an external TTL logic gate, or external contact closure.

69435A Pulse Counter Card. This card totalizes logic-level or contact closure pulses. Count-up and count-down inputs are provided. The count can be read without disturbing the counting process, and the counter can be preset under software control. As a totalizer, the card is used to count objects on production lines, to accumulate counts for a-c power meters, and to monitor units under test. Figure 4–10 shows some typical counter and totalizer applications. Figure 4–10 also shows an elapsed time clock application where the pulse counter card is used with a frequency reference card. With two pulse counter cards as shown, the resolution is from 10 μs to 1 s. The connections and programming required for both frequency and time-interval measurement using the pulse counter card are discussed further in Chapter 5.

69335A Stepping Motor Control Card. This card produces a programmable number of pulses at either of two outputs to drive stepping motor translators, and other actuators that respond to pulse train inputs (such as a rotary actuator, Sec. 2–14.2). Figure 4–11 is a simplified block diagram. The pulse outputs of this card are also used in testing sequential logic circuitry and subassemblies. The card can be programmed to generate from 0 to 2047 square-wave pulses at either of the two output terminals. The user may also configure the card to produce from 0 to 4095 square-wave pulses. When applied to a stepping motor translator (such as a Superior Electric Co. ST101) these pulses are converted to clockwise and counterclockwise drive pulses for an associated stepping motor. The square-wave outputs of the card can also be used for pulse-train update of supervisory control stations.

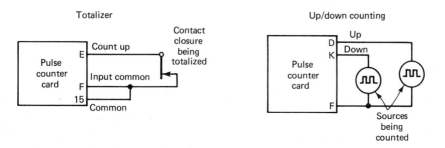

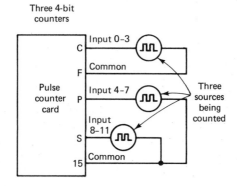

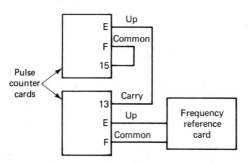

FIGURE 4-10 Typical counter and totalizer applications using pulse counter card.

4-2.4 Digital Output Cards

These cards provide general-purpose digital output functions. The cards include a digital output, an open-collector output, a relay output, and a relay output with readback card.

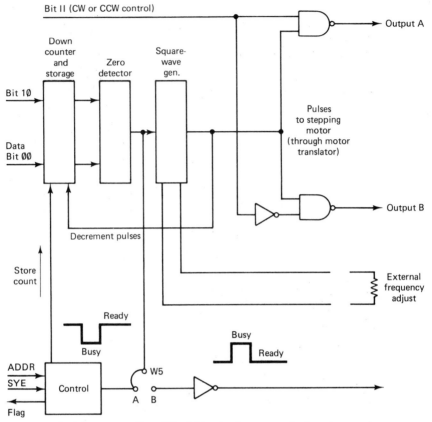

FIGURE 4-11 Simplified block diagram of stepping motor control card.

69331A Digital Output Card. This general-purpose output card has discrete transistor outputs that can provide 5- or 12-V logic levels to instruments, solenoid drive circuits, and solid-state a-c switches. The card has storage for 12 output bits, power-on preset circuits, system enable/disable capability, and gate/flag handshake capability to ensure orderly transfer of data to external digital devices. The card provides 12 bits with TTL/DTL-compatible logic levels as its output. The card uses the gate/flag timing method of digital data transfer. A maximum of 15 digital output cards may be used in any one mainframe.

69332A Open-Collector Output Card. This card is similar to the 69331A, except that the 69332A has open-collector outputs and can switch more voltage and current than the 69331A. Figure 4-12 shows the basic differences between the 69331A and 69332A cards. The outputs for the 69332A are not under gate/flag control, and are random at power-on. The 69332A is designed to drive lamps and relay coils using an external power source, as shown in Fig. 4–12. Digital storage circuits on the cards allow a single controller I/O channel to control up to 2880 lamps or relay coils with a chain of 16 mainframes. Twelve IC buffers on the card act as switches for voltages up to 30 V (dc) and currents up to 40 mA.

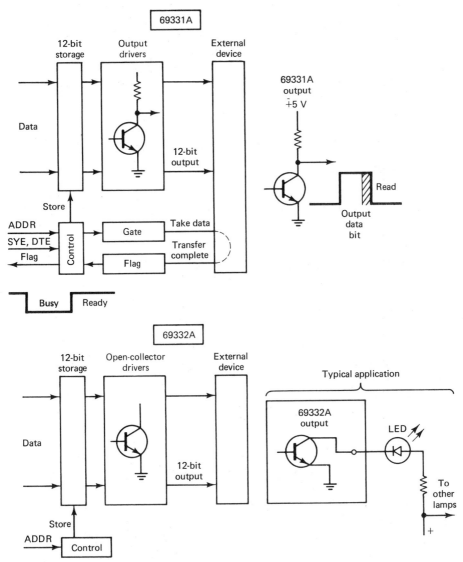

FIGURE 4–12 Basic differences between the 69331A and 69332A cards.

69330A Relay Output Card. This card provides 12, independent, single-pole single-throw (SPST), normally open, mercury-wetted contact pairs. A maximum of 15 cards may be used in any one mainframe, producing 180 independent sets of contacts available for switching or control functions. Two additional relays are provided for external circuit gate/flag operation. The gate/flag handshake capability of this card makes it useful for controlling instruments that are programmed with contact closures. Handshaking guarantees that the 12 data relays have had sufficient time to operate before the gate relay is actuated.

69433A Relay Output with Readback Card. This card provides the same 12 contact pairs as the 69330A. Figure 4–13 shows the basic differences between the 69330A and 69433A. In addition, the 69433A allows the controller to examine the status of the relay coil drive circuits on the card, before and after the contacts are actually changed. The 69433A is well suited for *analog scanning applications*. Timing circuits on the card assure that the relays are closed before a measurement is taken with an A/D card. The ability to read back contact status means that subroutines can check the state of the contacts before programming a change. Distribution trees and matrices can be easily wired with this card. No external handshaking is available with the 69433A.

4-2.5 Digital Input Cards

These cards provide general-purpose digital input functions. The cards include a standard digital input card and an isolated digital input card.

69431A Digital Input Card. This general-purpose input card has storage, gate/flag handshake capability, and the ability to interrupt the controller when the flag line is set by the external device. The card is used to read data from digital instruments, switches, ICs, contacts, and other digital data sources. Figure 4–14 is a simplified block diagram. As shown, the card can accept inputs from open-collector outputs or from TTL/DTL digital circuits, depending on the option selected. The card allows the controller to read 12 bits of logic level or contact closure that is referenced to the controller logic common (a-c earth ground).

Gate/Flag Handshaking: Handshaking is necessary in many digital input operations where an orderly exchange of control data is important. For example, suppose that a controller is programmed to read a BCD number that an industrial test station operator has set on a thumbwheel switch register. The interface must be made so that the computer does not read the register at the moment the operator is changing the switches. One way to do this is to connect the gate line of the input card to a light-emitting diode lamp next to the thumbwheel, and to connect the flag line of the card to a pushbutton next to the

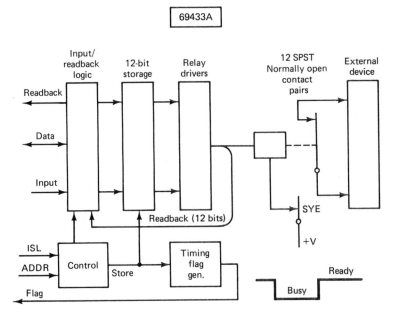

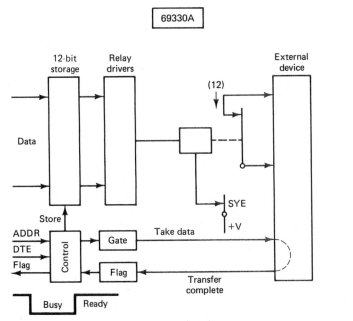

FIGURE 4-13 Basic differences between the 69330A and 69444A cards.

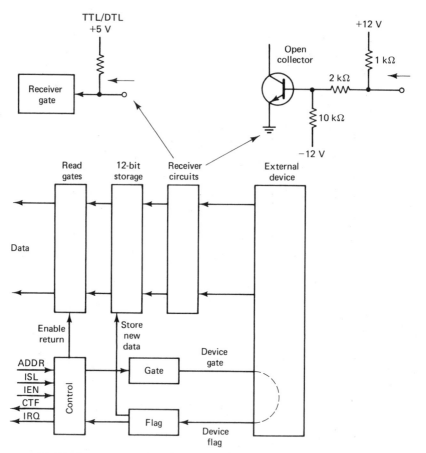

FIGURE 4-14   Simplified block diagram of digital input card.

thumbwheel. The 12 data bits of the card (and bits from as many other cards are necessary for large numbers) are connected to the BCD outputs of the thumbwheel.

The computer addresses the input card, causing the gate lamp to light as a signal that the operator may now change the thumbwheel settings. After changing the thumbwheels, the opertor pushes the flag pushbutton to let the computer know that normal operation may resume. Pressing the flag pushbutton automatically stores data on the card, turns off the gate lamp (because the controller has not yet read the new data), and can even interrupt the computer if the program has been written to respond to the interrupt. Handshaking is not always necessary in switch reading and other digital input control applications, but is nearly always used for reliable communication between digital instruments and computers. When not used, the gate and flag on the card are simply wired together.

69430A Isolated Digital Input Card.   This card is similar to the 69431A, but is used when digital signals in the control and instrumentation system must remain isolated from ground and from each other. Figure 4–15 is a simplified block diagram. The 69430A uses the *opto-couplers* described in Sec. 2–14.4. The external digital lines to be read must be capable of supplying at least 3 mA to each opto-coupler on the card. This card has no storage or gate/flag hand-shake capability.

Ground loops are one of the most persistent and annoying problems in control and instrumentation systems. The 69430A card breaks the path of

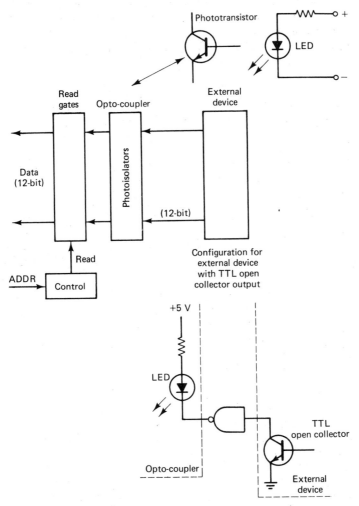

FIGURE 4-15 Simplified block diagram of isolated digital input card.

potential ground loops by using the opto-couplers (called *photoisolators* in the card literature) in each input line. Isolation between earth-grounded I/O and external circuits is necessary when the circuits being monitored are biased by power supplies that are isolated from earth ground (for safety or noise-immunity purposes) or that are floating up the 100 V (dc) above a-c earth ground.

Since the need for isolation arises from power supply grounding problems, the card is designed to monitor only circuits that are active, not passive. Simple relay contacts that have no connection to a power supply are inherently isolated, and there is no further need for isolation. Relay contacts that are "dry" (no voltage or current) are monitored with other cards. Dry contacts cannot be monitored with the 69430A. The card may be ordered with any of eight different options (different voltages, ground-true, positive-true, etc.).

4-2.6 Interrupt Cards

These cards provide for system interrupt when certain events in the control or instrumentation process occur, or when certain process control words do not match those programmed by the controller. The cards include an event sense card, and a process interrupt card.

69434A Event Sense Card. This card interrupts the controller when the 12-bit digital external word being monitored is unequal to the 12-bit reference stored on the card by the controller. Jumpers on the card can be positioned to generate the interrupt when the external word is unequal to, equal to, greater than, or less than the 12-bit reference word. This flexibility allows the multiprogrammer to act as an alarm sensor, freeing the controller to perform other tasks during nonalarm conditions. Signal conditioning circuits for each input line discriminate between true contact changes and noise or contact "bounce."

Filters on each input line make the card ideal for use in relay contact monitoring applications. The card has storage for 12 external lines. The interrupting bit (or bits) are identified. This card is for word-oriented contact closure events, while the 69436A process interrupt card is for bit-oriented TTL events.

69436A Process Interrupt Card. This card interrupts the controller when any one or more of 12 lines being monitored change state. The card has storage for 12 external lines. Up to 24 lines can be monitored by one card if identification of the interrupting line is not needed. The card stores data bits that last for 100 ns or more. The interrupting bit (or bits) are identified. The cards can be programmed to store events that occur while the interrupt system is off.

4-2.7 Breadboard Cards

Each breadboard card has space on it for mounting custom user-designed circuitry. The various power supplies of the multiprogrammer may be tapped through the breadboard cards to power external circuitry. The major differences between the three breadboard models are as follows:

The 69480A has input buffer gates for driving the multiprogrammer with input data.

The 69380A has output storage buffers for using multiprogrammer output data to drive external or custom circuits.

The 69280A has no circuits at all, only provisions for mounting and connecting circuit parts.

4-3 MULTIPROGRAMMER CAPABILITIES

Figure 4-16 summarizes the multiprogrammer capabilities. The following paragraphs provide brief descriptions of these capabilities.

4-3.1 Stimulus

Programmable D-c Voltage and Current. The output voltage (up to 100 V) and current (up to 1000 A) of 40 different Hewlett-Packard power supplies can be programmed to provide bias in automatic test systems or control of electromechanical process equipment. The resistance output cards 69501A to 69513A are used.

Digital-to-Analog Conversion (DAC). 12-bit voltage and current DACs provide outputs for strip chart, X–Y, and analog tape recordings, as well as control of analog programmable instruments and process control devices with 0- to 5-V or 4- to 20-mA inputs. The voltage DAC 69321B, quad DAC 69322A, current DAC 69370A, and voltage regulator 69351B cards are used.

Time and Frequency Reference. One-shot timing pulses, programmable from 1 μs to 40 days, and crystal-controlled pulse trains in fixed frequencies of 1, 10, 100, 1k, 10k, and 100 kHz serve as time-base references for control measurement, and data acquisition equipment. The timer 69600B and frequency reference 69601B cards are used.

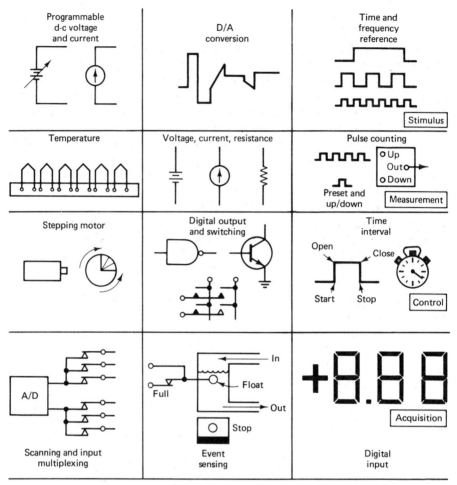

FIGURE 4-16 Summary of multiprogrammer capabilities.

4-3.2 Measurement

Temperature Measurement. The low-level A/D and scanner card 69423A is used primarily for temperature measurement. Up to six thermocouples can be connected to one card. The reference junction temperature is read from a seventh channel on the card.

Voltage, Current, and Resistance Measurements. The 69422A high-speed A/D card measures voltages in the presence of 100 V of common mode noise. Connecting a resistor across the input permits current measurement for 4- to 20-mA current loops used in many control applications. For resistance measurements, the voltage and current (69370A) A/D cards are combined.

Pulse Counting Preset and Up/Down. The 69435A pulse counter may be preset to any value within a count range of 0 to 4095. The program can examine the counter without disturbing the counting process (read-on-the-fly).

4-3.3 *Control*

Stepping Motor Control. One computer word applied to the 69335A stepping motor control card produces from 1 to 2047 square-wave pulses at either of two outputs (CW or CCW) to control motor translators. These output pulses can also be used for pulse-train update of supervisory control stations.

Digital Output and Switching. Twelve bits of data in TTL, open collector, or SPST relay-contact form provide digital control of instruments, indicators, and solid-state a-c relays. The TTL 69331A, open-collector 69332A, mercury-wetted relay 69330A, and relay output/readback 69433A cards are used.

Time-Interval Measurement. Elapsed time between two control events can be measured in the range of $10\,\mu s$ to 1 h by counting a known frequency over the unknown interval. The program divides the accumulated count by the known frequency to determine the interval. The 69435A pulse counter and 69601B frequency reference cards are used.

4-3.4 *Data Acquisition*

Scanning and Input Multiplexing. Simple single-ended switches or multiwire scanner matrices are formed by interconnecting relays on the 69433A relay output/readback card. Such scanners act as input multiplexers (MUX) for A/D, pulse counter, and digital input cards.

Event Sensing. It is often necessary for a control and instrumentation system to respond quickly to alarm conditions, operator intervention, or other requests for immediate service. This service request is made via a program interrupt generated by either the 69434A event sense card or the 69436A process interrupt card.

Digital Input. The 69431A digital input and 69430A isolated digital input cards accept 12 bits of data from digital measuring instruments, pushbuttons, switches, relays, and other digital devices in the form of logic levels or contact closures. Digital data sources with more than 12 bits of data use several digital input cards.

4-4   MULTIPROGRAMMER APPLICATIONS

The following paragraphs summarize a few typical applications for the multi-programmer.

4-4.1   *Production Testing*

IC Testing.   Figure 4–17 shows the basic relationships for functional test of ICs. As shown, functional testing of digital ICs involves the use of 69331A digital output cards to establish predetermined logic states at the inputs to the IC, and 69431A digital input cards to read the IC output back to the controller for comparison with expected results. Analog ICs are stimulated with pro-grammed voltage levels from the 69321B D/A voltage converter or 69370A D/A current converter. The analog IC outputs are measured with the 69422A high-speed A/D card. These tests are often performed on semiconductor

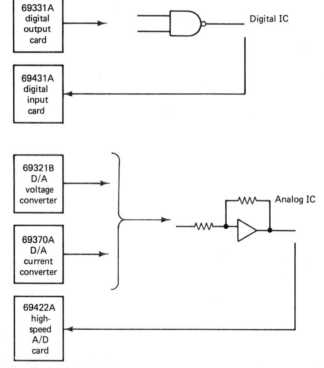

FIGURE 4-17   Multiprogrammer cards used for functional test of digital and analog ICs.

wafers as part of the IC manufacturing process, and repeated on the packaged IC for final inspection.

Electronic Subassembly Testing. Figure 4–18 shows the basic relationships for test of electronic subassemblies. The digital and analog inputs and outputs of the multiprogrammer are connected through fixtures to printed circuit modules, cables, and other assemblies such as D/A and A/D converters, filters, and oscillators for incoming inspection, production, calibration, and troubleshooting. During the test, the 69501A resistance output cards can control the outputs of d-c power supplies that bias the subassembly. Adjustment of critical circuits is performed by the 69335A stepping motor control card that operates a motor, translator, and flexible shaft as an automatic screwdriver. Multiconductor cables are tested for continuity with 69331A digital output and 69431A digital input cards.

Electromechanical Component Testing. Figure 4–19 shows the basic relationships for test of electromechanical components. A wide variety of tests on relays and solenoids are performed by the multiprogrammer, including operational tests in which the 69332A open-collector card applies power to the coil, and the 69431 digital input cards check for proper contact action. Hysteresis in the relay is often measured by generating a staircase function from a programmable power supply under the control of a 69501A resistance output

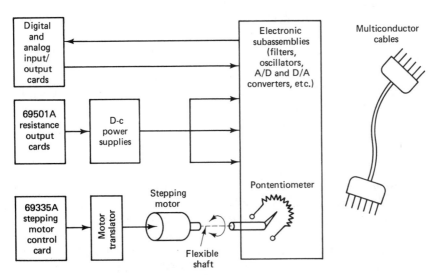

FIGURE 4-18 Multiprogrammer cards used for functional test of electronic subassemblies.

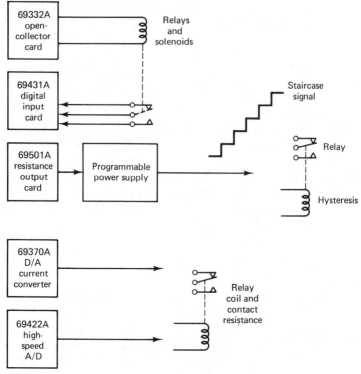

FIGURE 4-19   Multiprogrammer cards used for functional test of electromechanical components.

card. Time delays are measured with a 69435A counter card and 69601B frequency reference card. Contact and coil resistance at various current levels are measured using a 69370A D/A current converter or constant-current d-c power supply and the 69422A high-speed D/A card. Production tests of other electromechanical devices such as control valves, flowmeters, tachometers, gauges, switches, and detectors can also be performed using various configurations of the multiprogrammer.

Instrument Quality Control Testing.   Figure 4–20 shows the basic relationships for test of instrument quality control. Complete instruments such as modular power supplies are checked for conformance with line and load regulation, accuracy, transient response, and other specifications by using the multiprogrammer to control programmable loads through the 69321B D/A voltage converter cards, to set the sampling time of a DVM with a 69600B programmable timer card, and to control an a-c line regulator with 69330A relay output cards. Digital panel meters, set-point controllers, and other instruments with

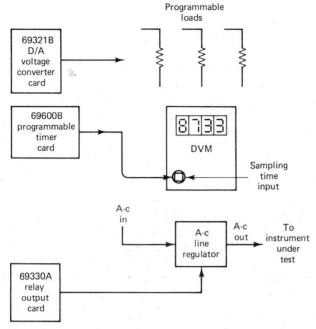

FIGURE 4-20 Multiprogrammer cards used for quality control tests of instruments.

digital or analog inputs or outputs are tested for accuracy, linearity, and operation under stress conditions using the multiprogrammer.

4-4.2 Research and Development: Environmental Testing

Figure 4-21 shows the basic relationships for environmental testing. Multiprogrammer I/O cards are not only capable of operating analog and digital instruments under environmental test, and measuring their performance, but are also well suited to control of environmental chamber parameters such as temperature, pressure, and humidity during the test cycle. In other types of environmental testing, such as operation of shake tables for small structures, and control of hydraulic rams for large structures and vehicles, 69321B D/A voltage converters can be programmed to synthesize the waveforms that simulate actual transportation and shock conditions. Designers can alter parameters during the lab test to analyze the effect of severe stresses and abusive treatment. Temperature of the test chamber and various parts of the unit can be measured with the 69423A low-level A/D scanner. Margin testing, life testing, and component evaluation can be done in the same way as environmental testing.

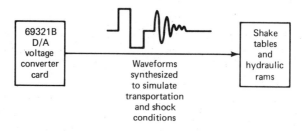

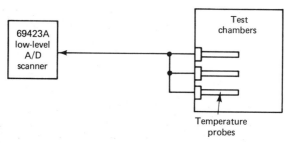

FIGURE 4-21   Multiprogrammer cards used for environmental testing.

4-4.3   Monitoring and Control

Power Management.   Figure 4–22 shows the basic realtionships for power management and control. Power companies calculate demand charges on the basis of peak power consumed. Connection of the 69435A counter card to the contact outputs of the wattmeter, and connection of the 69434A event sense card to the time interval contact at the wattmeter provide the information needed to sense an impending abnormal peak interval and temporarily shut down sheddable loads such as heating and ventilating equipment. Temperature is measured with the 69423A low-level A/D and scanner. 69331A digital output cards are used to operate solid-state a-c switches or electromechanical interposing control circuits for sheddable loads. When the demand charge portion of the total energy bill is not large enough to justify investment in a demand-limiting system, the multiprogrammer can be used in a system that automatically turns off loads when they are not needed.

Process Automation.   Multiprogrammer capabilities are used to interface with conventional process controllers (solenoid-operated valves, relays, electronic control devices, etc.) by using the 0- to 20-mA output of the 69370A D/A current converter card, or pulses from the 69335A stepping motor control card to adjust the set point in supervisory control systems. Multiprogrammers

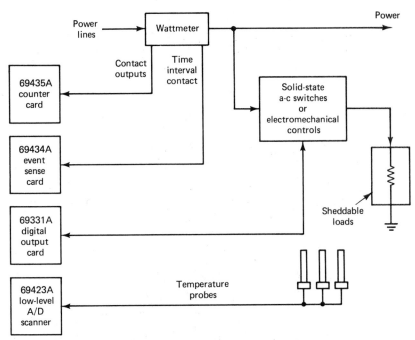

FIGURE 4-22 Multiprogrammer cards used for power management.

are also used in direct digital control systems where conventional analog control loops are replaced by multiprogrammer analog and digital I/O cards operating with a software algorithm for proportional, rate, and reset control. The flexibility and expandability of the multiprogrammer is particularly useful for pilot plant automation and process experiments that may require many changes in configuration during installation and development of the final system.

Data Acquisition and Signal Distribution. Figure 4–23 shows the basic relationships in data acquisition and signal distribution systems. Data acquisition systems use a 69433A relay output card as a scanner for routing analog signals to the 69422A high-speed A/D card for measurement. Temperature can be measured with the 69423A low-level A/D and scanner. Digital input cards monitor d-c logic levels directly, or are connected to optically isolated signal conditioners for monitoring 115– and 230–V a-c signals. Control signals up to 100 V are distributed directly to the process with 69433A or 69330A relay output cards, while 69331A digital output cards control solid-state relays for controlling voltages above 100 V. The multiprogrammer mainframes can be separated by up to 100 ft., so that proper location of mainframes used for scanning and distribution can significantly reduce cabling costs to sensors and indicators.

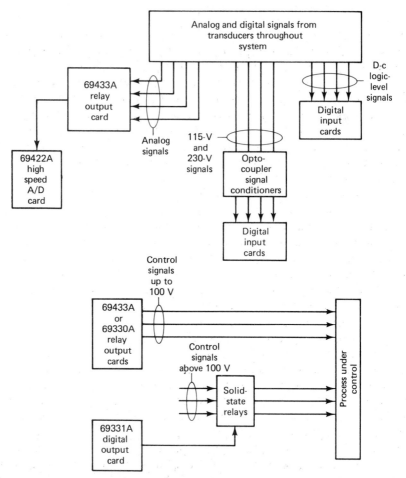

FIGURE 4-23 Multiprogrammer cards used in data acquisition and signal distribution systems.

4-5 MULTIPROGRAMMER OPERATING FEATURES

The following paragraphs summarize some basic operating features of the multiprogrammer. Sections 4–6 and 4–7 describe the multiprogrammer operating principles in greater detail.

4-5.1 Input/Output Expansion

The multiprogrammer expands a single 16-bit input, 16-bit output register of a controller (computer or calculator) to control up to 240 12-bit input or output channels. As shown in Fig. 4–24, four types of 16-bit words are exchanged between the controller and the multiprogrammer to achieve this expansion.

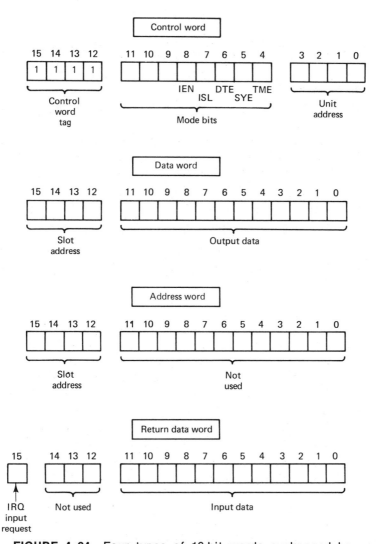

FIGURE 4-24 Four types of 16-bit words exchanged between the controller and multiprogrammer.

Control Word. A control word is sent from the controller to the multiprogrammer to select one of several output or input modes of operation, and to specify which mainframe (in a chain of one mainframe and up to 15 extenders) is to respond to subsequent words from the controller. The four most significant bits in a control word are always a logic 1. The multiprogrammer stores the unit address portion of a control word that specifies one of the 16 mainframe units, and also stores the mode information contained in bits 4 to 8 of the control word. The following are brief descriptions of each bit in the control word illustrated in Fig. 4-24.

Bits 0, 1, 2, 3: Unit Address: These bits select which unit (mainframe or extender) in a chain of up to 16 receives the data words that follow.

Bit 4: Timing Mode Enable (TME):   When programmed to a logic 0, data bits are transferred to the multiprogrammer at the maximum possible rate. When bit 4 is programmed to a logic 1, the controller waits until the multiprogrammer cards have finished their operation before proceeding to program the next data transfer.

Bit 5: System Enable (SYE):   Programming bit 5 (SYE) to logic 1 enables the outputs of most models of output cards to assume their programmed values. Setting SYE to zero disables the outputs.

Bit 6: Data Transfer Enable (DTE):   By programming bit 6 (DTE) to a logic 1, any preprogrammed combination of output cards (such as those needed to drive an X-Y display) simultaneously update their output.

Bit 7: Input Select (ISL):   Programming bit 7 (ISL) to a logic 1 allows subsequently addressed input cards to send 12 bits of input data to the controller. The ISL bit is programmed to a logic 0 when output cards are to be addressed.

Bit 8: Interrupt Enable (IEN):   When bit 8 (IEN) is set to a logic 1, cards that have interrupt capability and have been armed to generate interrupts are allowed to send interrupts to the controller.

Bits 12, 13, 14, 15:   These bits are all at a logic 1 to distinguish control words from the other types of words.

Data Word.   A data word is sent from the controller to an output card in the particular mainframe unit selected by a previous control word. The four most significant bits of the data word represent the slot address of the output that stores the other 12 bits of the data word. The slot address of an output card is determined by its physical location in one of the 15 input/output slots in each mainframe.

The data portion of the data word is stored on the output card to establish the desired magnitude of digital or analog output in the form of contact closures, bit patterns, pulses, resistance, voltage, or current (to operate solenoid valves, actuators, motors, etc.).

Address Word.   An address word selects a slot that holds an input card in the mainframe unit specified by the previous control word. Only the four most significant bits of an address word are used to specify the physical slot location of the input card. The 12 least significant bits are ignored by the input card in the input mode.

Return Data Word.   When an input card is addressed from the controller output register with an address word, the input card sends data back to the input register of the controller with a return data word. The 12 least significant bits of this word contain the input data. If the input card is the one that had generated an interrupt to the controller (via the multiprogrammer flag line), the most significant bit of the return data word (bit 15, IRQ) will be a logic 1.

To summarize input/output expansion, the multiprogrammer accepts control words to select mainframes and modes of operation, data words to select and control output cards and address words to select input cards that send data back to the controller with return data words.

4-5.2   Noise Immunity

Systems using the multiprogrammer may often be located in electrically noisy environments, such as manufacturing plants. The multiprogrammer deals with this situation in two ways. First, the maximum data transmission rate (50 μs per transmission) is fast enough to allow efficient operation with most controllers and output devices, but yet is not so fast that extreme noise sensitivity is a problem. Second, the particular method of data transfer used (gate/flag) greatly reduces noise sensitivity.

A typical data transmission sequence using the gate/flag method is as follows. First, the data lines are set in the controller to represent the data word being transmitted (these lines are set in the d-c sense and do not carry pulses). Second, the gate (encode) line is set at the controller to indicate the presence of valid data and to request that the data bits be stored. The multiprogrammer then waits about 5 μs to ensure that all data lines have settled firmly into their assigned states. Next, the data lines are sampled within the multiprogrammer and the bits are stored. Since all information is being sent as d-c level changes through bandlimited input circuits, the system is relatively insensitive to externally introduced noise pulses.

4-5.3   Internal Storage

As a means of saving programming time, the multiprogrammer system has a 12-bit storage register on each output card. This register maintains the last data word transmitted, allowing the program writer to forget about an output channel once it is set. Data bits are needed from the controller only when one of the output cards is to be set to a new value. Many of the digital input cards also have internal storage. Some input cards (such as the isolated digital input card) have no storage so that "live" or real-time inputs can be continuously monitored by the controller.

4-5.4   Dual-Rank Storage

A common problem in high-speed systems is the difficulty of simultaneously updating output channels. The voltage and current D/A cards provide dual-rank storage (shown in Fig. 4-25) to handle this problem. With these cards, a

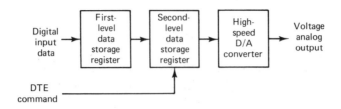

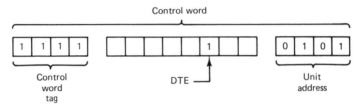

FIGURE 4-25   Dual-rank storage.

previously set output value can be maintained on the output by means of one data register, while new data bytes are stored on another register. Transfer of the stored data to the output is done by making use of the control word. The seventh least significant bit in the word (bit 6) is assigned the name "data transfer enable" or DTE. When this bit is set to 1, a signal is sent through the system which causes all cards having dual-rank storage to transfer the new data into the second storage register, thus simultaneously changing the output of all such cards to the previously stored new values.

4-5.5   *System Protection*

A common characteristic of instruments for generating stimuli and control is that of a high potential for causing damage. Consider a power supply programmed to provide 5 V for typical microcircuits. If the power supply gets set to 15 V (for whatever reason) during system turn-on, the higher voltage will cause mass destruction. The multiprogrammer system contains a controlled system turn-on function to handle this problem.

Each output card is provided with a protection circuit that keeps the card output in a safe state until a special command is transmitted by the controlling computer, regardless of the data stored on the card. For example, resistance cards (used to program power supplies) are provided with a normally closed pair of relay contacts connected directly across the output terminals. When the relay is not energized, the output of the card (and thus the power supply output) is maintained safely at zero. A single data line running throughout the system controls this relay and similar protective devices on other output cards. The line is automatically set to the safe (0) state at initial system turn-on.

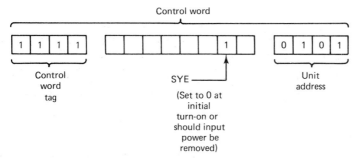

FIGURE 4-26 System protection scheme for all output cards.

The computer controls the relay line by again making use of the control word. As shown in Fig. 4–26, the sixth least significant bit (bit 5) in the control word is assigned the name ''system enable'' or SYE. When this bit is set to 1, all output cards in the system are enabled. Thus, it is possible to preset the data stored on each of the cards to the desired initial value and then activate the entire system by transmitting a single control word. The system enable function also provides protection against various other system failures. In addition to being under computer control, the SYE bit is automatically set to the safe (0) state if input power is removed from the system, if the data input cable is unplugged, or if the internal mainframe power supply shorts.

4-5.6 Automatic Timing

In a typical test system, the test program follows the sequence of first setting test conditions (supply voltages, load conditions, etc.), and then causing appropriate measurements to be made. This sequence ordinarily requires the programmer to know how much time is required to set up the outputs so as to prevent any measurements from being made before the system is ready. However, in the multiprogrammer system, the timing is a function of the hardware and not a concern of the programmer.

Automatic timing is done as follows. The resistance output, stepping motor, and D/A cards are provided with adjustable timing circuits that are triggered whenever the card outputs are programmed. The timing period can be set to match the response time of almost any device that might be connected to the multiprogrammer. The relay and digital output cards are provided with gate outputs (a contact pair and a logic-level line, respectively) for triggering an external timing circuit. After one or more output cards have been programmed with data words, the controller sends a control word with bit 4, TME (timing mode enable) turned on (as shown in Fig. 4–27). The flag line from the multiprogrammer to the controller now indicates when the programmed outputs have timed out.

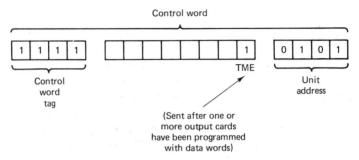

FIGURE 4-27 Automatic timing scheme control.

4-5.7 *Isolation of Input/Output Signals*

Figure 4–28 shows two basic techniques for isolation of input and output signals for the multiprogrammer. In many cases, it is desirable to provide analog output signals which do not share a common ground with the data input. This is particularly true when power supplies are controlled by a D/A card. Depending upon which of the power supply output terminals is grounded, it is possible to end up with the common side of the analog output connected to the high-voltage output of the power supply. The multiprogrammer eliminates this

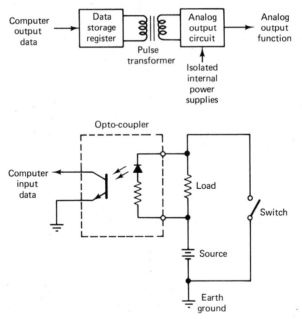

FIGURE 4-28 Two basic techniques for isolation of multiprogrammer input and output signals.

problem by providing complete isolation between analog outputs and data inputs. This isolation is achieved through the use of relays or pulse transformers, depending on the particular card. Also, *four isolated power supplies* are provided in each mainframe to independently power the output circuitry of up to four groups of analog output or input cards with a separate ground for each group if desired. In the case where digital inputs must be applied to the multiprogrammer, and these inputs must be isolated, opto-couplers are used, as shown in Fig. 4–28. This arrangement permits monitoring of active circuits at potentials that are referenced above or below computer ground.

4-5.8 Polling and Interrupting

Many types of digital inputs are initiated by the controller. To read the status of switches in a network under test, for example, the controller issues a control word with ISL, input select bit 7 (Sec. 4–5.1) on, and then sends an address word to a digital input card. The multiprogrammer then sends the data to the computer using a return data word. This is called *polling.*

Polling is not practical for certain types of alarm inputs or momentary transient inputs. When rapid system response to a digital input is necessary, continuous rapid polling may consume large amounts of controller time, and is an unnecessary burden for the software author. To solve these problems, the multiprogrammer uses cards (such as the event sense card) to generate a controller interrupt via the multiprogrammer flag when digital inputs being monitored change state. A control word with IEN (interrupt enable) and TME (timing mode enable) (Sec. 4–5.1) both turned on is an important part of the procedure that enables the event sense card to interrupt. Only when an interrupt is detected is the controller required to poll the cards, resulting in considerable savings of both controller time and software writing effort.

4-5.9 Troubleshooting

A primary aid in troubleshooting is the *manual switch register* on the front panel of the multiprogrammer (Fig. 4–1). These switches permit entering data by hand. This allows the controller, program, and interface (between the controller and multiprogrammer) to be eliminated as possible trouble sources. In the simplest of terms, if the multiprogrammer and cards perform their function when a control is set in manually with the switches, but fail to perform with the controller connected, there is a problem with the controller or its program, or possibly a problem in the interface.

In addition to data entry, the front-panel switches allow manual duplication of all normally computer controlled functions. As a result, this feature is useful not only in troubleshooting but also in initial checkout of a system.

4-6 MULTIPROGRAMMER BASIC PRINCIPLES OF OPERATION

This section describes the basic principles of operation for the multiprogrammer. Although these descriptions do not provide a complete hardware analysis showing every signal and circuit, they are quite comprehensive and provide the reader with a good understanding of the multiprogrammer system capabilities. A full circuit-by-circuit study of the multiprogrammer is found in the manufacturer's operating and service manual.

4-6.1 Introduction

In the most general sense, the multiprogrammer functions as a multichannel bidirectional interface between a controller and the real-world environment to which command signals are sent, and from which status signals are received. For the purposes of this discussion, the controller is the calculator (Fig. 4–3) equipped with an HP–IB interface card. As discussed in Sec. 4–1, the calculator can be used with a GPIO interface which provides a 16-bit word directly to the multiprogrammer. The HP–IB interface provides an 8-bit ASCII-coded output which must be converted to the 16-bit format required by the multiprogrammer. When operating on the HP–IB, a 59500A interface unit must be used to convert the ASCII code to the multiprogrammer format. Operation of the 59500A interface is described in Sec. 4–7.

Communications between the multiprogrammer and the external environment is realized via plug-in I/O cards. Data transfers between the multiprogrammer mainframe and I/O cards are digital (12 data bits). Transfer between the cards and external devices can be either digital (again, 12 data bits) or analog (voltages, currents, etc.). Cards with analog I/O capability have on-card converters that permit them to transmit data to and from the mainframe in digital form.

4-6.2 Data Transfers

Data transfers between the multiprogrammer and the controller (calculator) take the form of a 16-bit output word (from the controller to the multiprogrammer) and a 13-bit (12 data bits plus one status bit) return data word (from the multiprogrammer to the controller). All data transfers are 12-bit (from the standpoint of the I/O card–mainframe interface). However, the controller is required to output a 16-bit word in order to bring about the 12-bit communication. This reduction in word length provides the mechanism by which the multiprogrammer functions as a multiplexer, effectively expanding a single duplex I/O channel into many bidirectional I/O channels. The cards themselves generally act in one capacity (input or output) to the exclusion of the other, but either card type may be used in any I/O channel.

4-6.3 Data Transfer Synchronization

Two additional signal lines $\overline{GTE}$ and $\overline{FLA}$ facilitate a "handshake," permitting a synchronization of data transfers. The gate signal $\overline{GTE}$ is sent by the controller to indicate that the controller has valid data for the multiprogrammer to accept, while the flag signal $\overline{FLA}$ permits the multiprogrammer to indicate that (1) the multiprogrammer is processing data, and (2) has completed processing.

Figure 4-29 shows the sequence of a handshake cycle. A data transfer cycle is not finished unless the handshake is also completed, in which case the controller may begin a new transaction. In some operating modes, completion of the handshake may take considerable time, particularly when compared to the period required by the controller to execute a program step. If this situation is known to exist, the controller may be directed to proceed with other portions of the program (data reduction, communication with other peripherals, etc.), returning periodically to test the progress of the handshake. Once a transfer cycle is begun by means of the gate signal, failure of the system to provide both edges of the flag signal creates a "hang-up" situation in which the control is unable to initiate new communications with the multiprogrammer unless the handshake is terminated by special programming commands.

Handshake capability may be extended through the multiprogrammer mainframe to the I/O card in certain modes of operation, thereby altering the period (but not the sequence) of the handshake to suit the timing requirements of the particular card. In addition, some cards permit the handshake to be ex-

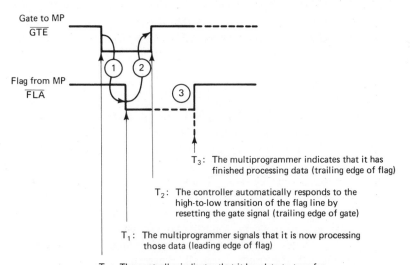

T_3: The multiprogrammer indicates that it has finished processing data (trailing edge of flag)

T_2: The controller automatically responds to the high-to-low transition of the flag line by resetting the gate signal (trailing edge of gate)

T_1: The multiprogrammer signals that it is now processing those data (leading edge of flag)

T_0: The controller indicates that it has data to transfer (leading edge of gate)

FIGURE 4-29 Sequence of handshake cycle between controller and multiprogrammer.

tended to the external device to ensure that the data transfers are accurate and complete. In either case, the mainframe no longer automatically returns the flag signal, but instead gives up control to the card and/or the external device.

Figure 4–30 shows an example of an extended handshake. The following is a brief description of the sequence. The controller (calculator) uses its gate to tell the multiprogrammer to take data (take it). The multiprogrammer uses a gate on one of its plug-in cards to tell an external instrument such as a printer or digitally controlled valve (which controls the flow of oil in our mythical petroleum refinery) to take the data (do it). When the external device is done, it uses the flag on the plug-in card to tell the multiprogrammer that the device is finished (I did it), and the multiprogrammer tells the calculator the operation is complete (we did it).

FIGURE 4-30 Extended handshake sequence between calculator and multiprogrammer.

4-6.4 Extender Units

Any number (none at all up to 15 total) of 6941B extender units may be included in a system as required. It is not possible, however, to use a 6941B without a 6940B in the system. Also, it is necessary that the 6940B be the first unit in the chain. A cabling diagram showing how a 6940B and one or more 6941B units are chained together in a system is illustrated in Fig. 4–31.

4-6.5 Slot and Unit Addresses

Each card slot automatically assumes a two-part address (whether or not 6941B extender units are used). This address uniquely specifies its location within the system. A card slot within either type of mainframe has a fixed address (slot 00 through slot 14) and may be accessed by means of a 4-bit binary code $\overline{B12}$ through $\overline{B15}$ as shown in Fig. 4–32. The sixteenth address (control word) accesses circuitry which is present in the 6940B mainframe only, and permits the controller to specify a unit select address, thereby providing the second part of the total address needed to access a particular I/O channel.

Like the slot address, the unit select address is specified by a 4-bit binary code B00 through B03, but in this case, all 16 possible combinations are interpreted as unit addresses. The address of a particular unit is automatically established by its position in the chain; the first 6941B becomes unit 01, the sec-

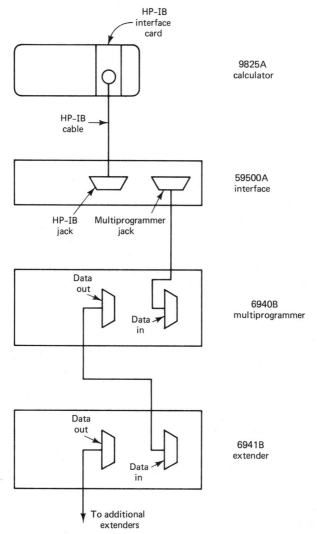

FIGURE 4-31 Cabling diagram showing how a 6940B and one or more 6941B units are chained together in a system.

ond becomes unit 02, and so on. The 6940B mainframe is always unit 00 and is specified when B00 through B03 are all at a logic 0.

Once a data transfer cycle with a control word is completed, both the mode of operation and the unit select address are stored by the 6940B mainframe, and subsequent operations are directed toward the particular unit addressed. Slot addresses, designated in succeeding words output by the controller, cannot access card slots except in the previously selected unit unless a

Address	B̄15	B̄14	B̄13	B̄12
Slot 00	0	0	0	0
01	0	0	0	1
02	0	0	1	0
03	0	0	1	1
04	0	1	0	0
05	0	1	0	1
06	0	1	1	0
07	0	1	1	1
08	1	0	0	0
09	1	0	0	1
10	1	0	1	0
11	1	0	1	1
12	1	1	0	0
13	1	1	0	1
14	1	1	1	0
Control word	1	1	1	1

FIGURE 4-32 Slot address codes.

new control word is sent specifying a different unit address. Similarly, if it is desired that the operating mode be changed but not the unit address, the new control word must respecify the particular unit address.

4-6.6 Block Diagram Description

At this point it is convenient to introduce both the functional block diagram and the concept of word format. Figure 4–33 shows the 6940B mainframe logic, the controller, a typical I/O card, and the significant connections between these segments of the total system. Although several signal lines between the mainframe and the I/O card are omitted in order to simplify the block diagram, the connections remain faithful to the functional mechanisms of data transfer, and it may be assumed that the card could be located in any I/O channel of the system.

The signal lines shown in Fig. 4–33 between the multiprogrammer and the controller correspond exactly to the hardware with the single exception that the SYE (system enable) jumper connection is not included. This feature serves only to provide an interlock on the SYE control line such that a cable must be connected between the multiprogrammer and the controller before SYE can be sent to the cards. Certain cards are deactivated to a "safe" state in the absence of the SYE signal.

Figure 4–24 shows the format, or structure, or a data word (as well as control, address, and return data words). The data word is the most general of the three formats used for the 16-bit output word sent from the controller to the multiprogrammer (data, control, and address). Bits $\overline{B12}$ through $\overline{B15}$ of the data word specify the card slot address, while the remaining 12 bits are used to transfer data. Note that the hardware organization as shown in the block diagram of Fig. 4–33 complements the format of the data word (the address and data portions of the word are processed separately by the mainframe logic).

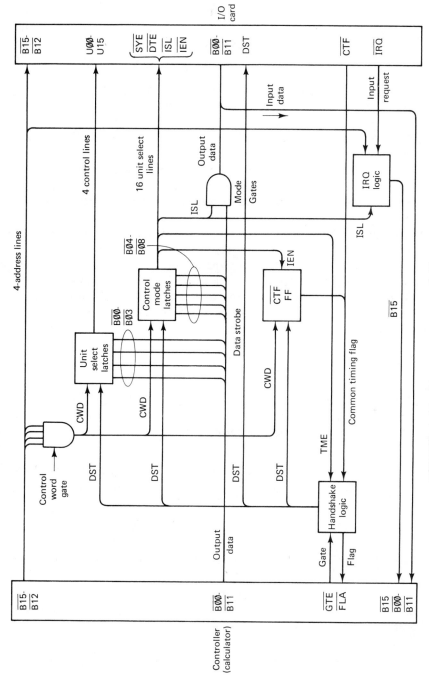

FIGURE 4-33 Multiprogrammer block diagram.

As shown in Fig. 4–33, the data signal lines are distributed to the unit select latches BØØ through BØ3, the control mode latches BØ4 through BØ8, and the mode gates (all 12 bits) which, depending on the mode of operation, either terminate the signals or transmit them in parallel to every card slot in the system.

Data signals sent to the unit select and control mode latches are ignored except when a control word is programmed and detected by a control word gate. As shown in Fig. 4–24, a control word is specified by the presence of logic 1 on all four address lines, and is considered as a special case of data word.

The address signal lines are sent to the control word gate (Fig. 4–33) and to each of the I/O card slots where a combination of hardwired logic in the mainframe and address decode gates (similar to the control word gate) on the cards permit the addressed card, and only the addressed card, to be partially enabled. A card is completely enabled when (1) the card slot address sent by the controller matches the address of the slot in which the card is located, (2) the unit address is similarly correct, and (3) the appropriate control signals are received by the card. One additional signal (data strobe or DST) is required whenever data bits are transferred from the controller to the multiprogrammer. Depending on card model and the system operating mode, the start of the data strobe initiates one of several possible responses to data present on lines BØØ through B11.

4-6.7 Basic Data Transfer Cycle

Data strobe is a function of the gate signal sent by the controller and is developed by the handshake logic. Referring back to Fig. 4–29, the most basic form of the data transfer cycle takes place as follows:

1. The controller transfers data to its output register, placing that data on the 16 lines (4 address and 12 data) that connect to the multiprogrammer input circuits. To indicate that it wishes to initiate a data transfer, the controller drives the gate $\overline{GTE}$ line low.

2. About 2 μ after the leading edge of GTE, handshake logic generates the data strobe. At some point in time after the beginning of DST, the handshake logic returns the leading edge of flag $\overline{FLA}$, indicating that processing has begun.

3. The controller responds to the leading edge of flag by resetting the gate line to the high state.

4. The handshake logic detects the resetting of the gate signal and terminates DST. When the multiprogrammer has finished processing, the handshake logic returns the trailing edge of flag, thereby concluding the transfer cycle.

The sequence of events just outlined is typical of all data transfers in the output and control modes. Information transferred in this manner (either to a card or to the unit select and control mode latches) remains stored until the particular address is again specified and a transfer cycle is initiated by the controller. Input operations (transfer of data from multiprogrammer to the controller) do not necessarily require use of the gate signal and subsequent handshake cycle. Note also that the sequence outlined above is general enough to describe either the *automatic handshake* or the *extended handshake*. Detailed descriptions of both handshake sequences are found in the following section.

4-6.8 Control Mode Bits

Control signals are distributed throughout the entire system and are totally independent of the slot and unit select address functions discussed in Sec. 4-6.5. The following paragraphs summarize the effects of control mode bits on the multiprogrammer. Figure 4-33 shows distribution of the bits.

System Enable (SYE). The absence of this signal automatically deactivates certain cards to a "safe" state. The SYE signal affects operation of output cards only. With the exception of a few cards (unaffected by SYE), the SYE signal provides a systemwide control of output cards which acts independently of the address function. In effect, the SYE signal influences operation of cards whether or not they are addressed.

When SYE is on, output cards are enabled to transmit any data currently latched in local (on-card) storage registers. If SYE is off, data connections between output cards and the external environment are open-circuited or otherwise disabled. The SYE circuitry on individual cards has no control over the address and storage functions, meaning that card outputs may be inhibited without affecting the controller's ability to address and load data into on-card registers. If SYE is programmed on after a number of cards have been loaded with data in this manner, the cards simultaneously output those data to external devices when the control word is gated.

Preset circuitry in the 6940B mainframe ensures that SYE is held off when the system is first powered up. Additional preset circuitry on the individual cards disables outputs (even if SYE is programmed on) until the card is addressed and strobed for the first time. Also, as explained previously, the SYE signal is used to protect against possible damage in the event that a cable is accidentally disconnected. If the connection is broken in the middle of a chain of mainframes, all units downstream from the break are disabled. Cards within these units retain previously programmed data, and output those data once the connection is restored.

If a mainframe in the midst of a chain is powered down, the SYE signal is again disabled, inhibiting outputs from that unit and from any units downstream. Once power is restored, all outputs resume as previously programmed except in the unit that was turned off. Cards in that mainframe will be preset, requiring that they be individually addressed with data and strobed before the system is fully returned to the state that existed just prior to the power-off condition. In all cases, absence of the SYE signal serves to prevent uncontrolled output, thus reducing the possibility of stimulating external devices (solenoid valves, actuators, motors, etc.) with undesired contact closures, excessive voltages, and so on.

Data Transfer Enable ($\overline{\text{DTE}}$).   The $\overline{\text{DTE}}$ signal controls data transfer and timing signals (extended handshake) on certain output cards. $\overline{\text{DTE}}$ provides a mechanism for synchronizing outputs from several cards. The $\overline{\text{DTE}}$ signal influences operation of four card models, all of which function as output devices. Two of these, the voltage and current D/A cards, have *dual-rank storage registers,* as shown in Fig. 4–34. The first register accepts data from the mainframe when the card is addressed with the DST signal. The second register receives data from the first and outputs the data to the D/A converter, but does not accept these new data unless $\overline{\text{DTE}}$ is programmed on.

Since the converter is connected directly to the external device (if SYE is on), outputs from several D/A cards can be held constant while new data bits are loaded into first-rank storage on each of the cards. $\overline{\text{DTE}}$ can then be pro-

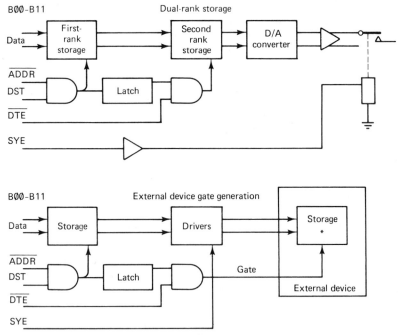

*The external device needs storage capability if the full dual-rank function of $\overline{\text{DTE}}$ is desired.

FIGURE 4-34   Data transfer enable ($\overline{\text{DTE}}$) circuits.

grammed on, simultaneously transferring data on each of the cards from first-to second-rank storage, thus changing the outputs of all such cards in unison. This feature can be defeated by programming $\overline{DTE}$ on prior to loading data into the first register. Data sent and gated under these circumstances immediately passes through first-rank storage to the second rank and then to the D/A converter.

The two other cards affected by $\overline{DTE}$ do not have dual-rank storage, but instead have a *gate/flag interface* with the external device, as shown in Fig. 4–34. These cards inhibit this gate signal unless $\overline{DTE}$ is on. The controller may address cards in sequence, and load data into on-card storage with the DST signal. If SYE is on, the data bits are transferred to the external device, but the gate signal to the external device is suppressed until $\overline{DTE}$ is programmed on and latched with DST, at which time all loaded cards simultaneously generate gate signals. If $\overline{DTE}$ is programmed on first, each card generates its gate signal when addressed and strobed. The gate signals may be used to enable storage circuits (if any) in the external device. In this case, the combination of the external storage circuits and the storage circuits on the cards provides a dual-rank storage system.

Input Select ($\overline{ISL}$). The $\overline{ISL}$ signal terminates output data in the mode gates, thus permitting input data to be returned to the controller from an addressed input card. $\overline{ISL}$ causes the most fundamental change in system operating mode. By terminating output data in the mode gates, the $\overline{ISL}$ signal effectively converts the mainframe from an output multiplexer to an input multiplexer. The address portion of the output word remains functional, and when combined with $\overline{ISL}$ on an input card, enables the addressed card to return data to the controller. The output word sent by the controller when the system is in the input mode is called an *address word* and has the format shown in Fig. 4–24.

Figure 4–24 also shows the format of the *return data word*. The 12 data bit lines $\overline{B00}$ through $\overline{B11}$ follow the state of the corresponding output data bits as long as $\overline{ISL}$ is off. When $\overline{ISL}$ is on, the bits are driven by the addressed card. Bits $\overline{B12}$ through $\overline{B14}$ are not used in the return data word, but $\overline{B15}$ is, and functions in a manner similar to the 12 data bits. Referring back to Fig. 4–33, the $\overline{IRQ}$ (input request) logic selects the source of the $\overline{B15}$ signal according to the state of $\overline{ISL}$. If $\overline{ISL}$ is off, $\overline{B15}$ of the output word is returned to the controller. If $\overline{ISL}$ is on, however, $\overline{B15}$ of the return data word no longer follows the state of the output bit, but instead reflects the state of the $\overline{IRQ}$ signal line.

The $\overline{IRQ}$ line is returned from every I/O slot in the system and may be driven by the currently addressed card, provided that that card is one of the models equipped with $\overline{IRQ}$ drive circuitry. The $\overline{IRQ}$ signal indicates whether or not the addressed card has completed a data transfer cycle with the external device, and is used as the basis for a status polling routine which is part of the interrupt input mode programming sequence (Sec. 4–6.11).

Timing Mode Enable (TME) and Interrupt Enable ($\overline{\text{IEN}}$). The TME signal modifies action of the handshake logic by suppressing the automatic flag and causing the $\overline{\text{FLA}}$ signal to follow the state of the $\overline{\text{CTF}}$ (common timing flag signal). The $\overline{\text{IEN}}$ signal is used in conjunction with TME to modify the action of the hanshake logic during input operations.

Up to this point, explanations of the handshake cycle have stressed the sequence of events without much reference to the factors controlling those events. An expanded discussion of these factors is necessary if operation of the TME and IEN control signals is to be understood. Figure 4–35 shows a portion of the functional block diagram given in Fig. 4–33. Only those elements affecting the handshake are shown, and have been slightly rearranged in order to clarify the following discussion.

Automatic Handshake: The TME signal determines whether the multiprogrammer operates in the automatic or extended handshake mode. When TME is off (automatic handshake), the handshake logic is the source of the flag signal returned to the controller. The DST signal, which is generated by the handshake logic in response to the controller gate $\overline{\text{GTE}}$, causes the handshake logic to return the leading edge of flag $\overline{\text{FLA}}$. When the controller resets $\overline{\text{GTE}}$, DST is terminated and the handshake logic returns the trailing edge of flag, completing the transfer cycle. In the automatic handshake mode of operation, *both edges* of $\overline{\text{FLA}}$ are an automatic response to the controller gate. The handshake logic has absolute control of the flag signal, and together with the controller form the complete circuit necessary to synchronize a data transfer.

Extended Handshake: When TME is on, the automatic handshake just described is suppressed, and the circuit elements shown to the right of the handshake logic in Fig. 4–35 assume control of the flag signal. The data strobe (DST) and the gate signal sent to the external device ($\overline{\text{GAT}}$) act as extensions of the

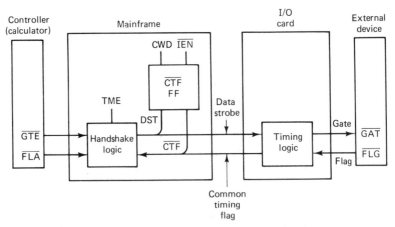

FIGURE 4-35   Extended handshake circuitry.

controller gate $\overline{\text{GTE}}$. In a corresponding manner, the flag returned from the external device ($\overline{\text{FLG}}$) and the common timing flag ($\overline{\text{CTF}}$) become the source of the flag returned to the controller $\overline{\text{FLA}}$. The six signals shown in Fig. 4–35 are used to implement the extended handshake. Since a number of card models do not have a gate/flag interface with the external device, the complete circuit is not always used. However, the $\overline{\text{FLA}}$ signal always follows the state of the common timing flag $\overline{\text{CTF}}$ when TME is on.

The $\overline{\text{CTF}}$ signal line is returned to the handshake logic from the $\overline{\text{CTF}}$ flip-flop and from all I/O slots in the system. The entire circuit is arranged in a wired-OR configuration such that any single source (a card or the $\overline{\text{CTF}}$ flip-flop) can drive the $\overline{\text{CTF}}$ line to a low state. It is not unusual for $\overline{\text{CTF}}$ to be driven by several sources at the same time, in which case $\overline{\text{CTF}}$ remains low as long as any one drive source is present. As long as $\overline{\text{CTF}}$ is low, $\overline{\text{FLA}}$ is also held low. The controller interprets the low state of the $\overline{\text{FLA}}$ signal as an indication that the multiprogrammer is processing data and therefore is "busy."

Except in the unique situation when the $\overline{\text{IEN}}$ control signal is used to arm input cards that have the W6 arming jumper option installed (arming operation is discussed in Sec. 4–6.11), no source can drive $\overline{\text{CTF}}$ unless the source has been addressed and gated with DST. In most cases, additional conditions (which vary from one card model to another) must be satisified before the source is fully activated. Since the $\overline{\text{FLA}}$ signal returned to the controller depends on the state of the $\overline{\text{CTF}}$ line when the multiprogrammer is in the extended handshake mode, care must be taken to ensure that one or more sources are or can be activated whenever the controller gates the system.

The $\overline{\text{CTF}}$ flip-flop is always activated when a control word (in which $\overline{\text{IEN}}$ is off) is programmed and gated. The only function of the $\overline{\text{CTF}}$ flip-flop is to guarantee that a flag is returned to the controller at the time a control word with TME on is gated and either of two situations exists:

1. No card has previously been activated to drive $\overline{\text{CTF}}$, or

2. All previously activated cards have completed their transfer cycles and have returned to a deactivated state.

When a control word with $\overline{\text{IEN}}$ on is gated, the action of the $\overline{\text{CTF}}$ flip-flop is suppressed. This control state is established as part of a specific sequence used during the interrupt input mode of operation and should not be programmed except as part of that sequence. The interrupt mode is described in Sec. 4–6.11.

4-6.9 Programming Sequences

Although the exact order in which control modes are established and card activated depends in part on the particular application, certain generalized programming sequences can be identified and explained. Figure 4–36 shows the

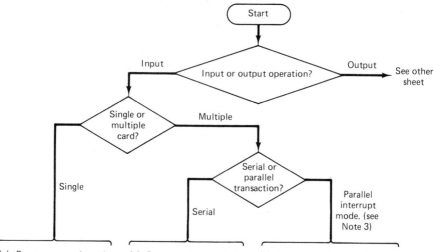

(a) Program control word
   with $\overline{ISL}$ and $\overline{TME}$ on.

(b) Send gate ($\overline{CTF}$ FF).

(c) Address card.

(d) Send gate (activated
   card).

(e) Wait for trailing edge
   of flag.

(f) Input data.

(a) Program control word
   with $\overline{ISL}$ and $\overline{TME}$ on.

(b) Send gate ($\overline{CTF}$ FF).

(c) Address card.

(d) Send gate (activated
   card).

(e) Wait for trailing edge
   of flag.

(f) Input data.

(g) Repeat steps (c)–(f)
   for other cards
   included in transaction.
   Return to step (a) if
   different unit address
   must be specified.

(a) Program control word
   with $\overline{ISL}$ and $\overline{TME}$ off.

(b) Send gate (auto flag).

(c) Address card.

(d) Send gate (activated card).

(e) Repeat (c) and (d) for other
   cards included in transaction.
   Return to step (a) if
   different unit address must
   be specified.

(f) Program control word with
   $\overline{IEN}$ and $\overline{TME}$ on.

(g) Send gate (any activated card).

(h) Wait for both edges of flag.

(i) Proceed to $\overline{IRQ}$ polling routine
   (see Note 4).

or

(a) Program control word
   with $\overline{IEN}$ and $\overline{TME}$ on.

(b) Send gate (any activated card).

(c) Wait for both edges of flag.

(d) Proceed to $\overline{IRQ}$ polling routine.

Notes:

1. It is assumed that SYE is on.

2. The source of the flag signal is given
   in brackets whenever a gating operation
   is indicated.

3. Only those input cards having interrupt
   capability can be used in this mode.

4. The W6 jumper must be installed on all
   cards used in the transaction.

FIGURE 4-36   Programming sequences in the timing mode

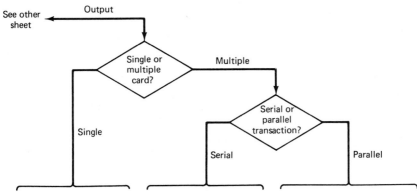

(a) Program control word with $\overline{DTE}$ and $\overline{TME}$ on.

(b) Send gate ($\overline{CTF}$ FF).

(c) Address card with data.

(d) Send gate (activated card).

(e) Wait for trailing edge of flag.

(a) Program control word with $\overline{DTE}$ and $\overline{TME}$ on.

(b) Send gate ($\overline{CTF}$ FF).

(c) Address card with data.

(d) Send gate (activated card).

(e) Wait for trailing edge of flag.

(f) Repeat steps (c)–(e) for other cards included in transaction. Return to step (a) if a different unit address must be specified.

(a) Program control word with $\overline{DTE}$ on and $\overline{TME}$ off.

(b) Send gate (auto flag).

(c) Address card with data.

(d) Send gate (auto flag).

(e) Repeat (c) and (d) for other cards included in transaction. Return to step (a) if a different unit address must be specified.

(f) Program control word with $\overline{TME}$ on.

(g) Send gate (all activated cards).

(h) Wait for trailing edge of flag.

or

(a) Program control word with $\overline{DTE}$ and $\overline{TME}$ off.

(b) Send gate (auto flag).

(c) Address card with data.

(d) Send gate (auto flag).

(e) Repeat (c) and (d) for other cards in transaction. Return to step (a) if a different unit address must be specified.

(f) Program control word with $\overline{DTE}$ and $\overline{TME}$ on.

(g) Send gate (all activated cards).

(h) Wait for trailing edge of flag.

FIGURE 4-36   (*Continued*)

sequences applicable to the basic classes of operation in the TME mode. These classes may be distinguished from one another by the answers to three questions:

1. Is the transaction an input or an output operation?
2. Is one card used in the transaction or are several cards used?
3. If several cards are used, do complete transactions occur in sequence (serially) or do they occur concurrently (in parallel)?

For the purposes of the following explanations, it is assumed that SYE has been programmed on previously and that no cards are activated when the programming sequence is started. Note that the source of the $\overline{\text{CTF}}$ signal used to control $\overline{\text{FLA}}$ is given in brackets whenever Fig. 4–36 indicates that a gate is sent by the controller. Timing diagrams showing the transitions of the $\overline{\text{GTE}}$ and $\overline{\text{FLA}}$ signals in both the automatic and the extended handshake modes are provided in Fig. 4–37. Arrows indicate that a given transition automatically brings about the transition immediately following.

Automatic handshake (TME off)

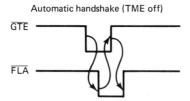

Extended handshake — output and input modes (TME on)

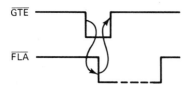

Extended handshake — interrupt mode (TME, IEN on)

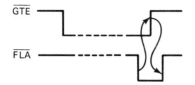

FIGURE 4-37 Handshake timing.

4-6.10   Output Operations

The following paragraphs describe typical output operations for single, serial, and parallel transactions, using the sequences shown in Fig. 4–36.

Single Transaction.   An output transaction with a single card is the least complicated data transfer operation. The output mode is first established by programming and gating a control word with $\overline{DTE}$ and TME on. $\overline{ISL}$ and $\overline{IEN}$ are off. $\overline{DTE}$ need not be on if the particular card is not controlled by $\overline{DTE}$, but no harm is done if $\overline{DTE}$ is on. It is generally good practice to program TME and $\overline{DTE}$ on together during output operations since many output cards cannot drive $\overline{CTF}$ unless $\overline{DTE}$ is on. The card is then addressed and gated, and immediately returns the leading edge of $\overline{CTF}$. Depending on the card model, the trailing edge of $\overline{CTF}$ is controlled by circuits on the card itself, or by the external device. In either case, the transaction is concluded when the trailing edge of $\overline{CTF}$ is detected by the handshake logic and returned to the controller as the trailing edge of $\overline{FLA}$.

Serial Transactions.   Serial transactions with output cards may be programmed by simply repeating the sequence just described for each card in turn. The serial method is disadvantageous when the number of cards is large and the periods of the successive handshake cycles are long. The controller must wait for each card to return the trailing edge of flag before it can proceed to the next card, with the result that the total operation consumes an unnecessarily large amount of time and makes inefficient use of the controller's processing capability. Consequently, the serial method should not be used unless a strict sequential operation is required by a particular application.

Parallel Transactions.   The two programming sequences for parallel output transactions shown in Fig. 4–36 solve the problem by *not* programming TME on *until all* the cards have been activated in the automatic handshake mode. This high-speed approach is possible since TME has no effect on the activation of cards and their subsequent control of $\overline{CTF}$, but only determines whether or not the $\overline{FLA}$ signal returned to the controller by the handshake logic will follow the state of the common timing flag. Once all cards have been activated, a control word with TME on is programmed and gated. The $\overline{CTF}$ flip-flop returns the leading edge of the flag when the control word is gated, but the wired-OR nature of the $\overline{CTF}$ circuitry suppresses the trailing edge until all the activated cards have timed out.

The two parallel output sequences differ from one another in the manner in which $\overline{DTE}$ is used. The first programming sequence is somewhat faster in execution because each card begins its transfer cycle as soon as it is addressed and gated. Cards with long transfer cycles can be activated early in the sequence, while cards with short cycles can be activated last, thus minimizing the time used for the complete transaction. The second sequence sacrifices speed in order to provide full parallel output capability. This method uses only those card models controlled by the $\overline{\text{DTE}}$ signal and is identical to the first except that neither TME nor $\overline{\text{DTE}}$ is programmed on until all cards have been addressed and gated. Since $\overline{\text{DTE}}$ must be on for these card models to be fully activated, they are not able to drive the $\overline{\text{CTF}}$ line, but do remain in a partially activated state even when they are no longer addressed. When the control word with TME and $\overline{\text{DTE}}$ on is programmed and gated, all cards are simultaneously enabled to output new data and fully activated to drive the $\overline{\text{CTF}}$ line.

If TME is not programmed on, all output cards (including those without $\overline{\text{CTF}}$ drive circuitry) may be operated in any of the four programming sequences discussed thus far. The distinction between the serial sequence and the first parallel sequence is no longer significant, however, since the flag is now returned automatically by the handshake logic. The second parallel sequence is different only because it makes use of the $\overline{\text{DTE}}$ function to synchronize outputs to the external environment.

4-6.11 Input Operations

The following paragraphs describe typical input operations for parallel (interrupt mode), $\overline{\text{IRQ}}$ poll, single, and serial transactions, using the sequences shown in Fig. 4-36.

Certain input cards may also be operated in the output mode, and are generally programmed using the single or serial sequences with TME off. Just as there are input cards that may be used in the output mode, so there are output cards which have a secondary function that is used in the input mode.

(Note: Unlike output operations, where a gate signal is always required to strobe data into local storage registers, use of the gate depends on the particular card model during input transactions.)

Cards with input capability have circuitry for driving either the $\overline{\text{IRQ}}$ signal line, some or all of the 12 return data lines, or for driving all 13 lines. Any card in this group is enabled to drive the return data bus if it is addressed with $\overline{\text{ISL}}$ on, regardless of whether or not the card is gated. Cards without $\overline{\text{CTF}}$ circuitry must not be gated if TME is also on, and are usually operated without a gate in the automatic handshake mode where TME is off and the possibility of a system "hang-up" is eliminated. The remaining cards with input capability may be used in this mode or in one or more of the input programming sequences given in Fig. 4-36.

Parallel (Interrupt Mode) Transactions. Cards that function in the parallel input mode (interrupt mode) are the only cards able to drive the $\overline{\text{IRQ}}$ signal line. These cards also have $\overline{\text{CTF}}$ drive circuitry and, with the exception of the 69431A digital input card (Sec. 4-2.5), respond to and act on data when addressed and gated in the output mode. Only one card (the 69600 timer card,

Sec. 4-2.3) actually transmits data to the external environment. However, the other cards use data received in the output mode to modify the manner in which they react to input signals. All cards with interrupt capability must be *armed* before they are enabled to drive either the $\overline{\text{IRQ}}$ or $\overline{\text{CTF}}$ signal lines in the interrupt mode.

Individual arming is done by addressing and gating the card when the system is in the input mode (a control word with $\overline{\text{ISL}}$ on must have been programmed and gated previously). *Group arming* is made possible by a hardware option available on all cards with $\overline{\text{IRQ}}$ circuitry. When installed, a jumper (W6) permits the controller to arm cards by programming the interrupt mode (a control word with $\overline{\text{IEN}}$ and TME on is programmed and gated). As they are armed, the cards are enabled to begin a data transfer cycle with the external device and to drive the $\overline{\text{IRQ}}$ signal line.

As shown in Fig. 4-36, steps (a) through (g) given in the first parallel input programming sequence, and steps (a) and (b) given in the second sequence, arm the cards and place the system in the interrupt mode. Since the $\overline{\text{IEN}}$ control signal suppresses the $\overline{\text{CTF}}$ flip-flop and TME suppresses the automatic handshake, the controller depends on the armed cards to return the leading edge of flag.

When operated in the interrupt mode, cards do not return a leading edge of flag until they have completed a data transfer cycle with the external device. The first card to complete transfer drives $\overline{\text{CTF}}$ low and causes the handshake logic to return the leading edge of flag, whereupon the controller resets $\overline{\text{GTE}}$ and the handshake logic responds by terminating DST. Once the data strobe is terminated, the $\overline{\text{CTF}}$ circuitry on all armed cards is disabled and the trailing edge of flag is returned to the controller, indicating that an interrupt has occurred. Unlike the parallel output mode, where the trailing edge of flag is controlled by the last card to complete its operation, the interrupt mode flag is controlled by the first card.

$\overline{\text{IRQ}}$ Poll. At this point the controller polls all armed cards by addressing them in sequence without a gate in the input mode ($\overline{\text{ISL}}$ is on and TME is off) and examining the $\overline{\text{IRQ}}$ bit (bit 15 of the return data word) returned from each card as it is addressed in order to determine which card completed its transfer cycle and generated the interrupt. If the addressed card has completed a transfer cycle, the $\overline{\text{IRQ}}$ signal is returned to the controller in the low (true), state. If the transfer cycle is not complete, the $\overline{\text{IRQ}}$ signal is high (false). Depending on the card model, a high state on the $\overline{\text{IRQ}}$ line means that the data transaction is still in process. For other card models, a high on the $\overline{\text{IRQ}}$ line indicates that the addressed card has not detected a change of state in the external device. Since it is possible that several cards have completed their transfer cycles, the order in which cards are polled establishes an interrupt priority system in software.

When an interrupting card is found, the controller may process the return data word according to the demands of the particular program. Once this is completed, the controller must either recycle or disarm the interrupting card since the card generates an interrupt as soon as the system is again gated with $\overline{\text{IEN}}$ on unless the card is reset. (The requirements for interrupting, recycling, and disarming are different for each card model, and are explained in detail in Chapter 5.) If a card recycles, the card remains armed but does not generate an interrupt until another transfer cycle has been completed. If the card is disarmed, the card becomes inoperative in the interrupt mode until the card is again armed. Recycling or disarming should be considered part of any gated data input sequence since cards with interrupt capability must be reset in one way or the other whenever they are used, regardless of whether the system is in the interrupt mode.

Once the interrupting card is reset, the controller may continue with the poll, or may reestablish the interrupt mode by gating the system with $\overline{\text{IEN}}$ on. If the first interrupt is generated by several cards at the same time, or if a card completes the transfer cycle while the polling routine is conducted, a new interrupt is generated immediately. (The 69434A event sense card is an exception since it cannot detect or store an event unless both DST and $\overline{\text{IEN}}$ are on.) If the interrupt is produced by only one card, and the interrupt is not completed during polling, the controller will wait for both edges of the flag. The controller may also reestablish the interrupt mode, proceed to a totally unrelated operation, and then return to the polling sequence at some later time, either as the interrupt occurs (if the controller has a hardware interrupt system) or when directed to do so by the program.

The entire interrupt sequence may be terminated after an interrupt has occurred provided that the system has not been gated again with $\overline{\text{IEN}}$ on. Even if the gate has been sent, the mode may still be aborted, but the controller gate must now be reset by a program command. In either case, it is a good policy to disarm any active cards.

The W6 jumper option should be used with caution. All cards in the system which have W6 installed are armed whenever $\overline{\text{IEN}}$ is programmed on and gated. This situation can create difficulties if the programmer is now fully aware of the implications. For instance, the $\overline{\text{IRQ}}$ polling routine must be conducted with $\overline{\text{ISL}}$ on and TME off, but $\overline{\text{IEN}}$ has no influence during this operation and may either be left on or turned off. If $\overline{\text{IEN}}$ is turned off, however, and the interrupting card is disarmed, the interrupt mode cannot be programmed back on without rearming the card. The problem may be solved by leaving $\overline{\text{IEN}}$ on during the polling and disarming operation. Similarly, cards with W6 installed may not be individually armed, but must instead be selectively disarmed after $\overline{\text{IEN}}$ is programmed on.

Single-card and Serial Transactions.   Returning to Fig. 4–36, it may be seen that single-card and serial input transactions are related (in the same sense that single-card and serial output transactions are related, Sec. 4–6.10). That is, the serial process is a repetition of the single-card operation. Assuming that all cards involved are able to drive the $\overline{\text{CTF}}$ line, the input and extended handshake modes are established by programming and gating a control word with $\overline{\text{ISL}}$ and TME on. The first card is then addressed, gated, and immediately drives $\overline{\text{CTF}}$ low, returning the leading edge of flag. Once the data transfer between the external device and the card is complete, the card stops driving $\overline{\text{CTF}}$ and the trailing edge of flag is detected and returned to the controller by the handshake logic. Thus informed that the data transfer has taken place, the controller maintains the card address and reads back the input word on the return data bus. Card models having the necessary drive circuitry also return $\overline{\text{IRQ}}$ while addressed, but the controller need not test that bit since the trailing edge of flag is returned only when the data transfer is complete and therefore is synonymous with $\overline{\text{IRQ}}$ true. Regardless of whether the total operation involves one card or many, transactions are completed with a single card at a time, and the $\overline{\text{IRQ}}$ function is not used. As discussed, cards with $\overline{\text{IRQ}}$ circuitry are armed when gated with $\overline{\text{ISL}}$ on and should be disarmed once the transaction is completed.

4-6.12 Flowchart for Main Programming Sequences

Figure 4–38 presents, in flowchart form, the programming sequences given in Fig. 4–36. The automatic handshake modes are also shown in Fig. 4–38. Note that the relationship between single-card and serial transactions is made more apparent by combining the two modes into a single sequence which incorporates a "last card" decision box. When the transaction involves a single card only, the "yes" condition is satisified on the first pass through the sequence, and the flow proceeds directly to the end of operation (EOP). The "no" condition is satisified during serial transactions until the last card has been programmed.

The "last card" decision box also implies the possibility of a different unit address. In such cases, the flow must return to "start" and proceed from there back to the same branch sequence after a control word with the new unit address and appropriate control bits is programmed and gated.

A "flag" decision box is shown immediately after each gating operation. The trailing edge of flag is required to satisfy the "yes" condition. The "no" condition is thus sustained until the handshake is complete and provides a "wait for flag" loop.

4-6.13 Flowchart for $\overline{\text{IRQ}}$ Polling Sequence

As shown in Fig. 4–38, the interrupt mode programming sequence does not conclude with an end-of-operation box, but proceeds to the $\overline{\text{IRQ}}$ polling routine. A flowchart for that sequence is given in Fig. 4–39, and is arranged as a self-contained subroutine.

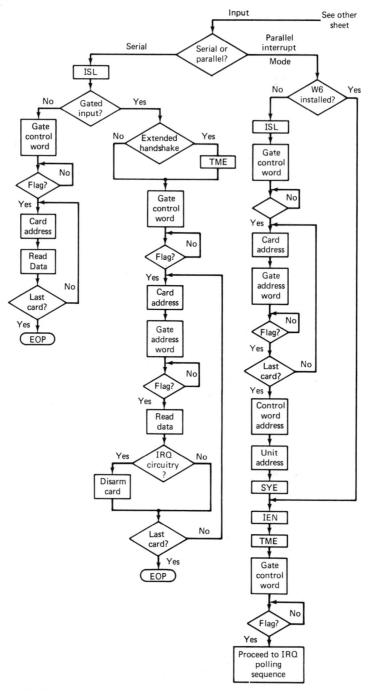

FIGURE 4-38 Flowchart for programming sequences.

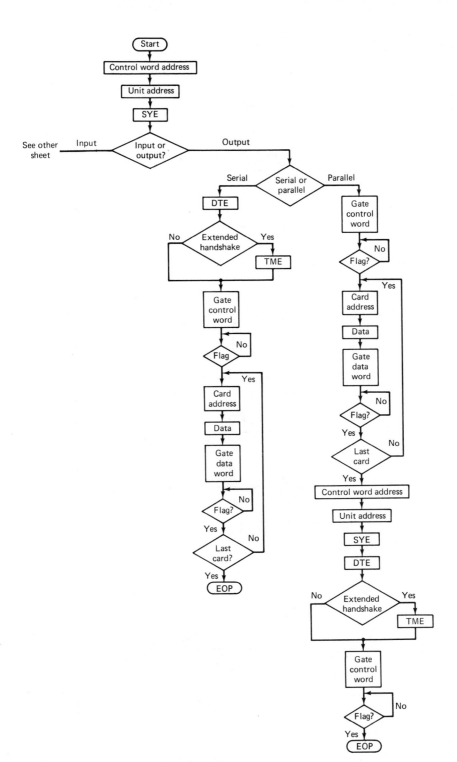

FIGURE 4-38 (*Continued*)

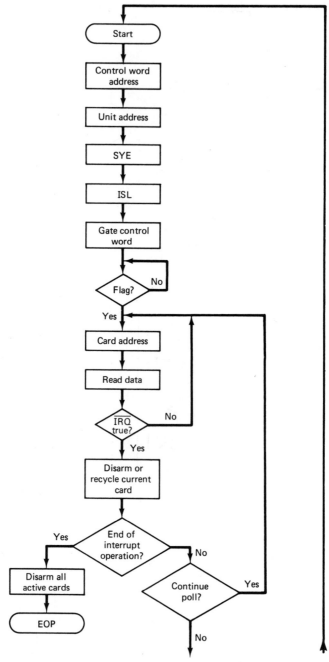

FIGURE 4-39 Flowchart for IRQ polling sequence.

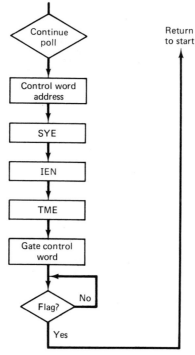

FIGURE 4-39 *(Continued)*

4-6.14   *Local Operation with Front-Panel Controls*

The 6940B mainframe is provided with a front-panel switch register (Fig. 4-1) which is enabled when the data source switch is set to local position. The switches (with the exception of the data source and power switches) are proximity types (Sec. 2-14.4) actuated by body capacitance and have integral indicator lamps. These lamps monitor the state of the various signal lines (the lamp is on when the signal is in the true state) in both the local and remote operating modes.

The 16 switch/indicators in the top row monitor and/or drive the data signal lines that connect between the multiprogrammer and the controller. If the mainframe is in the output mode ($\overline{ISL}$ is off), the switch register displays the data word either as sent by the controller or as manually programmed on the switches (assuming that the data source switch is set to the local mode). If the input mode is selected ($\overline{ISL}$ is on and a control word address is not specified), the display is a combination of the address word and the return data word. The switches corresponding to bits $\overline{B00}$ through $\overline{B11}$ are not enabled when local operation is selected in the input mode, but the switches for bits $\overline{B12}$ through $\overline{B15}$ are enabled and may be used to specify the card address.

4-6.15 Return Data Circuit

The $\overline{IRQ}$ signal is not displayed as bit $\overline{B15}$ on the switch register, but is instead displayed on the return data indicator. The return data switch/indicator also displays and/or drives the $\overline{FLA}$ signal line. Figure 4-40 shows the circuitry used to implement these functions. The return data indicator displays the state of $\overline{FLA}$ regardless of the system operating mode (the lamp is on when $\overline{FLA}$ is low). The return data circuit also displays the state of the $\overline{IRQ}$ line if $\overline{ISL}$ is also on (the lamp is on if $\overline{IRQ}$ is true). The switch function is enabled only in the local mode, in which case the handshake logic is prevented from driving the $\overline{FLA}$ line and the return data switch becomes the only source for $\overline{FLA}$. The exact reverse situation is in effect when remote operation is selected.

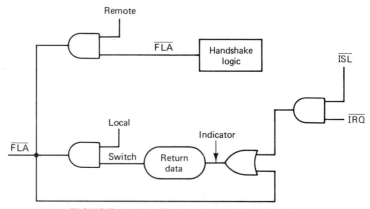

FIGURE 4-40 Basic return data circuit.

The load output indicator monitors the controller gate (the lamp is on when $\overline{GTE}$ is low). The associated switch drives the $\overline{GTE}$ line when the local operating mode is selected. The clear register switch returns all data switches to their off state and is provided as an operator convenience.

4-7 INTERFACE BASIC PRINCIPLES OF OPERATION

This section describes the basic principles of operation for the interface. The 59500A multiprogrammer interface permits bidirectional operation of the 6940B multiprogrammer and any associated 6941B multiprogrammer extenders on the Hewlett-Packard Interface Bus HP-IB. Programming fundamentals for the interface (when used with the HP-IB) are described in Chapter 5. In this section we concentrate on a basic description of the operation and functions performed by the interface, and on the relationship of the interface to the HP–IB and multiprogrammer.

4-7.1 Interface Connections

Figure 4–41 illustrates the signal flow on the HP–IB between the controller (calculator) and the interface. The major signal flow between the interface and multiprogrammer units is also shown.

Data bits are transferred over the bus on data input/output lines D101 through D108 using the byte serial technique (Chapter 3). Each byte (character) of information, 8-bits in parallel, is transferred onto the bus in serial fashion. Lines D101 through D107 accommodate the 7 bits (one character) of the ASCII code. Line D108 is not used by the multiprogrammer system but can be used by other bus instruments.

The state of the attention (ATN) line, controlled by the calculator, determines how the data lines are interpreted. The ATN line is constantly monitored by the interface and all other devices on the bus. When ATN is true, the bus devices (in this case the interface) interpret the data on lines D101–D108 as instructions (commands) from the calculator. Assume that a command is sent which enables the interface to listen in preparation to receive data from a talker (in this case the calculator). Multiprogrammer operations can only be initiated when the interface is listening. When the ATN line is false, data bits are transferred from the calculator to the interface.

The interface converts the serial ASCII characters from the calculator into the 16-bit word format required by the multiprogrammer. Depending on the data received, the multiprogrammer performs either an output or an input operation as described in Sec. 4–6. If the timing mode is not used, the calculator can send additional data to the interface. However, if the timing mode is used, the calculator is prevented from sending the interface additional data until the multiprogrammer has completed operation. When an input operation is performed by the multiprogrammer, a return data word is stored in the interface. In order for the calculator to receive these data, the calculator must set ATN true, command the interface to talk, and the calculator to listen. When ATN is false, the interface converts the multiprogrammer return data word into serial ASCII characters for processing by the calculator.

The service request (SRQ) line is used by the interface to indicate that the multiprogrammer requires service. The SRQ line is enabled whenever the multiprogrammer is operating in the timing mode and is set when the multiprogrammer completes an operation or requests an interruption of the current programming sequence. Control signals from the multiprogrammer to the interface implement the service request function. The interface also responds to the interface clear (IFC) control signal from the calculator. The IFC signal is used by the calculator to terminate activity on the HP–IB. The interface does not respond to the REN (remote enable) and EOI (end or identify) control bus lines.

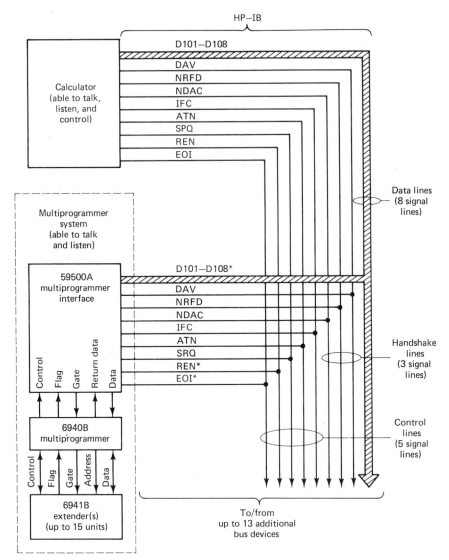

*Data bus line D108 and control signal bus lines REN and EOI
are not used by multiprogrammer system.

FIGURE 4-41   Signal flow on HP-IB.

A three-wire handshake process occurs with each character transferred on the HP–IB. A three-wire handshake cycle takes place when the interface is receiving a character and when it is sending a character. The interface adapts the three-wire handshake process used on the HP–IB to the two-wire method (gate/flag) used by the multiprogrammer. The three-wire handshake is implemented by the DAV (data valid), NRFD (not ready for data), and the NDAC (data not accepted) bus lines, all shown in Fig. 4-41.

4-7.2 Interface Description

Figure 4-42 illustrates the major circuits and signal flow through the interface. All signal abbreviations (DAV, NDAC, etc.) on the block diagram refer to the true state of the corresponding signal line. The following paragraphs describe operation of the interface in the *command mode* and in the *listen* and *talk* modes. The three-wire handshake cycle, service request operation, and associated serial poll operation are also described.

4-7.3 Command Mode

When the ATN line goes true, the command decoder is enabled. The command decoder consists of a talk/listen decoder and a serial poll decoder. The talk/listen decoder receives data lines D107 (MSB) through D101 (LSB) from the HP-IB and the associated switches (slide switches located on the rear of the interface). When the ATN line is true, the talk/listen decoder controls the talk and/or listen latches when any one of the following ASCII characters is decoded:

1. Unlisten command ("?"): Resets the listen latch inhibiting the interface from functioning as a listener.
2. Multiprogrammer listen address (suggested listen address is "7"): Sets the listen latch and resets the talk latch. The interface can function as a listener but not a talker.
3. Multiprogrammer talk address (suggested talk address is "W"): Sets the talk latch and resets the listen latch. The interface can function as a talker but not as a listener. The address switches select talk and listen addresses in pairs; a talk address of "W" corresponds to a listen address of "7."
4. Another bus device talk address or an untalk command ("-"): Resets the talk latch, inhibiting the multiprogrammer system from functioning as a talker.

After one of the commands or addresses listed above is decoded, the interface is enabled to function as a listener or as a talker; or is inhibited from functioning as either. The talk and listen latches remain either both reset, or one set and the other reset, until another command is decoded. The talk or listen latch (whichever is set) is reset when the interface clear (IFC) bus line is true. The IFC line is used by the calculator to clear all devices on the HP-IB.

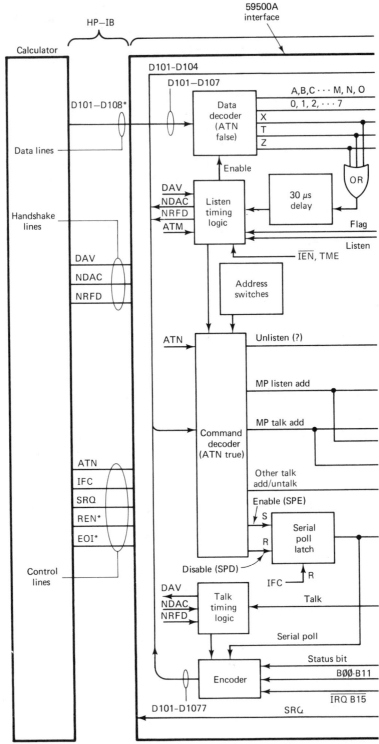

FIGURE 4-42 Basic block diagram of interface.

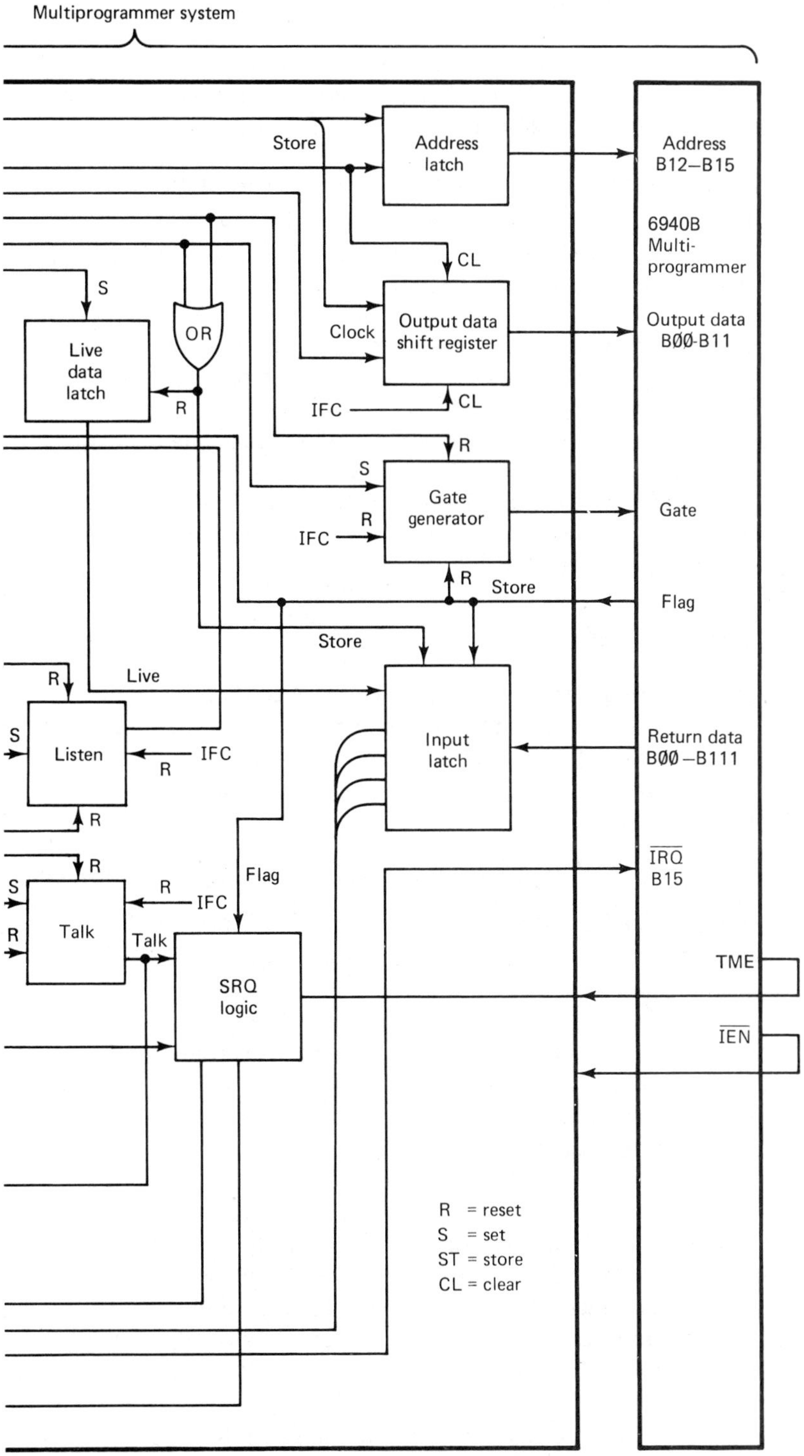

FIGURE 4-42 (Continued)

The serial poll decoder also receives data lines D107 through D101 from the HP–IB. When the ATN line is true, the serial poll decoder controls the serial poll latch if one of the following commands is decoded:

Serial poll enable: Sets the serial poll latch enabling the interface to operate in the serial poll mode.

Serial poll disable: Resets the serial poll latch, inhibiting the interface from operating in the serial poll mode.

Serial polling is a method of sequentially determining which device connected to the HP–IB has requested service. Service requests and serial polling operations are described in Sec. 4–7.7.

A three-wire handshake cycle occurs with each command character that is transferred from the calculator to every device on the HP–IB. In the command mode (ATN line true), the handshake cycle is automatically implemented by the timing and logic (listen) circuits in the interface. The three-wire handshake process is described in Sec. 4–7.8.

4-7.4   Listen Mode

When the interface listen address has been received (listen latch is set) and the ATN line goes false, the interface interprets alpha and numeric ASCII characters from the HP–IB as data, and processes them accordingly. The data decoder (five separate decoders) decodes ASCII characters on data bus lines D107 through D101 as follows:

Letter decoder: Decodes "@" sign and letters from "A" through "O."

Number decoder: Decodes numbers from "0" through "7."

"T," "X," "Z" decoders: Decode gate codes "T," "X," and "Z," respectively.

When any one of the foregoing characters is received, it is decoded and a handshake cycle between the interface and the calculator takes place. Unrecognized characters are ignored, but a handshake cycle between the interface and calculator occurs anyway (Sec. 4–7.8).

Letter Decoder.   When D107, 6, and 5 specify the ASCII code for an "@" sign or a letter from "A" through "O," the letter decoder stores the remaining 4 bits (D104 to D101) in the address latch. In addition, a clear signal is generated which presets the output data shift register to zero. The bits stored in the address latch represent a multiprogrammer card slot address or designate a multiprogrammer control word. The bits derived from the ASCII codes for "@" and "A" through "N" represent multiprogrammer card slot addresses 400 through 414, respectively. The bits derived from the ASCII code for "O" designate a multiprogrammer control word. If another "A" through "O" or "@" character is received, the new character replaces the previous character stored in the address latch.

Number Decoder.   When D107, 6, 5, and 4 specify the ASCII code for a number in the range from "0" through "7," the number decoder generates a clock pulse which loads bits D103 through D101 into the bottom three positions of the shift register. As succeeding numbers are received by the number decoder, the data present in the data shift register is shifted up, 3 bits at a time, as the new data (number) is loaded in. Numbers are shifted in from the bottom up as they are received. Thus, the first 3 bits (octal number) received are the most significant output bits in the register.

The data shift register holds 12 bits of data $\overline{B11}$ (MSB) through $\overline{B00}$ (LSB) representing data input to the multiprogrammer. Thus, after four numbers (3 bits each) are received, the data shift register is filled. If less than four numbers are received by the decoder, the most significant bits of the data shift register are logical zeros because of the prior clearing of the shift register (as discussed for the letter decoder). Since some calculators do not transmit leading zeros, this feature of the shift register makes the transmission of leading zeros optional as they have no effect. If more than four numbers are received, they continue to be shifted into the data shift register. However, since only 12 bits can be retained, only the last four decoded numbers are present and all previous numbers are lost. The shift register is cleared when the IFC line is true.

"T," "X," and "Z" Decoders.   As ASCII "T," "X," or "Z" gate code is decoded on data bus lines D107 through D101 by the applicable decoder. The "T" code, included in all control and data words, generates the multiprogrammer gate signal. The control or data word bits $\overline{B15} - \overline{B00}$ (contents of the address latch and output data shift register) are sent to the multiprogrammer along with the gate. The gate signal initiates the multiprogrammer data storage and/or processing functions specified by the associated control and data words. The "T" code can also be used in an address word to initiate a data strobe to activate the addressed input card, and then store return data bits $\overline{B11} - \overline{B00}$ from the addressed input card in the interface input latch. Thus, when the "T" code is used in an address word, the "T" code designates a "read with gate" function.

The "X" code (read without gate) is used in an address word when it is desired to store data from the addressed input card without gating (strobing) the card. When the "X" is received, the return data ($\overline{B11} - \overline{B00}$) form and addressed input card is stored in the input latch. The "Z" code (read live data) is used in an address word to allow return data ($\overline{B11} - \overline{B00}$) from the addressed card to pass continually through the input latch to the encoder.

The "Z" code (read live data) is used in an address word to allow return data ($\overline{B11} - \overline{B00}$) from the addressed card to continually pass through the input latch to the encoder. When the "Z" code is received, the input latch is enabled and remains enabled until a "T" or "X" is received. Thus, the "Z" code allows the contents of the input latch (encoder input) to be updated continually to reflect the return data from the addressed multiprogrammer input card. Control data, address words, and the uses of the "T," "X," and "Z" gate codes are described in detail in Chapter 5.

The three-wire handshake cycle for a "T," "X," or "Z" character is delayed 30 μs. When a "T," "X," or "Z" is decoded, the timing logic holds the NRFD bus line true for 30 μs preventing the calculator from sending another character until NRFD goes false. The delay allows the multiprogrammer time to process the data before the calculator sends new data. Note that if a "T" is received, the receipt of another character could be delayed for more than 30 μs since the multiprogrammer flag overrides the 30 μs delay (Sec. 4–7.8).

If a "T" is decoded, the gate generator is set and the live data latch is reset. When set, the gate generator produces the multiprogrammer gate signal which strobes bits $\overline{B15} - \overline{B00}$ into the multiprogrammer. The multiprogrammer gate can only be generated when a "T" is decoded. The leading edge of the multiprogrammer flag resets the gate generator and the trailing edge stores the return data bits ($\overline{B11} - \overline{B00}$) in the input latch. The flag is also applied to the timing logic (listen) circuit to control the NRFD bus signal. In effect, when a "T" is decoded, the HP-IB three-wire handshake is converted to the multiprogrammer two-wire handshake (Sec. 4–7.8).

If an "X" is decoded, the gate generator is reset, data bits present on the return data bit lines ($\overline{B11} - \overline{B00}$) are stored in the input latch, and the live data latch is reset. The ability to reset the gate generator with an "X" becomes necessary if the gate generator remains set when the multiprogrammer is operating in the interrupt mode. During the interrupt mode, the trailing edge of the flag signal (indicating an interrupt condition) resets the gate generator and activates the service request (SRQ) bus line. If the trailing edge of the flag is not received, the interface will "hang up," waiting for an interrupt indication with the gate generator set and the SRQ line false. Consequently, if the interrupt indication (SRQ line goes true) does not occur as anticipated, the calculator can send an "X" to reset the gate generator, removing the "hang-up" condition. Conditions for setting the SRQ line true are described in Sec. 4–7.6.

When a "Z" is received, the live data latch is set causing the input latch to be continually enabled. For this condition, the input latch continually reflects the status of return data bits ($\overline{B11} - \overline{B00}$) from the addressed multiprogrammer input card.

4-7.5 Talk Mode

Before the interface is placed in the talk mode, a control word with a "T" gate code must have previously been received, defining the input mode of operation (ISL on). Also, an address word specifying a particular input card slot address, and an accompanying "T," "X," or "Z" gate code, must have been previously sent to the interface. After the multiprogrammer system is in the input mode (ISL on), and the address word and gate code have been received, the data stored in the interface input latch reflect the data returned ($\overline{B11} - \overline{B00}$) from the addressed input card. This information, together with bit $\overline{B15}$ (the multiprogrammer $\overline{IRQ}$ bit), is sent to the encoder. At this point, the direction of the data flow on the HP-IB must be reversed by commanding the calculator to listen and the interface to talk.

When the interface talk address is received (talk latch is set) and the ATN line goes false, the encoder translates bit 15 into one octal digit and bits $\overline{B11} -$ $\overline{B00}$ into four octal digits. Bit $\overline{B15}$ is encoded a 1 if $\overline{IRQ}$ is set, and a 0 if $\overline{IRQ}$ is not set. The $\overline{IRQ}$ bit is used by certain programmer inputs to indicate that they contain valid data. $\overline{IRQ}$ is also used to identify the interrupting card when multiple input cards are used in the interrupt mode.

Bits $\overline{B11} - \overline{B09}$, $\overline{B08} - \overline{B06}$, $\overline{B05} - \overline{B03}$, and $\overline{B02} - \overline{B00}$ are encoded into ASCII codes for numbers ranging from "1" to "7." Data bits are transmitted from the encoder onto the HP-IB in the order given above, starting with the octal digit representing bit $\overline{B15}$ and ending with the octal digit representing bits $\overline{B02} - \overline{B00}$. Carriage return and line feed are added after the last multiprogrammer octal digit ($\overline{B02} - \overline{B00}$) as an "end of record" indication to the calculator. As each character is transmitted, a three-wire handshake occurs between the interface and the calculator (Sec. 4-7.8).

4-7.6 Service Request

The service request (SRQ) line is used by the interface to notify the calculator that the multiprogrammer requires service. Whenever the multiprogrammer is operating in the timing mode (TME on), the SRQ logic circuit in the interface is enabled and sets the SRQ line true upon receipt of the trailing edge of the multiprogrammer flag. As discussed, a multiprogrammer flag is obtained only when a "T" gate code is received by the interface. The three possible conditions which determine when the trailing edge of the flag is received (with TME on) are as follows:

1. When using certain multiprogrammer input or output cards in serial (sequential) timing mode, TME must be programmed on (control word with a gate) before addressing a card with a gate. When the control word is received, the multiprogrammer generates a handshake flag, causing the interface to set the SRQ bus line true. Since this service request is caused by the control word, the request must be cleared (Sec. 4-7.7) before addressing the card with a gate. Once the card has been addressed with a gate, the card controls the flag line into the interface. When the interface receives the trailing edge of this flag, SRQ is set true as an indication that the card has completed a data transfer.

2. When using multiple output cards in parallel (simultaneously) TME

mode, the trailing edge of the multiprogrammer flag is not returned to the interface until the last output card completes its data-transfer operation.

3. When the multiprogrammer is in the interrupt mode (TME, $\overline{\text{IEN}}$ on), the multiprogrammer flag is not received until a multiprogrammer card generates an interrupt. Note that for this condition (TME, $\overline{\text{IEN}}$ on), the NRFD line is not a function of the multiprogrammer flag. The TME and $\overline{\text{IEN}}$ control signals are sent to the timing logic (listen) to prevent the multiprogrammer flag from controlling the NRFD line in the interrupt mode. Thus, when cards interrupt, the NRFD line is not affected by the resulting flag(s). However, the trailing edge of the flag from the first interrupting card sets the SRQ bus line true.

4-7.7 Serial Poll

Serial poll is a method used by the calculator to determine which bus device has requested service (set SRQ bus line true). Essentially, serial poll consists of interrogating bus devices in sequence and reading back a status byte from each device which is used to identify the device(s) requesting service. When addressed to talk in the serial poll mode, the interface (1) returns a status byte equal to decimal 64 if the interface is requesting service, or (2) returns a status byte of zero if the interface is not requesting service.

When a serial poll enable (SPE) command is received, the command is latched in and sent to the encoder and the SRQ logic circuits. The SRQ logic circuit sends a status bit which indicates the state of the service request to the encoder. A logic 1 status bit, indicating SRQ is true, is translated into a decimal 64 by the encoder. A logic 0 status bit, indicating SRQ is false, is translated into a decimal 0 by the encoder.

When the serial poll enable latch is set and the interface talk address is received, the interface is placed in the serial poll active state (SPAS). For this condition, the SRQ logic circuit is reset and further transmission of SRQ on the HP–IB is inhibited. In addition, the interface transmits the status byte (decimal 64 or 0) on data bus input/output lines D107 through D101.

When the interface receives a serial poll disable command (SPD), an untalk command at the listen address, or the talk address of another device, the serial poll active state is terminated, preventing further transmission of the status byte.

4-7.8 Three-Wire Handshake Process

A three-wire handshake cycle occurs with each character transferred over the HP–IB data lines. The following paragraphs describe the three-wire handshake process in greater detail. Figure 4–43 shows the interface with the DAV, NDAC, and NRFD HP–IB handshake lines. The handshake signal flow

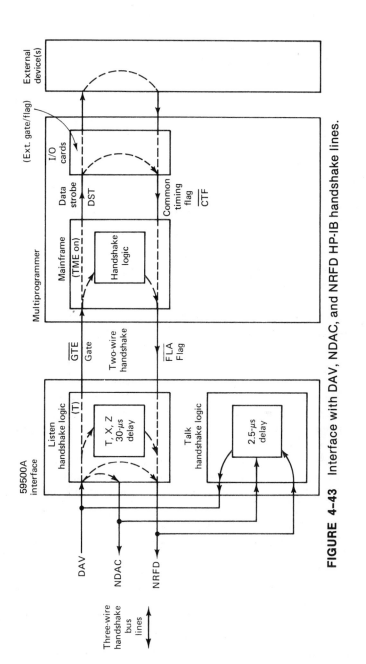

FIGURE 4-43 Interface with DAV, NDAC, and NRFD HP-IB handshake lines.

245

through the multiprogrammer system is also shown. The three-wire handshake cycle occurs when the interface is receiving characters (command and listen modes) and when the interface is sending data (talk mode).

Command Mode and Listen Mode Handshaking Process. When the HP–IB is in the command mode (ATN line true) or when the interface is in the listen mode (addressed to listen and ATN lines goes false), the listen handshake logic (Fig. 4–43) in the interface is enabled. As the interface receives each character (whether recognizable or not), a three-wire handshake cycle with the HP–IB occurs.

The cycle is initiated when DAV goes true. The NDAC signal is controlled directly by the DAV signal through the listen handshake logic circuit. However, control of the NRFD signal depends on the following conditions (Fig. 4–43):

1. If any character except a "T," "X," or "Z" is received, NRFD is controlled directly by the DAV signal. When the DAV signal goes true, a three-wire handshake cycle occurs automatically between the talker (assume the calculator) and the interface.

2. If a "T," "X," or "Z" gate code character is decoded, a delay circuit in the interface holds NRFD true for 30 μs. This delay prevents the calculator from inputting another character for 30 μs, allowing the multiprogrammer sufficient time to process and store the existing data. As shown in Fig. 4–33, a "T" code also generates the multiprogrammer gate which (when timing mode TME is off) results in an automatic flag from the multiprogrammer handshake logic. However, since the multiprogrammer handshake circuit provides a 30-μs (nominal) delay in parallel with the interface delay, the NRFD is still held true for 30 μs (nominal).

3. If the multiprogrammer is in the timing mode (TME on) and a "T" is received, the three-wire handshake cycle is not automatic but depends on the flag signal from the multiprogrammer. In the timing mode, the multiprogrammer gate $\overline{GTE}$, generated by the "T," is extended (DST, $\overline{GAT}$ signals) through the mainframe to the input/output cards and any associated external devices, as shown in Fig. 4–43. Timing circuits in the input/output cards or external devices will, upon receipt of the gate signal, generate a flag ($\overline{FLG}$, $\overline{CTF}$) which holds the NRFD bus line true until the input or output operations are completed. The flag line overrides the 30-μs delay in the interface if the operations are not completed within 30 μs. In many cases, the operations required a number of seconds before completion. When the operations are completed, the trailing edge of the flag causes NRFD to go false. In effect, by controlling the NRFD line with multiprogrammer flag, the multiprogrammer two-wire handshake (gate/flag) is converted to the HP–IB three-wire handshake process (DAV, NDAC, NRFD). The only time the multiprogrammer flag does not af-

fect the NRFD line is when the multiprogrammer is in the interrupt mode (TME, $\overline{\text{IEN}}$ both on). For this condition, NRFD is not a function of the flag line. The multiprogrammer automatic and extended handshake processes are described in Sec. 4–6.

A three-wire handshake cycle between the talker (calculator) and listener (interface) occurs in the following sequence, as shown by the timing diagram of Fig. 4–44.

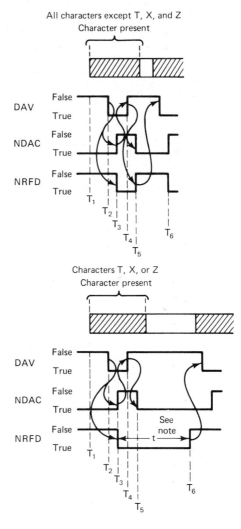

FIGURE 4-44 Timing diagram for three-wire handshake sequence.

Note: t = 30 μs for X, Z, or T (TME off)

t = 30 μs minimum for T (TME on)

T1: Initially, the interface is ready to accept data; NRFD is false, and NDAC is true.

T2: Calculator puts a character on the HP–IB and indicates that the character is valid by setting DAV true.

T3: Upon sending DAV true, the handshake logic (listen) circuit in the interface automatically sets NDAC false and NRFD true.

T4: Calculator senses NDAC false and sets DAV false, indicating that the character is no longer valid.

T5: Upon sensing DAV false, the handshake (listen) circuit in the interface automatically sets NDAC true and NTFD false (if character received is not a "T," "X," or "Z"). If a "T" (TME off), "X," or "Z" is received, the NRFD is held true for 30 μs. If a "T" (TME on) is received, NRFD is held true for 30 μs or more, depending on the time required to complete the input or output operations.

T6: With NRFD false, the calculator sets DAV true and another character is transferred (T3 through T5 are repeated).

Talk Mode Handshake Process.   When the interface is in the talk mode (addressed to talk and the ATN line goes false), the talk handshake logic is enabled. As each character is transferred from the interface to the calculator, a three-wire handshake cycle occurs. The sequence of operation is the same as described and shown in Fig. 4–44. However, in this case, the interface is the talker and the calculator is the listener. As shown in Fig. 4–43, setting DAV true is delayed 2.5 ms to allow for HP–IB delays.

5

MULTIPROGRAMMER FUNCTIONS AND PROGRAMMING FUNDAMENTALS

Now that we have introduced the basic multiprogrammer system in Chapter 4, let us discuss how the system can be programmed to perform the various control and instrumentation functions. We start with a block-diagram-level discussion of the system, covering both input and output modes. This is followed by a brief description of how the multiprogrammer system can be programmed with a calculator and an HP–IB interface bus. The remainder of the chapter is devoted to descriptions (functional descriptions, sample programs, etc.) for the various plug-in cards.

5-1 BASIC MULTIPROGRAMMER SYSTEM BLOCK DIAGRAM

Figure 5–1 is an overall block diagram of the multiprogrammer showing the four major circuits, together with the principal input and output signals of each circuit. The multiprogrammer is the master control and data distribution unit for the entire bidirectional system. Although the multiprogrammer operates bidirectionally, the first programming steps are always in the output direction to initialize the system and to establish operating modes. Computer (calculator) data bits are received in the form of 16-bit parallel words and applied to the in-

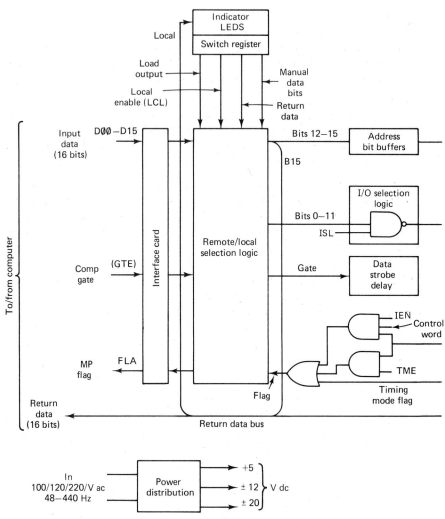

FIGURE 5-1 Overall block diagram of multiprogrammer.

terface card of the multiprogrammer. The interface card provides the proper termination for the calculator output circuits. The data-bit output of the interface card, together with a set of manually selected data bits from the local switch register, are applied to the remote/local selection logic circuit.

When LOCAL operation is selected, a local enable line (LCL) blocks the path for the calculator data and gates through the manually programmed data. When REMOTE operation is selected, the computer data words are gated

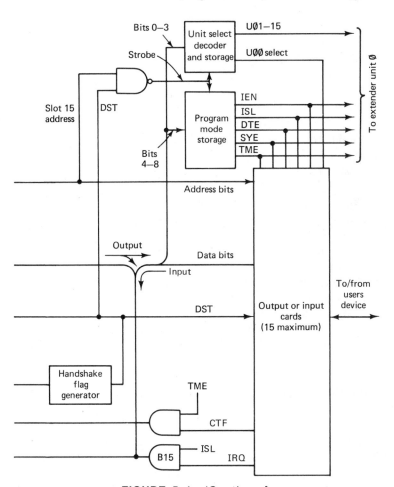

FIGURE 5-1 (*Continued*)

through and local data words are blocked. The 16 bits selected by the remote/local circuits are divided into two groups: address bits (bits 15, 14, 13, and 12) and data bits (11 through 0). The 4 address bits are applied to a set of buffer amplifiers which produce both the true and complemented forms ($B15/\overline{B15}$ through $B12/\overline{B12}$) of the address bits. Simultaneously, the 12 data bits are gated through I/O selection logic (since no modes have yet been programmed).

After an 8-μs software delay which allows the input data lines to settle, the calculator issues a gate signal. The calculator gate signal is interfaced and selected as described for the input data bits and applied to a data strobe delay circuit. Prior to the gate being issued by the calculator, the multiprogrammer is in a "wait" condition. The address and data bits are distributed to the 400-series accessory card slots and to the control word decoding and storage circuits, but do nothing while awaiting a data strobe. When the calculator gate appears, the data strobe delay circuit waits 2 μs and then generates a data strobe signal.

Assuming the calculator input to be a control word (as it must be for the first programming step), address bits 15, 14, 13, and 12 are all binary 1, signifying slot address 15. Slot address 15, combined with DST, strobes bits 0 through 3 into unit select storage registers and bits 4 through 8 into mode storage registers. Bits 0, 1, 2, and 3 are decoded by the unit select logic and energize one of 16 unit select lines (U00 through U15) according to the programmed address. The energized unit select line partially enables all 15 accessory card slots of the selected unit. The unit selection is stored and remains in effect until a new unit is addressed by a later control word.

From this point in the operation, the multiprogrammer either functions as an output device, supplying programmed data to selected output cards; or as an input device, reading digital data from selected input cards and returning these data to the calculator. The output/input status depends on the programmed state of the input select (ISL) mode bit.

5-2 MULTIPROGRAMMER OUTPUT MODES

In the absence of an input mode selection, the multiprogrammer functions as an output device, applying signals to actuators and other control elements of a control and instrumentation system. Two of the five programmable modes, SYE and DTE, relate exclusively to output functions; TME is used for both output and input modes. Each of these three functions is covered briefly in the following paragraphs.

5-2.1 System Enable Mode

The system enable mode (SYE) is selected when bit 5 of a control word is programmed to the 1 state. SYE is routed from the programmed mode storage circuits to all accessory card slots in the system. Prior to SYE's being programmed, the output circuits of all output cards are disabled; resistance outputs are short circuited, voltage outputs are held at 0 V, current outputs are opened, relay contact outputs are held open, and TTL outputs are at logic 0. In effect, the control function of the system is disabled. When SYE is programmed, the output cards are allowed to respond to programmed data. SYE is reset by programming bit 5 = 0, by removing power, or by removing card A3. As an added safety feature, a jumper on input data plug P1 completes the SYE path to all card slots, making it necessary to have input calculator data connected in order to enable the output cards in the system.

5-2.2 Timing Mode

The timing mode (TME) is used for both output and input operations. TME is selected by programming bit 4 of a control word to the 1 state. For output functions, TME causes the flag signal returned to the calculator to be held in the busy state until the programmed output cards have completed processing their last data input. The busy state of the flag signals the calculator not to input new data. TME is distributed to all timing mode flag circuits of all units in the system. The mode remains in effect until programmed out of the mode by bit $4 = 0$.

5-2.3 Data Transfer Enable Mode

The data transfer enable mode (DTE) is selected by programming bit $6 = 1$. DTE is wired to accessory card slots of the system, but is used only by output cards having dual-rank storage, by relay output cards, and by TTL output cards. As discussed, output cards with dual-rank storage have two sets of storage registers. The first set stores the programmed data bits as they are strobed in by DST. The second set of registers receives the data from the first set, and applies the data bits to the output conversion circuits only when DTE is programmed.

For output cards with dual-rank storage, the DTE mode is normally used in either of two ways:

DTE Selected First and Latched. In this mode, output cards are addressed and programmed one at a time. Since DTE is present, the programmed data bits are transferred immediately from the first set of registers to the second set of registers and on to the conversion circuits. Each card thus produces an output proportional to the programmed data, as the card receives the data.

DTE Not Initially Selected. In this mode, the output cards are addressed and store the programmed data bits in the first set of registers, but do not transfer the data to the second set of registers, since DTE has not been programmed. This method permits the first registers of all cards of this type to be loaded with data first, then by programming DTE, the outputs of all the cards are simultaneously transferred to the control system. The output cards continue to hold the most recently programmed value after DTE is removed.

The digital (TTL) and relay output cards have only a single level of storage, and the output relays respond to data as the card is programmed. However, a gate line (or a contact closure available on each relay output card) is enabled only when DTE is programmed. The gate line (or contacts) can be used in the external control system to initiate two operations:

1. To simultaneously strobe the outputs of all digital and/or relay output cards into the external system.

2. To start a timing flag circuit in the external system that holds the flag line (returned to the multiprogrammer) in the busy state until the circuit times out. The delay provided by this circuit should coincide with the maximum time required for the control system to process the digital or data relay outputs.

5-2.4 Computer Data Input

For output modes, the output cards are programmed by 16-bit data words from the computer. A data word contains two types of information: slot address (bits 15, 14, 13, and 12 programmed to any number from 0000 to 1110) and data (bits 11 through 0). A unique combination of the 4 address bits is wired to each of the 15 card slots. Slot 400 receives address 0000, slot 401 receives 0001, slot 414 receives 1110, and so on.

The same slot address wiring is carried through in all units so that when a given slot address is programmed, all slots in the system having that address are partially enabled. However, only one unit of the system can be selected at a time, so only the slot of the unit selected by a previous control word is enabled to accept the data contained in bits 11 through 0. (Input-type cards require ISL in addition to the appropriate slot and unit addresses to be enabled.) The multiprogrammer is assigned unit number Ø0 (UØ0), while extender units are numbered consecutively from UØ1 up to U15.

5-2.5 Handshake Mode

Computer (calculator) data bits are entered into the multiprogrammer in either of two modes: the handshake mode or the timing mode. The return path to the calculator for the handshake flag is enabled when TME is programmed off, and blocked when TME is programmed on. An alternate path for the handshake flag is enabled when a control word is programmed, provided IEN (interrupt enable) is not being selected by that control word. For output modes, it can be assumed that IEN is always off and the alternate path is enabled for all control words, even if TME is on. The significance of the alternate path for control words is covered in Sec. 5-3.

In the handshake mode, the multiprogrammer accepts data at rates up to 20,000 words per second. A timing diagram of the data, gate flag, and data strobe signals for the handshake mode is given in Fig. 5-2. The significant multiprogrammer and calculator operations at each *time interval* are as follows. It

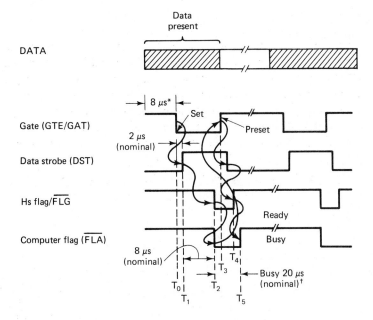

*Software delay.
† Computer flag line is held busy for 20 µs by
the multiprogrammer flag stretcher circuit.

FIGURE 5-2 Timing diagram for handshake mode.

should be noted that because the multiprogrammer system is designed to operate with up to 100 ft of cabling between each unit, an 8-µs software delay is required between data output to the multiprogrammer and setting the gate signal.

Time interval T_0: Following the 8-µs software delay, the gate signal from the calculator goes low, indicating that a word is available on the 16 data input lines. The gate signal is applied to a data strobe delay circuit in the multiprogrammer, and to identical circuits in all extender units of the system.

T_1: Following a 2-µs delay, the data strobe delay circuit switches DST to a high level. This level loads the programmed data into the control word decoding logic (if a control word code is present) or into an addressed output card.

T_2: After a delay of approximately 8 µs from the start of the gate, the handshake flag generator sets the handshake (H.S.) flag low (which is applied to a flag stretcher circuit in the multiprogrammer), setting the flag line ($\overline{FLA}$) back to the calculator low (busy). This indicates to the calculator that the data input operation has been completed. The calculator must reset the gate at this time. Data bits may be removed after the gate is reset.

T_3: The gate line is reset (goes high) in preparation for the next data output operation.

T_4: When the gate line is reset, the data strobe delay circuit resets DST and the handshake generator resets the H.S. flag ($\overline{FLG}$ goes high), allowing the calculator flag (FLA) to go high. Note that the multiprogrammer flag stretcher circuit (Sec. 5-2.7) holds the $\overline{FLA}$ signal low (busy) for 20 µs.

T_5: The calculator flag (FLA) goes high (ready). The calculator may initiate a new data output cycle any time after T_5.

5-2.6 Timing Mode

Whenever an output card is addressed and data are strobed in, a CTF pulse is produced by a timing circuit on the address card or a timing circuit on the device attached to the address card. This flag pulse (Fig. 5–3) is initiated by DST, but

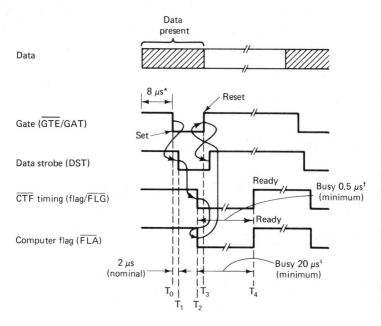

*Software delay.

†Duration of $\overline{CTF}$ busy depends on the timing circuits on the individual output cards or related external devices.

‡Computer flag line is held busy for a minimum of 20 µs by the multiprogrammer flag stretcher circuit.

FIGURE 5-3 Timing diagram for timing mode.

the pulse duration depends on the timing circuit of the individual output cards or related external device. The timing flag duration for a particular output card is selected on the basis of maximum time required for the card, or the external device connected to the card, to complete processing data before the card can accept new data. The timing flag output of the individual cards are ORed together to become the common timing flag (CTF). When the timing mode is not programmed, CTF is still generated by the output cards but has no effect on the flag line back to the calculator. When TME is programmed, the CTF pulse becomes the flag to the calculator. In the timing mode, the flag is held busy until the timing flag pulses from the individual output cards have timed out. The flag stretcher circuit in the multiprogrammer holds the calculator flag ($\overline{FLA}$) line busy for a minimum of $20\mu s$.

5-2.7 Extender Unit Flags

Every extender unit in the system has a flag circuit similar to the mainframe flag circuit. Figure 5-4 is a block diagram showing the interconnection between flag circuits. As can be seen from Fig. 5-4, a handshake or timing flag generated by an extender unit is ORed through each unit in the system to the mainframe or master unit. The mainframe receives the flag line signal (designated as FOR) and returns the signal to the calculator (via the flag stretcher circuit) as the system flag. Operation of the extnder unit flag circuits is identical to the master (mainframe) unit flag circuit.

5-3 MULTIPROGRAMMER INPUT MODES

There are two primary input modes and a number of secondary variations of these modes involving both hardware and software options. The two primary modes are designated: (1) the dedicated input mode and (2) the interrupt search mode. The basic theory of operation for input functions is described here in terms of the two primary input modes, as related to a typical digital input card.

5-3.1 Dedicated Input Mode

In this mode, the calculator reads data from input cards on an individual card basis. Until the calculator completes its operation on the currently addressed card, the calculator should not go to another input card. The dedicated input mode is normally used in either of two ways: *ungated* or the *timing mode*.

Ungated Input Mode. This is the most basic method of reading data from an input card. The procedure is done in two programming steps: (1) programming a control word with ISL = 1, IEN = 0, and TME = 0, and (2) programming the desired card address and *not* using a calculator gate signal. Note

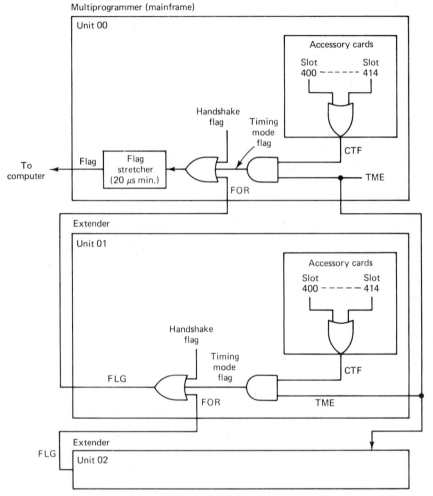

FIGURE 5-4 Block diagram of interconnection between flag circuits.

that because the multiprogrammer system is designed to operate with up to 100 ft of cabling between each unit, a software delay must be incorporated between addressing an input card and reading the data without a gate.

In step (1), ISL = 0 simply turns the 12-data bit lines of the multiprogrammer in the direction of the calculator. Although ISL is also applied to the input cards, ISL has no effect on their operation in the ungated mode.

In step (2), the 12-data bits currently stored on the addressed input card are placed on the return data lines and remain there for as long as the card address is present. Since a calculator gate is not issued in this mode, the multiprogrammer does not produce a data strobe (DST) and the addressed card is not armed. (CTF and IRQ are neither generated nor required in the ungated mode.)

Timing Mode. This mode is also programmed in two steps: (1) a control word is programmed with ISL = 1, IEN = 0, and TME = 1, and (2) the desired card address is issued together with a computer gate signal.

Step 1 sets up three initial conditions for this mode: First, ISL reverses the direction of the 12 data bit lines; second, ISL is applied to all input cards as a condition necessary to enable (arm) an input card when the card is addressed and data strobed; and third, TME enables the common timing flag (CTF) return path from the input cards to the calculator.

In step 2, the address of the desired input card is programmed together with a calculator gate. Upon receipt of the address bits, the selected input card immediately places 12 bits of data on the return data bus to the calculator. However, the calculator should not accept these data until the multiprogrammer signals (via the trailing edge of CTF) that the input data from the addressed card have been updated and are now ready to be read.

Within the selected input card, the combination of ISL, DST, and the card address sends a gate signal to the external device and simultaneously resets the flag flip-flop on the input card. Resetting the flag causes the CTF line back to the multiprogrammer to switch to the busy state. When the external device is ready with new data, the external device signals the input card via the trailing edge of the device flag. This edge sets the input card flag flip-flop, which returns the CTF line to the ready state. At the same time new data are strobed into the storage registers on the input card. The calculator interprets the trailing edge of CTF as permission to read the return data.

Before going on to an interrupt-search mode, previously armed cards whose flag flip-flops have been set should either be rearmed (by programming ADDR DST ISL) or disarmed (by programming ADDR DST $\overline{\text{ISL}}$), with either operation done in the handshake mode.

5-3.2 *Interrupt-Search Mode*

The interrupt-search mode offers an efficient means of retrieving data from groups of input cards. There is a hardware option available which adds versatility to the interrupt-search mode by allowing all digital input cards with jumper W6 installed (Sec. 4-6.11) to be armed as a group. However, in order to keep this explanation simple, the multiprogrammer operation in the interrupt-search mode is described here in terms of four basic programming steps, with W6 not installed.

1. Establish initial mode conditions by programming a control word with ISL = 1, IEN = 0, and TME = 0.

2. Arm desired input cards by programming card addresses. (A calculator gate must accompany each address as the address is programmed.)

3. Select the interrupt enable mode by programming a control word with IEN = 1, TME = 1, and ISL = X (X = doesn't care).

4. Wait for the multiprogrammer CTF flag to indicate that one or more addressed input cards have valid data ready. Then, poll the input cards (by issuing their addresses) in a software-determined order. Do not issue a computer gate while polling. A programmed delay (wait time) must be incorporated between addressing each input card and reading the data without a gate. The delay time depends on the multiprogrammer unit number (0–15) of the card addressed. Examine bit 15 of each return data word in the calculator and accept data only when bit 15 = 1. (The state of bit 15 is determined by IRQ from the addressed input card; when the addressed input card has valid data available, IRQ makes bit 15 = 1.)

Step 1 establishes two initial conditions for this mode: First, ISL reverses the direction of the 12 data bit lines; and second, ISL is applied to all input cards as a condition necessary to enable (arm) an input card when it is addressed and data strobed. Since the timing mode has been programmed off in this step, subsequent data transfers between the calculator and the multiprogrammer are done in the handshake mode.

In step 2, the address of the desired input card is programmed together with a calculator gate. Upon receipt of the address bits, the selected input card momentarily places 12 bits of data on the return data bus to the calculator. The computer should ignore this data.

As in the dedicated input timing mode, the combination of ISL and DST and the card address arm the addressed card. As a result, a gate is sent to the external device and the flag flip-flop on the card is reset. When the device is ready with new data, the device signals the input card via the trailing edge of the device flag. This edge sets the flag flip-flop and strobes new data into the storage registers on the input card. When the interrupt mode is programmed in the next step, the "set" flag flip-flop on this, or any other input card with new data ready, generates an interrupt. Also, when the input cards are polled in the search mode, any card whose flag flip-flop is set causes IRQ (and thus bit 15 is returned to the calculator) to be true.

Step 3 establishes conditions for enabling interrupts from previously armed input cards which now have data available. Together with the control word containing IEN = 1 and TME = 1, the calculator must also issue a gate signal. When the control word containing IEN = 1 is programmed, a handshake flag is not generated. The calculator should now wait for a transition of the CTF line from an input card to signal an interrupt. Within the input cards,

IEN and DST (derived from the calculator gate) are logically ANDed with the output of the flag flip-flop, which is true when the external device has data ready. When all three conditions are true on any input card, the CTF line is set to the busy state. This transition of the CTF line to the busy state signals the calculator to reset the gate, which, in turn, resets DST. With DST reset, the CTF AND gate within the input cards is inhibited, causing CTF to return to the ready state. The calculator interprets this transition as an interrupt request.

In step 4, the address of each input card of the selected group is programmed in a program-assigned order, without a calculator gate. As each card is addressed, the card places the 12 data bits on the return data bus. The card address is also ANDed with the output of the flag flip-flop on the input card, and when both are true (signifying that the addressed input card has new data) the IRQ signal is made true. IRQ directly controls the state of bit 15 returned to the calculator; when bit 15 is true, the calculator should accept the associated 12 data bits.

5-4 HP-IB PROGRAMMING FUNDAMENTALS

This section outlines the fundamentals of programming the multiprogrammer system with a 9825A calculator using an HP-IB interface. Included in this section are multiprogrammer compatibility with the HP-IB and how to program the basic word formats. Programming for specific plug-in cards is discussed in the remaining sections of this chapter.

5-4.1 HP-IB Interface Functions

The multiprogrammer system (Models 59500A and 6940B/6941B) is capable of performing the following functions on the HP-IB: *talk, listen, service request, and serial poll.* Conversely, the multiprogrammer system cannot act as a controller, extended talker, or extended listener, and will not respond to remote-local, parallel poll, device clear, or device trigger commands.

5-4.2 Multiprogrammer Word Formats

The remainder of this section is devoted to the fundamentals of communicating between the calculator and the multiprogrammer system. For calculator-to-multiprogrammer exchanges, three different types of codes (words) can be sent. For multiprogrammer-to-calculator exchanges, two types of words can be received. The following paragraphs describe the basic construction and purpose of each word type, showing how to send the output words or read in the input words. Each word type is treated separately without too much regard for the programming sequences which can be used to do a specific task. Programming examples for individual cards are described in the remaining sections of this chapter.

5-4.3 Calculator Output Words

Three types of output words are sent from the calculator to the multiprogrammer system: control words, data words, and address words.

Multiprogrammer Listen Address.   Before any of these words are sent, the multiprogrammer must first be established as the *listener*. Throughout this section it is assumed that the HP–IB interface card has been assigned a standard select code of "7" and that the multiprogrammer system has been assigned listen and talk address of "7" and "W," respectively. Note that "7" and "W" correspond to an address of "23" as defined in the calculator manual. Using these addresses, the addressing sequence appears as shown in Fig. 5–5 (addressing the multiprogrammer to listen).

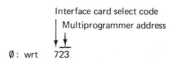

Interface card select code

Multiprogrammer address

Ø : wrt   723

FIGURE 5-5   Addressing the multiprogrammer to listen.

Control Word.   Usually, the first word sent to a multiprogrammer system is the control word, which specifies a *unit address* and the *operating mode* of the multiprogrammer system. The unit address portion selects which mainframe in the chain (of one mainframe and up to 15 extenders) will respond to subsequent data or address words from the calculator. The operating mode portion of the word selects one of several output or input modes of multiprogrammer operation (system enable, timing mode enable, input select, etc.). How the multiprogrammer system responds to these various control word modes is described in Sec. 4–6. Keep in mind that the multiprogrammer manual provides much more detailed information concerning the control word functions. Here, we are concerned with understanding the basic multiprogrammer word formats, so that you will be able to follow the plug-in card descriptions and programs that follow in this chapter.

Figure 5–6 shows the structure of a control word as transmitted on the HP–IB. The six control word characters are transmitted and obeyed in the order written, from left to right. The address character "0" is the control word tag that tells the multiprogrammer that the data characters that follow are to be interpreted as control mode and unit address information.

The data field consists of four octal numbers. The most significant digit, D_4, conveys no information in a control word and can be sent as a "Ø" or not transmitted at all. (Because of the way the multiprogrammer system processes

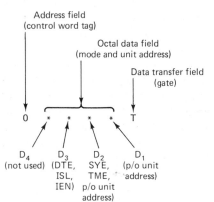

Address field
(control word tag)

Octal data field
(mode and unit address)

Data transfer field
(gate)

D_4 (not used) D_3 (DTE, ISL, IEN) D_2 (SYE, TME, p/o unit address) D_1 (p/o unit address)

FIGURE 5-6 Structure of control word as transmitted on the HP-IB.

octal characters in a data field, any leading Ø's need not be sent. Of course, trailing Ø's must be transmitted.) Digits D_3 and D_2 specify the operating mode (SYE on, SYE off, etc.).

Digits D_2 and D_1 specify the unit address. The first unit in the chain (main-frame or master) has an address of ØØ, the second unit (extender) has an address of Ø1, and so on, up to a unit address of 15. The two unit address digits are simply added (in octal) to the last two control mode digits to obtain the final data field code. The last character in a control word must be a "T." The multi-programmer system interprets this character as a "gate" which initiates the gate/flag handshake sequence within the multiprogrammer.

A typical control word, with DTE and SYE on, is sent as shown in Fig. 5-7. Note the format statement used. The "c" specifies a character field, while "z" is used to suppress the carriage return/line feed codes at the end of the write statement. Suppression of the carriage return/line feed codes is essential when using the multiprogrammer in the timing mode. The reason for this is that the calculator must receive handshake flags with the carriage return/line feed codes in order to continue with the program. Thus, by suppressing the carriage return/line feed codes, the calculator can continue to the next statement in the program while the multiprogrammer is still timing out. Note that all write statements shown in this chapter reference a format (fmt) containing "z," even those used in the nontiming mode (TME off). It does no harm to do this, and it helps avoid potential problems.

Control word tag

DYE, SYE on;
unit ØØ address

Multiprogrammer
gate

FIGURE 5-7 Typical control word with DTE and SYE on.

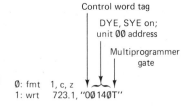

Ø: fmt   1, c, z
1: wrt   723.1, "ØØ140T"

Data Word. Data words select and control output cards and a few "special-purpose" input cards. The data word selects an individual card within the mainframe previously specified by a control word.

Figure 5-8 shows the basic construction of a data word sent from the calculator. The address character selects the particular card (one of 15 slots in a mainframe) that receives the four "control" digits in the data field portion of the word. The data field consists of four octal digits that can be of any value between 0000 and 7777. As in a control word, leading 0s need not be sent in the data field. A data word with 0000 in the data field could be sent with just an address and a gate (T). The data transfer character must always be a "T" (gate) in a data word, the same as in a control word.

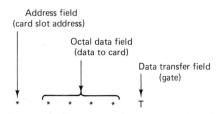

FIGURE 5-8   Basic construction of a data word sent from the calculator.

Figure 5-9 shows a write (output) statement using a typical data word preceded by the same sample control word used in Fig. 5-7. In the example of Fig. 5-9, an output card (in slot 401, unit 00) is being directed to output data represented by the octal number "7777."

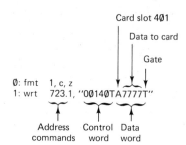

FIGURE 5-9   A write (output) statement using a typical data word.

Address Word. An address word selects the input card that is to send data (a return data word) back to the calculator. Before an address word can be sent, a control word must have first selected an input operating mode (and the unit address). Notice also that before the addressed input card can send a return data word back to the calculator, the multiprogrammer system must be placed in the talk mode (Sec. 5-4.4).

An address word contains just two characters, as shown in Fig. 5-10. The address character specifies one of 15 possible input card slot addresses. The data transfer field character can be a "T" (read with gate), an "X" (read without gate), or a "Z" (read live data). Which character to use depends on the

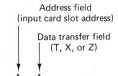

Address field
(input card slot address)

Data transfer field
(T, X, or Z)

FIGURE 5-10 Address word
containing two characters.

specific application and the input card type. A "T" always results in the generation of a "gate" to the addressed input card, and the data from the input card
(return data word) are stored in the 59500A interface on the trailing edge of the
flag from the multiprogrammer. Thus, a "T" character is used when it is
desired to wait for the completion of a gate/flag sequence before storing the
return data word in the interface. As previously mentioned, to obtain the return
data information after an address word is sent, the user must address the multiprogrammer to talk and read the data into the calculator.

An "X" character is sent when it is necessary to store the return data word
from the addressed card immediately, without initiating a multiprogrammer
gate/flag cycle. The "X" character itself stores the return data in the interface
as soon as all data bits are received from the input card. The "Z" character
allows the return data from the addressed card to pass continuously through the
interface to the output encoder, without being stored. When using the "Z"
character, the user must keep in mind that the return data may be continuously
passed and can therefore be difficult to interpret.

Figure 5-11 shows a typical address word sent to an input card installed in
multiprogrammer slot 402 (address character B). Notice that the preceding control word calls for an input mode of operation (ISL on), and the address word
"BX" specifies a read without gate sequence.

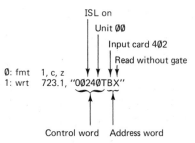

FIGURE 5-11 Typical address
word sent to an input card installed in multiprogrammer slot
402.

ISL on

Unit 00

Input card 402

Read without gate

0: fmt   1, c, z
1: wrt   723.1, "00240TBX"

Control word   Address word

5-4.4 Calculator Input Words

Two types of input words are sent to the calculator from the multiprogrammer
system: return data words and status characters (bytes).

Multiprogrammer Talk Address. Before the multiprogrammer can send
a return data word, a statement must be sent directing the multiprogrammer to
talk. Figure 5-12 shows the necessary address commands.

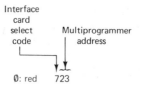

FIGURE 5-12 Addressing the multiprogrammer to talk.

Return Data Word.   Return data words contain information from an input card previously selected by an address word. As shown in Fig. 5-13, each word contains an input request character, four octal data characters, and a carriage return/line feed (not shown in Fig. 5-13).

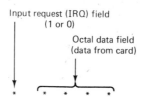

FIGURE 5-13 Return data word.

The input request (IRQ) character can be either a "1" or a "∅." A "1" indicates that the input card has returned a flag and the input data bits are valid. Moreover, during an interrupt sequence (TME and IEN on), a "1" in the IRQ field indicates that this card has generated an interrupt. A "∅" indicates that (1) the input card has not returned a flag (card is still busy or has not interrupted) and the data are not valid, or (2) the card does not contain an IRQ function. Some input cards, such as the voltage monitor card, do not contain an IRQ function, and a "∅" in the IRQ field can be ignored.

The four data characters, representing the input information from the multiprogrammer card, can be any octal number between ∅∅∅∅ and 7777. Thus, a return data word with all "7"s in the data field and a "1" in the IRQ field appears as a 17777 on the calculator display.

Figure 5-14 shows how to read in a return data word and store the word in variable "X." First, a write statement is sent containing a control word with ISL on. Next, an address word is sent to select the input card in slot 4∅2 (unit ∅∅) to return the data. Finally, a read statement directs the multiprogrammer to talk and allows the calculator to read the data into variable "X." The return data bits in variable "X" can be used directly unless they are obtained from a card that contains the IRQ function. In these cases, the return data must first be

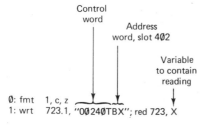

FIGURE 5-14 How to read in a return data word and store the word in variable "X."

checked to determine if there is a "1" in the IRQ field. If the IRQ character is a "1," the character must be subtracted from the input data before continuing with the program.

Status Bytes. The 59500A of the multiprogrammer system returns an 8-bit status byte to the calculator in response to a serial poll routine. Serial polling is the method used by the calculator to determine which bus device has requested service (set SRQ true). The multiprogrammer requests service (set SRQ line) only in the timing mode (TME on) upon completion of a multiprogrammer flag. Both input and output card types can set SRQ. The specific operating conditions required for a service request to occur are discussed in Sec. 4–7.6.

The user has two options available to monitor the service request line (SRQ) of the bus. The program may be set to interrupt on SRQ, or *bus status checks* may be used. In either case, when a bus service request is detected, a serial poll of the bus can identify the device that has requested service. Briefly, doing a serial poll on the multiprogrammer system places the multiprogrammer in the serial poll mode, addresses the multiprogrammer to talk, and then reads the status byte into a variable on the calculator. The status byte, stored in the variable, has a decimal value of 64 if the multiprogrammer requested service, or to a value of 0 if no service request has been made. Doing a serial poll also clears the SRQ line so that the calculator can detect the presence of new service requests. For this reason, a serial poll should be done at the beginning of any program to ensure that the service request line starts out in a clear state.

Figure 5–15 illustrates serial polling of the multiprogrammer, and storing the status byte in variable "C" in the calculator.

Store in variable "C"

Ø: rds   (723) ⟶ C

FIGURE 5-15 Serial polling of the multiprogrammer and storing the status byte in variable "C."

5-5 PLUG-IN CARD DESCRIPTIONS AND PROGRAMS

The remainder of this chapter provides HP-IB interface programming examples for each type of plug-in card that can be presently used in a multiprogrammer control and instrumentation system. The cards are presented in numerical sequence according to the card model number. Also, a brief functional description and a sample test program are provided for each type of card. Block diagrams and input/output connections (if applicable) are provided as aids to understanding both the programming and card functions. In addition, some programming examples of typical control applications using certain card types are provided. Unless otherwise specified, all examples assume that the card is installed in unit Ø, slot 4Ø2 (B).

5-6   D/A VOLTAGE CONVERTER CARD, 69321B

As show in Fig. 5–16, this card is a 12-bit bipolar (two's complement) D/A converter which may be programmed to output a voltage in the range of –10.240 through + 10.235 V. The 12-bit binary word accepted by the D/A card allows for 4096 unique programmed codes. Since zero is one of the possibilities, however, the actual decimal values fall in the range 0 through 4095. Presented graphically, the range of output voltages and the corresponding decimal, octal, and binary values are as shown in Fig. 5–17.

5-6.1   Calculating Data Value

The following steps yield the octal data value required to program the card to a desired output voltage. Disregard the sign when making calculations.

1. Divide the desired output voltage in volts by 0.005 (the LSB).

2. For negative voltages only, subtract the absolute value yielded in step 1 from 4096.

3. Calculate the octal equivalent of the decimal value yielded in step 1 or 2. For example, to calculate the octal data value required for + 5 V: 5/0.005 = 1000; 1000 = 1750 in octal; or to calculate the octal data value required for –5 V: 5/0.005 = 1000; 4096 – 1000 = 3096; 3096 = 6030 in octal.

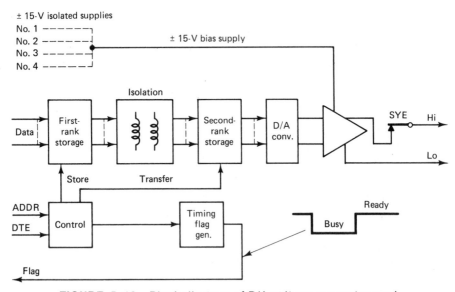

FIGURE 5-16   Block diagram of D/A voltage converter card.

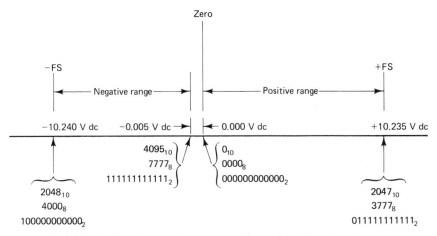

FIGURE 5-17 Range of output voltages for D/A voltage converter card.

5-6.2 Programming an Output Voltage

The following program illustrates using a data constant of 6030 (in octal) to program the output voltage of the card to –5 V. A control word is sent containing SYE and DTE, followed by a data word containing the card slot address and the data constant.

Ø: fmt   1, c, z

1: wrt   723.1, "0Ø14ØTB6Ø3ØT"

Although the card returns a CTF flag as a function of the internal timing circuit (Fig. 5-16), TME is not included in the control words of the programmed examples. This is because the period of the internal timing circuits on this card is shorter than the period of the multiprogrammer handshake flag (without TME). Therefore, TME is not useful when programming this card.

5-7 POWER SUPPLY/AMPLIFIER CONTROL CARDS, 69325A–69328A

As shown in Fig. 5-18, these resistance output cards are designed to control the gain, voltage, and current limit of Hewlett-Packard Bipolar Power Supply/Amplifiers (BPS/As).

Model 69325A controls the magnitude and polarity of the BPS/A output voltage. During the period that the resistance output of the card is changing, a *hold command* from the card causes the BPS/A voltage to remain constant, and then make a smooth transition to the new output voltage.

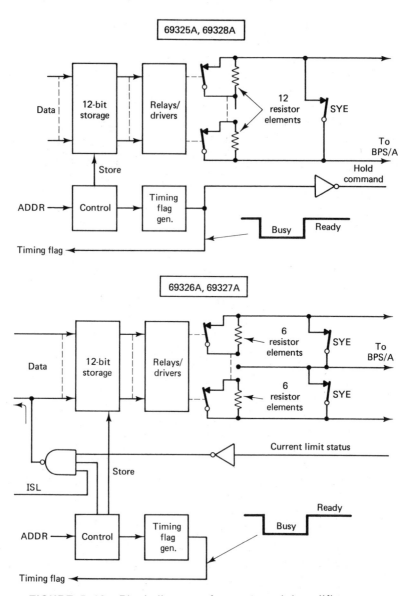

FIGURE 5-18   Block diagram of power supply/amplifier control cards.

The 69326A or 69327A card is used to control independently the positive and negative current limits of a BPS/A, and to monitor the status of the BPS/A current limit.

The 69328A is used to program the gain of the BPS/A from zero (no gain) to the full gain value of X2, X4, X8, X20, or X40, depending on the particular model of the BPS/A being controlled.

5-7.1   Resistance Outputs

Octal data bits are transmitted to program one 12-bit resistance output from a BPS/A control card as follows:

1. Voltage control card 69325A: 12 bits in two's-complement form program the resistance output which controls the voltage magnitude and polarity of a BPS/A.

2. Current control cards 69326A and 69327A: Each card provides two identical 6-bit resistance channels. Channel 1 controls the negative current limit and channel 2 controls the positive current limit of a BPS/A. The two least significant octal digits in the data field program the negative current limit (channel 1). The two most significant digits program the positive current limit (channel 2).

3. Gain control card 69328A: 12 bits program the gain of a BPS/A.

Tables in the multiprogrammer manual describe the procedures for calculating data values (in decimal) necessary to program the control cards to specific output resistances. The decimal value is then converted to an octal value before being transmitted from the calculator to the card through the multiprogrammer. For example, assume that it is desired to program the output resistance of a 69325A card to 12,000 Ω. Using the applicable table, the data value is calculated as follows:

$$D = \frac{12,000}{5} - 2048$$

$$= 2400 - 2048$$

$$= 352; \quad 352 = 540 \text{ in octal}$$

Corresponding programming formulas for voltage, current limit, and gain are given in the manual.

5-7.2   Programming Examples

The following program illustrates using a data constant of 2412 to program a BPS/A control card located in slot 402 (B).

```
0: fmt  1, c, z
1: wrt  723.1, "O0160TB2412TO0040T"
2: rds  (723) → C
```

5-7.3   Reading Status from 69326A/69327A Cards

As shown in Fig. 5–18, the 69326A and 69327A cards examine the *current limit status* of the BPS/A. The following program illustrates the format required to read the status. In this program, the return data word is input to variable "X" of the calculator. The return data word equals 1 if the BPS/A is in the current limit, or Ø if the current is out of limit.

Ø: fmt   1, c, z

1: wrt   723.1, "OØ24ØTBX"; red 723, X

5-8 RELAY OUTPUT CARD, 69330A

As shown in Fig. 5–19, this card provides 12 independent SPST normally open relays. Output from the card is in the form of relay closures to operate devices in the control system (solenoid valve actuators, etc.) Two additional relays are provided for external circuit gate/flag operation. An output connector is provided to route the 12 data outputs and the gate/flag signals to the external control device.

5-8.1 Operating Modes

This card has two basic modes of operation:

Automatic Handshake Mode (TME Off):   Used to send data to an external device when it is not necessary to handshake with the device.

Timing Mode (TME On):   Used to send data to an external device when the program requires an indication from the device that data bits have been accepted. The trailing edge of the multiprogrammer flag is returned upon completion of the data transfer, and can be used to generate an interrupt on the HP–IB interface, thereby notifying the calculator that the data transfer is complete. Note that when using this card without an external gate/flag timing circuit, the card gate output must be jumpered to the flag input.

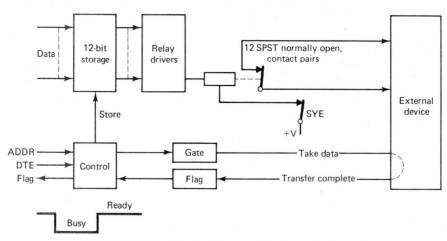

FIGURE 5-19 Block diagram of relay output card.

5-8.2 Automatic Handshake Mode

This mode requires sending a control word containing SYE and DTE only, followed by a data word containing the card slot address, and the output data desired. The following program illustrates using a data constant of 7777 (octal) to program the output of the card located in slot 402 (B).

```
0: fmt   1, c, z
1: wrt   723.1, "O0140TB7777T"
```

5-8.3 Timing Mode

The following program illustrates programming the card in the timing mode. First, an interrupt linkage is established between the appropriate interface and a service routine "done." Then a control word with DTE, SYE, and TME is sent to the multiprogrammer, followed by a data word which initiates a timing sequence with an external device. The appropriate interface is then enabled to receive interrupts. The main program continues execution from this point until the multiprogrammer completes the data transfer, returning the trailing edge of CTF flag and thereby generating an interrupt to the calculator. Note that DTE and TME must be programmed on together because the card cannot drive the CTF line unless DTE is on.

When an interrupt occurs, program control passes to service routine "done." Service routine "done" sends a control word to the multiprogrammer, turning off TME, prints "done" on the calculator to notify the user that the data transfer is complete, then returns program control to the main program. Of course, the actual action to be taken in response to an interrupt is decided by the user when writing a service routine.

```
0: rds   (723) → C
1: oni   7, "done"
2: fmt   1, c, z
3: wrt   723.1, "O0160T"; rds (723) → C
4: wrt   723.1, "B7777T"; eir 7
              .

              .

              .

20: "done": if rds (723)#64; gto "iret"
21: wrt   723.1, "O0040T"; prt "done"
22: "iret": iret
```

5-9 DIGITAL OUTPUT CARD, 69331A

As shown in Fig. 5–20, this card provides 12 bits with TTL/DTL-compatible logic levels as the output, and uses the gate/flag timing method of digital transfer with an external device. An output connector is provided to route the 12 output bits and gate/flag signals to the external device. The card operates in both the automatic handshake mode (TME off) and timing mode (TME on) in a manner almost identical to that of the relay output card described in Sec. 5–8. The only significant difference between the cards is that the digital output card produces TTL/DTL outputs, whereas the relay card produces relay closures.

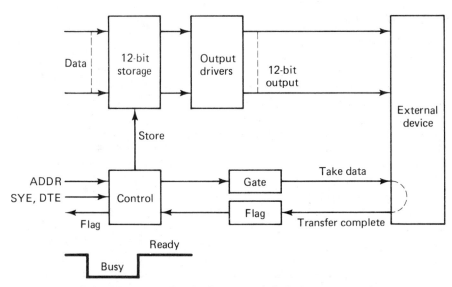

FIGURE 5–20   Block diagram of digital output card.

5-10 OPEN-COLLECTOR OUTPUT CARD, 69332A

As shown in Fig. 5–21, this card is designed to drive lamps and relay coils using an external d-c power source. Twelve separately programmable outputs are available, each of which is open-collector. The following program illustrates using a data constant of 7777 to program the output of the card located in slot 4∅2 (B). A control word is sent first, containing SYE only, followed by a data word containing the card slot address and the output data. Although SYE has no effect on this card, SYE is included in the control word to avoid disabling the outputs of output cards programmed previously.

```
∅: fmt   1, c, z
1: wrt   723.1, "O∅∅4∅TB7777T"
```

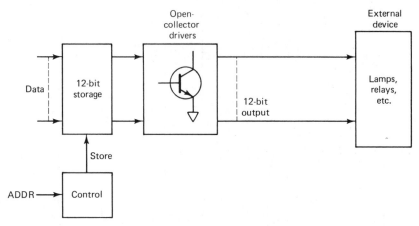

FIGURE 5-21   Block diagram of open-collector output card.

5-11 STEPPING MOTOR CONTROL CARD, 69335A

As shown in Fig. 5–22, this card can be programmed to generate from 1 to 2047 square-wave pulses at either of two output terminals. When applied to a stepping motor translator, these pulses are converted to clockwise and counterclockwise drive pulses for a stepping motor. The square-wave outputs of the card can also be used for pulse-train update of supervisory control stations.

5-11.1 Selecting Output Terminal and Number of Output Pulses

Data bits transmitted to this card are a combination of the number of output pulses desired and a user-selected output terminal. For values up to octal 3777 (decimal 2047) the output is from pin 1 of the output connector. If it is desired to obtain the output pulse train from pin 2, an octal 4000 must be added to the number of pulses desired (in octal). For example, 7777 (octal) will program 2047 pulses from pin 2.

5-11.2 Operating Modes

This card has two basic modes of operation.

Automatic Handshake Mode (TME Off).   This mode allows the user to program an output pulse train, consisting of a specified number of pulses, from either of two output circuits. Programmable selection of the appropriate out-

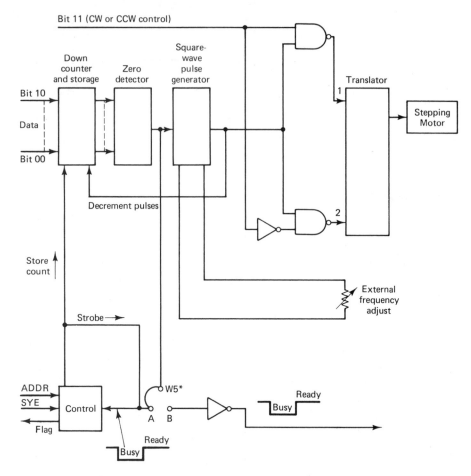

*In position A of W5, the timing flag signal returned to the
multiprogrammer stays "busy" for the duration of the output count.
In position B of W5, the timing flag is available at output
terminal 13, and a short-duration flag (about 2 μs) is returned
to the multiprogrammer.

FIGURE 5-22 Block diagram of stepping motor control
card.

put circuit allows the user to determine the direction of rotation of a stepping
motor. Since this mode does not control the trailing edge of the multiprogrammer flag, the mode does not provide an indication to the program (calculator)
that the output pulse train is complete.

Timing Mode (TME On).   This mode is used when the program requires
an indication from the multiprogrammer that the output pulse train has been
completed. The trailing edge of the multiprogrammer flag is returned upon
completion of the output pulse train, and can be used to generate an interrupt
on the HP–IB interface, thus notifying the calculator that the pulse train is

complete. In the case of the HP–IB, the service request line is set upon completion of the data transfer.

5-11.3 Automatic Handshake Mode

The following program illustrates using a data constant of 3777 (octal) to program 2047 output pulses from pin 1 of the card located in slot 402 (B). This mode requires sending a control word with SYE only, followed by a data word containing the card slot address and output data (number of pulses and output terminal) desired.

```
0: fmt  1, c, z
1; wrt  723.1, "O0040TB3777T"
```

5-11.4 Timing Mode

The following program illustrates programming the stepping motor card in the timing mode. First, an interrupt linkage is established between the appropriate interface and service routine "done." Then a control word with DTE, SYE, and TME is sent to the multiprogrammer, followed by a data word specifying 2047 pulses from pin 2 of the card (7777 in octal). The interface is then enabled to receive interrupts. The main program continues execution from this point until the pulse train is complete. At that time, a trailing edge of the multiprogrammer flag is returned, thus generating an interrupt to the calculator.

When an interrupt occurs, program control passes to service routine "done." The "done" service routine sends a control word to the multiprogrammer, turning off TME; prints "done" on the calculator to notify the user that the pulse train is complete, and then returns program control to the main program. Of course, the actual action to be taken in response to an interrupt is decided by the user when writing the service routine.

```
0: rds  (723) → C
1: oni  7, "done"
2: fmt  1, c, z
3: wrt  723.1, "O0160T"; rds (723) → C
4: wrt  723.1, "B7777T"; eir 7
         .

         .

         .

20: "done": if rds (723)#64; gto "iret"
21: wrt  723.1, "O0040T"; prt "done"
22: "iret": iret
```

5-12   D/A CURRENT CONVERTER CARD, 69370A

As shown in Fig. 5–23, this card provides a high-speed, constant-current output that is the analog equivalent of the digital input data. The output current range is from 0 to 20.475 mA with a minimum programmable step change of 5 μA. Current output levels are programmed in straight 12-bit binary form.

5-12.1   Calculating Data Value

The following steps yield the octal data value required to program the card to the desired output current.

1. Divide the desired output current in milliamperes by 0.005 (the LSB).
2. Calculate the octal equivalent value yielded in step 1.

For example, to calculate the octal data value required for 5 mA:

$$5/0.005 = 1000; \quad \text{octal equivalent of } 1000 = 1750$$

5-12.2   Programming an Output Current

The following program illustrates using a data constant of 1750 (octal) to program the output current to 5 mA. A control word is sent containing SYE and

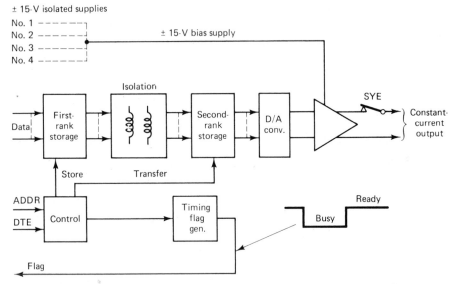

FIGURE 5-23   Block diagram of D/A current converter card.

DTE, followed by a data word containing the card slot address and the data constant. Although the card returns a CTF flag as a function of internal timing circuits (Fig. 5-23), TME is not included in the control words of the following program example. This is because the period of the internal timing circuits on this card is shorter than that period of the multiprogrammer handshake flag (without TME). Thus, TME is not useful when programming this card.

```
Ø: fmt   1, c, z
1: wrt   723.1, "OØ14ØTB175ØT"
```

5-13 BREADBOARD OUTPUT CARD, 69380A

As shown in Fig. 5-24, the breadboard card is a simple multiprogrammer interface card which allows the user to design, build, and control special output circuits through the multiprogrammer system. The following program uses a data constant of 7777 to program the output of the card located in slot 4Ø2 (B). A control word is sent first, containing SYE only, followed by a data word containing the card slot address and the output data. Although SYE has no effect on this card, SYE is included in the control word to avoid disabling the outputs of output cards previously programmed.

```
Ø: fmt   1, c, z
1: wrt   723.1, "OØØ4ØTB7777T"
```

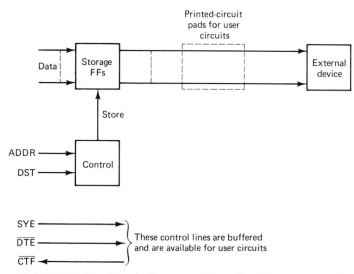

FIGURE 5-24   Block diagram of breadboard output card.

5-14   VOLTAGE MONITOR CARD, 69421A

As shown in Fig. 5-25, this input A/D card monitors bipolar d-c voltages in the range +10.235 to −10.240 V, and returns a 12-bit two's-complement digital word to indicate the magnitude and sign of the measured voltage. In addition, options are available which allow voltage measurements from +1.0235 to −1.0240 and +102.35 to −102.40 V.

The conversions required by this card are basically the inverse of those for the 69321B D/A card discussed in Sec. 5-6. However, the conversion process for the 69421A A/D card is simplified since the octal value returned to the calculator by the A/D card is always an integer in the range 0 through 7777 (octal). The octal-to-decimal function of the calculator converts this value to a decimal number in the range 0 to 4095. Since the 69421A is a bipolar device and produces a two's-complement code, the decimal number must be scaled and then multiplied by the analog equivalent value of the LSB in order to yield the actual decimal value of the applied voltage. This conversion is done as follows.

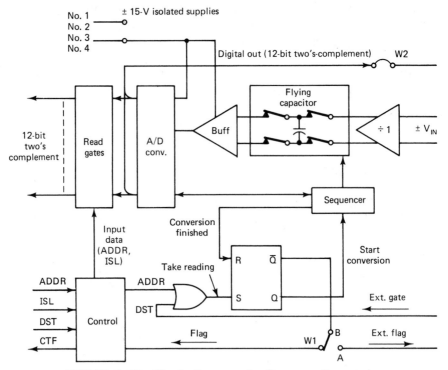

FIGURE 5-25   Block diagram of voltage monitor card.

1. If the decimal value is 2048 or larger, subtract 4096; for decimal values less than 2048, go directly to step 2.

2. Multiply the decimal value from step 1 by the analog equivalent value of the LSB.

For example:

$$6065 \text{ (octal)} = 3125 \text{ (decimal)}$$

$$
\begin{array}{r}
3125 \text{ (decimal)} \\
- \underline{4096} \\
- 971 \\
\times \underline{0.005} \\
- 4.855
\end{array}
$$

The following program shows the appropriate statements (program lines 2 and 3) for the operations performed above.

Ø: "meas": fmt 1, c, z; wrt 723.1, "O26ØTBTBX"

1: rds   (723) → C; red 723, X

2: ot   dX → X; if X > 2047; X-4Ø96 → X

3: .ØØ5X → X

4: fxd   3; dsp X, "VOLTS"; end

*13122

This programming example uses the timing mode of operation. A control word is transmitted specifying the input timing mode (ISL and TME on). Then the card is addressed with a gate. When the voltage monitor card receives a gate in the timing mode, the internal CTF circuits delay the trailing edge of the multiprogrammer flag until the voltage monitor card converts the analog input voltage into a digital equivalent. Attempting another multiprogrammer operation before the trailing edge of the flag is received causes the calculator to wait until the voltage monitor card completes the conversion (6 ms) and returns a CTF flag. When the trailing edge of flag is received by the calculator, the program continues. The voltage monitor card is then addressed without a gate and the octal equivalent of the analog voltage is read into variable "X" in the calculator.

In line 2 of the program, the octal data bits returned from the voltage monitor card in variable "X" is converted to a decimal value by use of the octal-to-decimal function of the calculator (otd). If the decimal value exceeds 2047, this indicates a negative voltage and requires a two's-complement number. This is done by subtracting 4096 from the decimal value. In either case (positive or negative), the final decimal value is then converted to a voltage value in line 3 by multiplying the decimal value stored in "X" by the LSB (in volts) of the voltage monitor card.

Notice that the first four lines of the program can be incorporated as a voltage-measuring subroutine in a user program merely by adding a return (ret) statement to the fourth line. When used in this way, subroutine "meas" returns variable "X" containing the measured voltage in volts.

5-15   ISOLATED DIGITAL INPUT CARD, 69430A

As shown in Fig. 5–26, this card allows the calculator to read 12 logic-level data bits that are isolated from a-c earth ground, thus eliminating ground loop problems in automatic test and control systems. The following program is a sample test program which allows the user to verify operation of the card by reading in and displaying data applied to the card. In this sample program, octal data bits are read into variable "X" in line 1. The first two lines of the program are all that is required to return data from this card. The user has the option of using the data in octal form, or using the octal-to-decimal (otd) function of the calculator to get the equivalent decimal value. The data inversion in line 2, as well as the (otd) function, are used in this example only to satisfy the requirements of subroutine "BIT" (which is described fully in the multiprogrammer manual).

The isolated digital input card is always read without a gate, as there is no storage or CTF drive capability on this card. The only requirements for reading

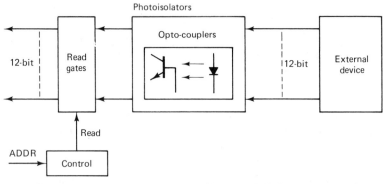

FIGURE 5-26   Block diagram of isolated digital input card.

data from this card are: (1) a control word with ISL on must have been sent previously, and (2) the card must be addressed.

Ø: fmt 1, c, z

1: wrt 723.1, "OØ24ØTBX"; red 723, C

2: 7777 X → X

3: ot dX → X; gsb "BIT"

4: end

*2114Ø

5-16 DIGITAL INPUT CARD, 69431A

As shown in Fig. 5–27, this card allows the calculator to read 12 logic-level or contact closure data bits that are referenced to the logic common (a-c earth ground). Gate/flag circuits are provided on each card to allow external devices to use the interrupt system of the calculator.

5-16.1 Operating Modes

This card has three basic operating modes:

Automatic Handshake Mode (TME Off). This mode is used to read data from an input card when it is not necessary to handshake with an external device.

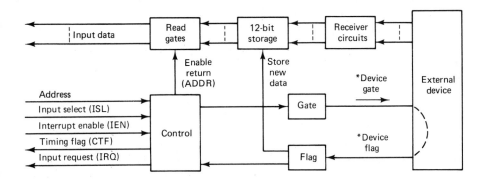

*Gate can be directly wired to flag if handshake is not needed.

FIGURE 5-27 Block diagram of digital input card.

Timing Mode (TME On).   This mode, also called the *dedicated input mode,* is used to read data from an input card when it is necessary for the card to handshake with an external device.

Interrupt Mode.   This mode is useful for activating many input cards simultaneously, then reading back data after a handshake is completed between an external device and one of the activated input cards.

Regardless of the mode used, the return data word is input in octal form to variable "X." The data bits can be used in octal form or can be converted to decimal by using the octal-to-decimal function (otd) of the calculator.

5-16.2   Automatic Handshake Mode

The following program illustrates reading back data in the automatic handshake mode (TME off). This mode is used when a handshake between the card and external device (data source) is not required.

```
0: fmt   1, c, z
1: wrt   723.1, "O0240TBT": red 723, X
2: X-10000 → X
```

5-16.3   Timing Mode

The following program illustrates reading back data in the timing mode (TME and ISL on). First, an interrupt linkage is established between the multiprogrammer interface and service routine "read." Then a control word with ISL and TME on is sent to the multiprogrammer, followed by an address word (with gate) to the appropriate card slot. The appropriate interface is then enabled to receive interrupts and the main program continues execution from this point until a calculator interrupt occurs.

When addressed with a gate, the card initiates a gate to the external device and does not read data until a flag is received indicating that data bits are ready. When the flag from the external device is returned, the card reads in the data and allows the multiprogrammer to return a trailing edge of the flag to the appropriate interface, thereby generating an interrupt to the calculator.

When an interrupt occurs, program control passes to service routine "read," which, in turn, stores data from the input card in variable "X" and prints the data on the calculator before returning program control to the main program. Of course, the actual action to be taken in response to an interrupt is decided by the user when writing a service routine.

Ø: rds (723) → C

1: oni 7, "read"

2: fmt 1, c, z

3: wrt 723.1, "OØ260T"; rds (723) → C

4: wrt 723.1, "BT"; eir 7

.

.

.

20: "read": if rds (723)#64; sto "iret"

21: red 723, X; X-10000 → X

22: fxd Ø; prt "data = ", X

23: "iret": iret

5-16.4 Interrupt Mode

The following program illustrates the interrupt mode of operation. Programming the digital input card in the interrupt mode consists of three basic steps:

1. The card must be armed using either one of the following methods:
Sending a control word with ISL on, followed by an address word (with gate) to the appropriate card slot, then another control word with IEN and TME on.
If jumper W6 is installed, simply send a control word with IEN and TME on.

2. When the external device returns a trailing edge of flag, the digital input card allows the programmer to return a trailing edge of flag to the appropriate interface, thus generating an interrupt to the calculator. (Of course, the interface must have previously been enabled to receive interrupts.) The card must then be addressed without a gate in the ISL mode and the return data word read in and examined for the presence of IRQ. If the input data word is equal to or greater than 10000, this indicates that the card has interrupted and has data ready.

3. The card should then be disarmed by sending a control word with ISL off, followed by an address word (with gate) to the appropriate card.

When an interrupt occurs, service routine "interrupt" reads the digital input card in slot 402 (B) (without gate) and examines the state of IRQ to be certain that the card has generated the interrupt. (This is very important when using multiple input cards in the interrupt mode.) A value of −1 is stored in variable "X" if the card in slot 402 (B) did not generate the interrupt. If the card has interrupted, valid data bits are stored in variable "X," and the card is disarmed by sending a control word with ISL off and addressing the card with gate. In either case, the calculator prints the value stored in "X" and returns program control to the main program.

```
0: rds  (723) → C
1: oni  7, "interrupt"
2: fmt  1, c, z
3: wrt  723.1, "O0240TBTO0460T"; eir 7
         .

         .

         .

20: "interrupt": if rds (723)#64; gto "iret"
21: wrt   723.1, "O0240TBX"; red 723, X
22: if X > 10000;-1 → X; gto "data"
23: X-10000 → X; wrt 723.1, "O0040TBT"
24: "data": prt "interrupt data = ", X
25: "iret": iret
```

5-17 RELAY OUTPUT WITH READBACK, 69433A

As shown in Fig. 5–28, this card provides 12 independent SPST normally open relays. Output is in the form of contact closures. In addition, the card allows the calculator to examine the status of the relay coil drive circuits on the card before and/or after the contacts are actually changed.

The following program illustrates using a data constant of 7777 (octal) to program the card located in slot 402 (B). A control word with SYE, DTE, and TME is sent, followed by a data word containing the card slot address and output data, then another control word with SYE only. Since TME has been turned on by the first control word, the calculator is forced to wait until the relay card returns a CTF flag (4 ms) before sending the second control word.

```
0: fmt  1, c, z
1: wrt   723.1, "O0160TB7777TO0040T"
2: rds (723) → C
```

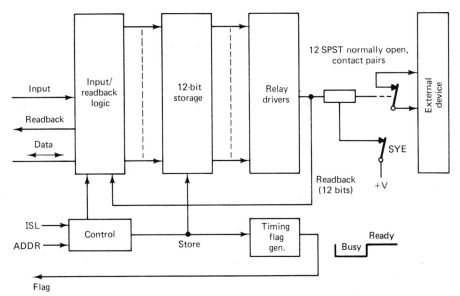

FIGURE 5-28 Block diagram of relay output with readback card.

5-17.1 Reading Relay Status

The user may examine the status of the relays at any time. The following program illustrates reading and storing the status of the relays in variable "X." A control word with ISL is sent to the multiprogrammer, followed by an address word (without gate) to the appropriate card slot. The return data word is then stored in "X." This card is always read without a gate.

Ø: fmt   1, c, z
1: wrt   723.1, "OØ24ØTBX"; red 723, X

5-18   EVENT SENSE CARD, 69434A

As shown in Fig. 5-29, this card monitors up to 12 external contact closures and can be used to interrupt the calculator when one or more contacts change for 20 ms or longer with respect to 12 reference bits stored on the card. The return data word is input (in octal form) to variable "X" of the calculator. It is then up to the user to process the data. For example, the data bits can be used in octal form or converted to decimal by the octal-to-decimal (otd) function of the calculator.

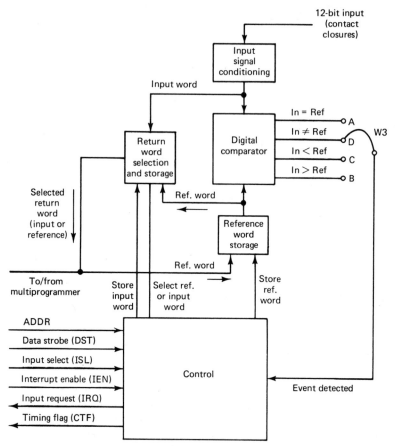

FIGURE 5-29 Block diagram of event sense card.

5-18.1 Interrupt Mode

Basically, this card is used only in the interrupt mode, either singly or with other cards having interrupt capability. The card generates an interrupt when any one of four conditions prevails. The interrupting condition is selected by jumper W3 (illustrated in Fig. 5-29) as follows:

W3 position	Interrupting condition
A	Input word = reference word
B	Input word > reference word
C	Input word < reference word
D	Input word ≠ reference word

The event sense card continually compares the input word with a reference word while the system is in the interrupt mode and stores the entire input word at the moment the event (interrupt) occurs. Both the interrupting input word and the reference word can be read back, after the event has occurred. As shipped from the factory, the event sense card does not store input data unless the multiprogrammer is in the interrupt mode with the gate set.

Programming the event sense card consists of four basic steps (which are covered fully in the manual and summarized here):

1. Loading the reference word to initialize the card.

2. Arming the card. This permits the card to control the multiprogrammer flag and thus generate an interrupt to the calculator.

3. Reading the card without a gate to return the interrupting word.

4. Disarming the card.

5-19 PULSE COUNTER CARD, 69435A

As shown in Fig. 5-30, this card counts pulses, up or down, in the range 0 to 4095. A carry or borrow pulse is generated as the count goes above 4095, or below 0, respectively. These carry and borrow pulses allow multiple counter

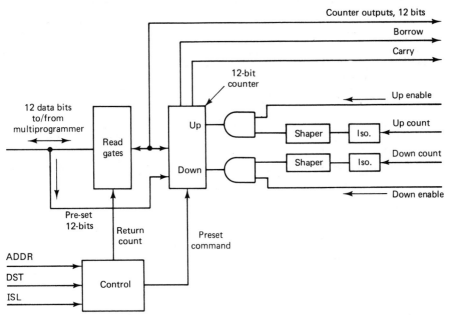

FIGURE 5-30 Block diagram of pulse counter card.

cards to be cascaded for greater counting capability, or they can serve as alarm signals. The card can also be used as a preset counter.

5-19.1   Programming the Card

Programming the pulse counter card consists of two basic steps (which are summarized here):

1. The card must first be preset by sending a control word to the multiprogrammer with ISL off, followed by a data word containing the card slot address and the data value to which the counter is to be set. The counter is then preset when the data word is gated into the multiprogrammer.

2. The pulse counter card can be read by sending a control word with ISL on, then addressing the card without a gate and storing the return data in the calculator. It is then up to the user to process the data.

5-20   PROCESS INTERRUPT CARD, 69436A

As shown in Fig. 5-31, this card provides TTL and open-collector-compatible edge detectors: one positive and one negative for each of 12 storage latches. Logic transitions lasting 100 nA or longer are detected, stored, and can be used

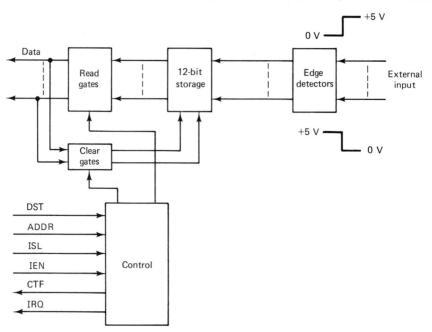

FIGURE 5-31   Block diagram of process interrupt card.

to interrupt the calculator. The return data word is input (in octal form) to variable "X." It is then up to the user to process the data.

5-20.1 Interrupt Mode

Basically, this card is used only in the interrupt mode, either singly or with other cards having interrupt capability. The card generates an interrupt when any one of the 24 edge detectors is toggled.

Programming the card consists of five basic steps (which are summarized here):

1. Initializing all edge detectors to a known (reset) state.

2. *Arming the card.* This permits the card to control the multiprogrammer flag and thus generate an interrupt to the calculator.

3. Reading the card without a gate to return the interrupting bits to the calculator.

4. Resetting the card to clear the bits that interrupted, and prepare the card for generating a new interrupt.

5. Disarming the card to prevent further interrupts.

5-21 BREADBOARD INPUT CARD, 69480A

As shown in Fig. 5-32, the breadboard input card is a simple multiprogrammer interface card which allows the user to design, build, and control special input circuits through the multiprogrammer system.

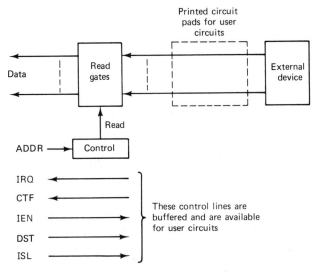

FIGURE 5-32 Block diagram of breadboard input card.

5-22 RESISTANCE OUTPUT CARDS, 69500A-69513A

As shown in Fig. 5–33, these cards provide a programmed value of resistance as their output. Twelve magnetically shielded mercury-wetted reed relays select the resistance values by modifying the value of a series string of high-accuracy binary-weighted resistors.

> Model 69500A is supplied without output resistors so that customers may select and load their own resistors if desired.

> Models 69501A–69506A are single-output 12-bit resolution cards designed to program the voltage output of a single Hewlett-Packard power supply equipped with Option 040.

> Models 69510A–69513A are dual-output 6-bit resolution cards designed to program the current outputs of two Hewlett-Packard power supplies equipped with Option 040.

A table in the manual describes the maximum resistance outputs and resolution for each card. Typically, the resistance outputs run from 8 Ω (with 2-Ω resolution) on up to 81,900 Ω (with 20-Ω resolution).

5-23 PROGRAMMABLE TIMER CARD, 69600B

As shown in Fig. 5–34, this card generates a crystal-controlled one-shot pulse each time a pulse is commanded by the program. The duration of the pulse is determined by the combination of two factors: (1) the number of programmed time increments, from 1 to 4095; and (2) the selected period of the increments, from 1 μs to 0.1 s. The number of time increments is programmable, but the actual period of the increments is selected by installing appropriate jumpers on the card.

At the option of the user, jumpers may be installed on this card to allow DTE or an external trigger signal to control the output from the card. When used this way, either DTE or an external trigger (depending on the jumper installed) may be used to generate timed outputs simultaneously from multiple cards.

There are three basic operating modes for this card:

1. *Automatic handshake mode:* This mode allows the user to program an output pulse of a specified duration, but does not provide an indication to the calculator when the pulse is complete.

2. *Timing mode (TME on):* This mode is used when the program requires an indication that the output pulse is complete. The trailing

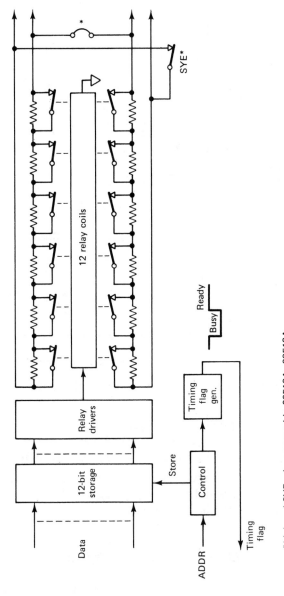

*Link and SYE relay removed in 69510A—69513A.

FIGURE 5-33 Block diagram of resistance output card.

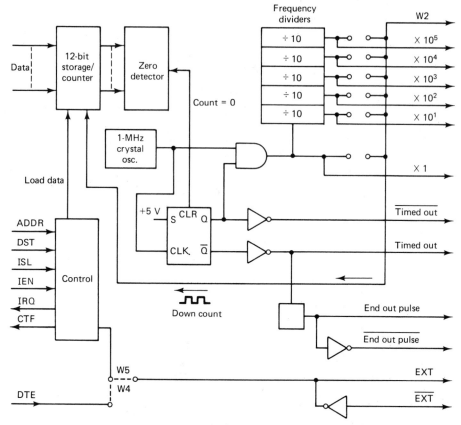

FIGURE 5-34 Block diagram of programmable timer card.

edge of the multiprogrammer flag is returned upon completion of the output pulse and can be used to generate an interrupt on the interface, thus notifying the program that the pulse is complete.

3. *Interrupt mode:* This mode allows the user to program output pulses from multiple cards and notifies the calculator, by means of an interrupt, when the first card has completed the output pulse.

5-24 FREQUENCY REFERENCE CARD, 69601B

As shown in Fig. 5-35, this card is not programmable, but can be used in conjunction with other plug-in cards. For example, the frequency reference card can be used with the pulse counter card (Sec. 5-19) for making time interval measurements (Secs. 2-13.5 and 5-28). Also, the frequency reference card can

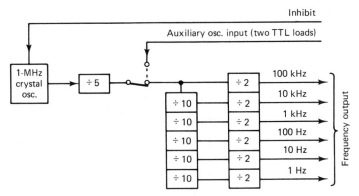

FIGURE 5-35 Block diagram of frequency reference card.

be used as a divider for TTL signals through use of the auxiliary oscillator input.

The frequency reference card provides six square-wave outputs at fixed frequencies of 1 Hz, 10 Hz, 100 Hz, 1 kHz, 10 kHz, and 100 kHz. The output frequencies are derived from an internal 1-MHz crystal oscillator and can be turned off by the low state of an external TTL logic gate or external contact closure between the inhibit and common pins on the card.

5-25 MULTIPLE-CARD PROGRAMS

The programs and explanations in the remainder of this chapter provide examples of typical measurement applications and methods using several types of multiprogrammer cards together. The techniques described are examples of how to solve certain common problems in control and instrumentation systems, and should not be considered as an exhaustive treatment of the subject. The examples given in the remaining sections (*voltage scanning* or *multiplexing, frequency measurement,* and *time-interval measurement*) may be used as stand-alone programs, or modified and incorporated as subroutines in a larger program.

5-26 VOLTAGE SCANNING AND MEASUREMENT (MULTIPLEXING)

Figure 5-36 and the following program illustrate using a 69421A voltage monitor card (Sec. 5-14) in conjunction with a 69433A relay output with readback card (Sec. 5-17) to measure six isolated voltages, store the measured values, and then print the values on the calculator. This application could be

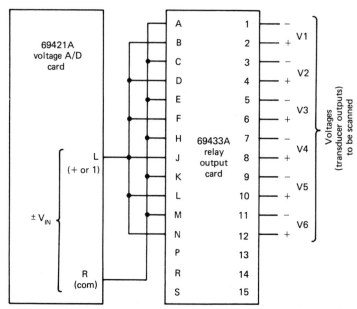

FIGURE 5-36 Voltage scanning and measurement (multiplexing) using voltage A/D and relay output cards.

used to monitor six transducers at various points in our imaginary petroleum refinery, and print out the results on the calculator for use by the refinery operator. If the voltages to be measured share a common reference, it is possible to use this card combination to measure 12 different voltages. Additional cards and appropriate modifications to the program may be used to expand the scanner array if desired.

The program example assumes that the relay card is installed in slot 4Ø1 (A) and the voltage monitor card is installed in slot 4Ø2 (B). It is further assumed that the voltages to be measured are in the range -10.240 through + 10.235 V, permitting use of a standard voltage monitor card. Note that there is an explanation given in Sec. 5-26.1 for each step of the program.

Ø: rds (723) → C

1: fmt 1, c, z; fmt 2, c, f4.Ø, c, z

2: for J = Ø to 1Ø by 2

3: dto (2↑J + 2↑ (J + 1)) → A

4: wrt 723.2, "OØ16ØTATA," A, "T"

5: gsb "meas"

6: X → r((J + 2)/2); next J

7: for J = 1 to 6

8: fxd 3; prt "VOLTAGE = ," rJ; next J

9: end

10: "meas": wrt 723.1, "O260TBTBX"

11: rds (723) → C; red 723, X

12: ot dX → X; if X> 2047: X-4096 → X

13: .005X → X; ret

*8478

5-26.1 Explanation of Program

0 Clears the service request line from the multiprogrammer at the beginning of the program.

1. Format statements for write statements in lines 4 and 10.

2. Establishes a "for/next" loop with line 6 in order to calculate and program the relay closures required to take the six voltage measurements.

3. An octal value representing appropriate relay closures is calculated and stored in variable A.

4. Control word with DTE, SYE, and TME establishes the output timing mode. The data word "AT" opens the previously closed relays before programming the next set of contact closures, thereby preventing the possibility of shorting voltages together. The second data word with variable A programs the appropriate relay closures for each of the six voltage measurements.

5. Calls the voltage measurement subroutine (lines 10–13), which returns to line 6 with a decimal value in volts stored in variable X.

6. The decimal value in volts is successively stored in variables r1 through r6 (corresponding to the voltage being measured).

7-8. Another "for/next" loop is established to print the six voltage values stored in r1 through r6.

9. End of program.

10-13. Voltage measurement subroutine: note that in line 11, the service request line (which is set in line 10 TME on) is cleared.

5-27 FREQUENCY MEASUREMENT

Figure 5–37 and the following program illustrate using a 69435A pulse counter card (Sec. 5–19) and a 69600B programmable timer card (Sec. 5–23) to measure the frequency of a pulse train, and then display the frequency on the calculator. The timer enables the counter for a programmed period of time, and the calculator divides the count by the time to determine frequency. This application could be used for any of the frequency measurement functions described in Chapter 2 (for example, to measure the output of the turbine flowmeter described in Sec. 2–4.1).

The following program assumes that the pulse counter card is installed in slot 401 (A) and the timer card is installed in slot 402 (B). The pulse train frequency being measured should not exceed 200 kHz. Note that there is an explanation given in Sec. 5–27.1 for each step of the program.

A primary consideration when measuring frequency with the technique described here is the capacity of the pulse counter card. The timer card output is connected to the count enable input of the counter card and is programmed to select the gate time for the frequency measurement. (Refer to Sec. 2–13.5). The user must select gate times so that the maximum count capacity of 4095 is not exceeded during the measurement period. This particular program automatically selects gate times as follows:

1. The initial gate time is 10 ms, which produces 2000 counts at the maximum input frequency of 2000 kHz.

2. Whenever the total count is less than 100, the time interval is increased by a factor of 10 and a new measurement is made. The maximum gate time in this program is 1 s.

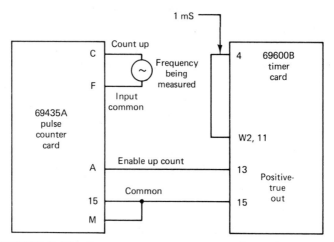

FIGURE 5-37 Frequency measurement using pulse counter and timer cards.

The timer card is used in the timing mode, requiring that jumper W3 be installed on the card. Instead of using the calculator interrupt system as an indication that the gate pulse is completed, the data word containing the pulse length is followed by a control word which turns TME off and ISL on prior to reading data from the counter card. The calculator does not send the control word with ISL on until the output pulse is complete and the timer card returns a CTF flag. As shown in Fig. 5-37, the pulse train to be measured (say from the turbine flowmeter) is applied between the appropriate count-up input and pin F (common) of the pulse counter card.

Ø: rds   (723) → C

1: fmt   1, c, z; fmt 2, c, f4.Ø, c, z

2: 1Ø → B; 1ØØØ → D

3: dto   B → A; wrt 723.1, "OØØ4ØTAT"

4: wrt   723.2, "OØ16ØTB," A, "TOØ24ØTAX"

5: red   723, X

6: B*1Ø → B; D/1Ø → D

7: if X < 144 and D > 1; jmp -4

8: ot   dX*D → X

9: dsp   "FREQUENCY = ," X, "HZ"

1Ø: rds   (723) → C; end

*36

5-27.1 *Explanation of Program*

Ø. Clears the service request line from the multiprogrammer at the beginning of the program.

1. Format statements for write statements in lines 3 and 4.

2. An initial gate time of 10 ms is stored in variable B; an initial frequency conversion multiplier (1ØØØØ), used to convert the pulse count to hertz in line 8, is stored in variable D.

3. Variable B is converted to octal and stored in variable A; the control word with SYE establishes the output mode; the data word "AT" presets the pulse counter card to zero.

4. A control word with DTE, SYE, and TME on establishes the output timing mode; the initial gate time is sent to the timer card; a control word with ISL on establishes the input mode upon completion of the gate pulse from the timer card.

5. The pulse counter card is read without a gate and the pulse count is stored in variable "X."

6. The gate time is increased by a factor of 10 and the frequency conversion multiplier is reduced by a factor of 10 to prepare for the next reading.

7. The total pulse count is tested for 100 (144 octal) and the frequency multiplier is tested for a value greater than 1 (10 or 100); if the count is less than 100 and the frequency multiplier is greater than 1 (indicating that the previous gate time was less than 1 s), the program returns to line 3 and a new measurement is made.

8-9. The pulse count is converted to a decimal value and multiplied by a frequency multiplier to determine the frequency in hertz; the frequency is displayed.

10. The service request line from the multiprogrammer is cleared; the program ends.

5-28 TIME-INTERVAL MEASUREMENT

Figure 5–38 and the following program illustrate using a 69435A pulse counter card (Sec. 5–19) and a 69601B frequency reference card (Sec. 5–24 to measure the *period* of a single positive pulse (Sec. 2–13.5), and then display the period (or time interval) on the calculator. The calculator divides the total count by the frequency output of the frequency reference card to determine the time interval. This application could be used for any of the time-interval measurement functions described in Chapter 2 (for example, to measure the time between a tank valve being opened, and the time a certain pressure is reached).

The following program assumes that the pulse counter card is installed in slot 401 (A) and the frequency reference card is installed in slot 402 (B). For the

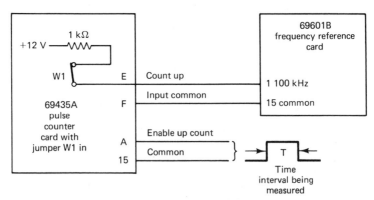

FIGURE 5-38 Time-interval measurement using pulse counter and frequency reference cards.

connections and calculations used in this particular example, the pulse duration should not exceed 40 ms. Note that there is an explanation given in Sec. 5-28.1 for each step of the program.

A primary consideration when measuring time intervals with the technique described here is the capacity of the pulse counter card. The user must select a reference frequency so that the maximum count capacity of 4095 is not exceeded during the longest time-interval measurement. Capability varies inversely with the reference frequency. For example, selection of a 1-kHz reference frequency permits measurement of time intervals with durations of approximately 4 s. Lower reference frequencies reduce the resolution of the measurement, however, so that some compromise is necessary either way. Longer intervals may be measured at high resolution by cascading counter cards in order to eliminate the overflow problem.

```
0: rds  (723) → C
1: fmt  1, c, z; wrt 723.1, "O0040TAT"
2: dsp  "ENTER PULSE"; stp
3: wrt  723.1, "O0240TAX"; red 723, X
4: ot   dX → X; X/100000→ X; fxd 6
5: dsp  "PULSE TIME =," X, "SECONDS"
6: end
  + 6801
```

5-28.1 Explanation of Program

0. Clears the service request line from the multiprogrammer at the beginning of the program.

1. A control word with SYE on establishes the output mode. The data word "AT" presets the pulse counter card to zero.

2. After the calculator stops, a pulse is applied to the enable up-count input of the pulse counter card.

3. A control word with ISL establishes the input mode. The pulse counter card is read without a gate and the pulse count is stored in variable "X."

4. The pulse count is converted to a decimal value and divided by the reference frequency to obtain the time interval in seconds.

5. The pulse time interval is displayed.

6. The program ends.

INDEX

A

AC to DC signal conditioning, 65
A/D (analog/digital) conversion, 68, 182
Acceleration sensors (accelerometer), 29
Accumulator, microcomputer, 128
Actuators, 2, 5, 86
Addresses, 212
   bus, 127
   word, 204
Alphanumeric codes, 104
ALU, 135
Amplifier signal conditioning, 66
Analog I/O, 177, 182
Angular motion sensors, 23
Architecture, 138
ASCII, 106

B

BCD, 104
Binary:
   conversion ladder, 71
   numbers, 103
Bits, 104
Branch instructions, 158
Breadboard circuits, 179, 193, 291
Bridge circuits, 15
Buffer, 133

Assembly:
   language, 164
   microcomputer, 154
Automatic timing, 207
Automation process, 200